Families, Young People, Physical Activity and Health

The family is an important site for the transmission of knowledge and cultural values. Amidst claims that young people are failing to follow health advice, dropping out of sport and at risk of an ever-expanding list of lifestyle diseases, families have become the target of government interventions. This book is the first to bring together critical sociological perspectives on how families do and do not function as a pedagogical site for health education, sport and physical activity practices.

This book focuses on the importance of families as sites of pedagogical work across a range of cultural and geographical contexts. It explores the relationships between families, education, health, physical activity and sport, and also offers reflections on the methodological and ethical issues arising from this research. Its chapters discuss key questions such as:

- how active living messages are taken up in families;
- how parents perceive the role of education, physical activity and sport;
- how culture, gender, religion and social class shape engagement in sport;
- how family pedagogies may influence health education, sport and physical activity now and in the future.

This book is essential reading for anyone with an interest in health, physical education, health education, family studies, sport pedagogy or the sociology of sport and exercise.

Symeon Dagkas is a Reader in Youth Sport and Physical Activity at the University of East London, UK, and an Honorary Senior Research Fellow in the School of Social Policy at the University of Birmingham, UK. He is currently interested in research examining intersections of race, ethnicity, culture and social class of young people and their families in relation to health and well being, sport (PE) and physical activity. Symeon is the editor of another Routledge book, *Inclusion and Exclusion through Youth Sport*.

Lisette Burrows is an Associate Professor in Physical Education Pedagogy at the School of Physical Education, University of Otago, New Zealand, where she has taught for over 20 years. Her research is primarily focused on understanding the place and meaning of health and physical culture in young people's lives. Health and Physical Education curriculum, issues around inclusion of young people with disabilities and critical obesity work are also part of her research agenda. She predominantly draws on post-structural theoretical resources in her writing and teaching.

Routledge Research in Sport, Culture and Society

For a full list of titles in this series, please visit www.routledge.com.

Families, Young People, Physical Activity and Health

Critical perspectives

Edited by
Symeon Dagkas and Lisette Burrows

Routledge
Taylor & Francis Group

LONDON AND NEW YORK

First published 2016
by Routledge
2 Park Square, Milton Park, Abingdon, Oxon OX14 4RN

and by Routledge
711 Third Avenue, New York, NY 10017

Routledge is an imprint of the Taylor & Francis Group, an informa business

British Library Cataloguing in Publication Data
A catalogue record for this book is available from the British Library

Library of Congress Cataloging in Publication Data
A catalog record for this book has been applied for

ISBN: 978-1-138-83818-5 (hbk)
ISBN: 978-1-315-73457-6 (ebk)

Typeset in Times New Roman
by Taylor & Francis Books

Contents

Illustrations

Figures

Tables

Contributors

Veronica Allan is a doctoral student within the Performance Lab for the Advancement of Youth in Sport, which is within the School of Kinesiology and Health Studies at Queen's University. Veronica's current research focuses on the contextual factors underlying coaches' roles in the youth sport environment, particularly in relation to positive youth development.

Louisa Allen is an Associate Professor in the Faculty of Education at the University of Auckland. She specializes in research in the areas of sexualities, young people and schooling and innovative research methodologies which seek to engage hard to reach research populations. She examines these areas most recently through the lenses of queer and feminist new materialist theoretical frameworks. She has written four books, the latest a co-edited with Mary Lou Rasmussen and Kathleen Quinlivan, entitled *Pleasure Bound*.

Whitney Babakus Curry is a Senior Lecturer in Physical Education and Sport Pedagogy at Edge Hill University. Her research interests include measuring physical activity and sedentary time using a mixed-methods approach. Her work focuses on using objective measurement and self-report methods among culturally and linguistically diverse groups to accurately and reliably measure physical activity and sedentary time.

Dean Barker is an Associate Professor at the Department of Food and Nutrition, and Sport Science, University of Gothenburg. He is co-ordinator of the Physical Education Teacher Education program and is involved in ongoing professional development for practising teachers. Dean's research has centred around sociocultural dimensions of learning in physical education (PE).

Lisette Burrows is a Professor in the School of Physical Education, Sport and Exercise Sciences at the University of Otago, New Zealand. She has been researching and teaching health and physical education pedagogy for over 20 years. Her research draws on post-structural theoretical tools and insights from the sociology of education, sociology of youth, curriculum studies and cultural studies' perspectives to explore the place and meaning of physical culture and health in young people's lives. She has become increasingly fascinated with the ways in which families are drawn into health enhancing projects both in public health and school-based pedagogies.

Jean Côté is a Professor and Director of the School of Kinesiology and Health Studies at Queen's University. As the head of the Performance Lab for the Advancement of Youth in Sport (PLAYS), Jean's research program focuses on the developmental and psychosocial factors that affect sport and physical activity performance and participation. Using a broad array of quantitative and qualitative methodologies, his research explores the complex interaction of youth, parents and coaches within sport to identify variables and behaviours that create favourable conditions for excellence and participation in sports.

Symeon Dagkas is a Reader in Youth Sport and Physical Activity at the University of East London, UK, and an Honorary Senior Research Fellow in the School of Social Policy at the University of Birmingham, UK. He is currently interested in research examining intersections of race, ethnicity, culture and social class of young people and their families in relation to health and well being, sport (PE) and physical activity. Symeon is the editor of another Routledge book, *Inclusion and Exclusion through Youth Sport*.

Fiona Dowling is a Professor of Education at the Department of Cultural and Social Studies at the Norwegian School of Sports Sciences. Her research interests include gender and PE/sport, education for social justice, teacher professionalism, and qualitative methodology (in particular, narrative enquiry). She is currently involved in research on race and (anti)racism in PE and teacher education.

Eimear Enright is a lecturer with the School of Human Movement and Nutrition Sciences at the University of Queensland. Eimear's teaching and research interests centre on 'youth voice', pedagogy, technology and physical culture. Her current work explores the limits and possibilities of using digital technology to develop relevant and student-driven ways of teaching health and physical education. She is also working on two Australian Research Council Discovery projects that examine teachers' work and policy in relation to health and globalization.

John Evans is Professor of Sociology of Education and Physical Education at Loughborough University, England. He teaches and writes on issues of equity, education policy, identity and processes of schooling. He has authored and edited many papers and books in the sociology of education and physical education including with Emma Rich, Rachel Allwood and Brian Davies (2008) *Education, Disordered Eating and Obesity Discourse*, Routledge, and with Brian Davies (2013) *New Directions in Social Theory, Education and Embodiment* (2013), Routledge.

Michael Blair Evans is a post-doctoral fellow within the Performance Lab for the Advancement of Youth in Sport, which is within the School of Kinesiology and Health Studies at Queen's University. He is interested in exploring how social relationships within small groups and organizations shape our interests and experiences in sport.

Hayley Fitzgerald is a Reader in Disability and Youth Sport at Leeds Beckett University and a Visiting Professor at the University of Worcester, England. Hayley's teaching and research reflects an ongoing commitment to explore the inequalities experienced by young disabled people in physical education and youth sport. Methodologically, Hayley's research has adopted a participatory student-centred approach in order to enable young people with multiple and severe disabilities to take a meaningful part in research. Theoretically, her work engages in a process of reconceptualizing social model critiques of disability and notions of inclusion.

Michael Gard is Associate Professor of Sport, Health and Physical Education in the School of Human Movement and Nutrition Sciences at the University of Queensland. He teaches, researches and writes about how the human body is and has been used, experienced, educated and governed.

Valerie Harwood is a Professor of Sociology of Education, Faculty of Social Sciences, University of Wollongong. She researches issues that affect inclusion and exclusion from education. In 2013 Valerie was awarded an Australian Research Council Future Fellowship to pursue research on educational inclusion and early childhood. Her most recent book, co-authored with Julie Allan, is *Psychopathology at School: Theorising Mental Disorders in Education*. Her book *Diagnosing Disorderly Children* was awarded runner-up for the UK Times Higher Education NASEN Academic Book Award (2006).

David Haycock is an independent researcher in the sociology of youth sport and leisure. He has worked as a lecturer on a number of taught undergraduate and postgraduate programmes focused on physical education, sport development and management and the sociology of sport at Edge Hill University, UK. He has also published a range of peer-reviewed articles in the sociology of physical education, sport, leisure and youth that appear in journals including *Leisure Studies, Sport, Education and Society*, and *British Journal of Sociology of Education*. David was awarded his PhD entitled *University Students' Sport Participation: The Significance of Sport and Leisure Careers* from the University of Chester in 2015.

Anna Hickey-Moody is the Co-Director of the Disability Research Centre and Head of the Centre for The Arts and Learning, at Goldsmiths. Her work focuses on the politics of disability, youth arts practices, gender and cultural geography. Recently she has been developing a concept of little public spheres, which theorises disadvantaged young people's creative practices as forms of civic participation. Anna also researches and publishes on masculinity and is interested in the politics and aesthetics of masculinity as embodied critique of institutionalized patterns of hegemony. She has edited a number of collected works, most recently an anthology on new materialism, arts practice and cultural resistance with Rowman and Littlefield, to be published later this year. She is currently completing a book on the politics of educational imaginaries, place and affect with Valerie Harwood and Samantha McMahon.

Rebecca Johnson is an experienced secondary health education teacher who graduated from the Queensland University of Technology in 2005. She has been involved in the implementation of the MindMatters mental health framework in South-East Queensland schools and, more recently, has developed contemporary sexuality and relationships education curriculum resources in partnership with Family Planning Queensland. Rebecca is currently a Research Officer in the School of Human Movement and Nutrition Sciences at the University of Queensland and is involved in the teacher education program.

Deana Leahy is a Senior Lecturer in the Faculty of Education at Monash University, Australia. Her research interests are framed by a concern about the political and moral work that is 'done' under the guise of improving the health of children and young people in educational settings. Her research draws from Foucauldian and post-Foucauldian writings on governmentality to consider the various mentalities that are assembled together in policy and curriculum and how they are translated into key pedagogical spaces.

Martin R. Lindley is Senior Lecturer in Human Biology and academic lead of the Translational Chemical Biology research group in the School of Sport Exercise and Health Science/Chemistry Department at Loughborough University. He also holds a Visiting Assistant Professor position in the Kinesiology Department at Indiana University, School of Public Health. Martin's research is concerned with diet and exercise and their impact upon inflammation (specifically dietary Omega 3 PUFAs [fish oil]); Martin's research group works as a collaborative network between synthetic and analytical chemists, biochemists and molecular biologists alongside exercise physiologists and nutritionists with a thread of genetics and epigenetics running through it.

Suzanne Lundvall is an Associate Professor at the Swedish School of Sport and Health Sciences, GIH, in Sweden. Her main research interest is teaching and learning processes in PE, organized sport and physical activity. At present she is involved in a project in collaboration with the National Agency of Education, aiming at identifying newly arrived immigrant students' knowledge of and experiences in PE and sport.

Doune Macdonald is a professor of Health and Physical Education and holds the position of Pro-Vice-Chancellor (Teaching and Learning) at the University of Queensland. She has recently completed the role of Lead Writer for the Australian Curriculum: Health and Physical Education and is currently chief investigator on Australian Research Council projects addressing questions of teachers' work and policy in relation to health and globalisation.

Louise McCuaig currently convenes the Health and Physical Education (HPE) teacher education program at the University of Queensland, School of Human Movement and Nutrition Sciences. Louise's teaching and research addresses the curriculum, pedagogical and assessment practices of school-based health education, and the impact of teacher education, caring teachers and health literacy curricula upon young people's healthy living journeys.

Samantha McMahon is a Research Fellow in the Faculty of Social Sciences, University of Wollongong, and an associate member of the Early Start Research Institute. Her research interests include sociology of education, preservice teacher epistemology and teacher education. Sam's PhD thesis used Foucauldian archaeological analytics to describe and problematize preservice teachers' knowledge of challenging behaviour. Her current research project focuses on AIME (the Australian Indigenous Mentoring Experience).

Moss Norman is in the Faculty of Kinesiology and Recreation Management at the University of Manitoba. He uses a qualitative lens to examine the relationship between physical culture, health and embodiment. Currently, he is using a community-based research design to explore contemporary and historical Indigenous physical cultural masculinities in Fisher River Cree Nation (Manitoba). Moss also maintains secondary, but active research interests in masculinity, fatness and health; rural youth and recreation; and biomedicalized constructions of youth, health and embodiment. He has numerous peer-reviewed publications, including in journals such as *Men and Masculinities, Gender, Place and Culture, Sport in Society, Sociology of Sport Journal,* and *The Journal of Rural Studies* (forthcoming).

LeAnne Petherick is in the Faculty of Kinesiology and Recreation Management at the University of Manitoba. She is a qualitative researcher who uses feminist post-structural approaches to disrupt dominant ways of thinking about the body in physical and health education. Focusing on the cycle of knowledge production, particularly in relation to school-based health promotion curricula, LeAnne examines how these initiatives are taught and taken up in everyday life and how they shape how students' and teachers' alike come to think about health, the body and human movement.

Jo Pike is Senior Lecturer in Childhood Studies at Leeds Beckett University. Her research is primarily related to the ways in which space is implicated in the production of children self-governing healthy subjects with a particular focus on school foodscapes. Her work seeks to explore the social, cultural, moral and affective dimensions attached to educative programmes and interventions which seek to shape the health behaviours and food choices of young people and their families. Her most recent book, *The Moral Geographies of Children, Young People and Food* with Peter Kelly, takes *Jamie's School Dinners* as a starting point for examining idealized views of parenting, nutrition, health and well-being as well as public health 'crises' such as obesity.

Carolyn Pluim (Vander Schee) is an Associate Professor and the Assistant Chair of the Department of Leadership, Educational Psychology and Foundations at Northern Illinois University in Dekalb, Illinois. Her research interests focus on the ways that health and physical education policies and practices are discursively positioned in formal and informal school mandates, influence students, the responsibilities and obligations of teachers, and the affective environment of schools.

Thomas Quarmby is a Senior Lecturer in Physical Education and Sport Pedagogy at Leeds Beckett University. Prior to his move to Leeds, he studied and taught at the University of Birmingham. His research interests broadly focus on the role of the family in young people's engagement in physical activity and, more specifically, with how children in care understand, value and access physical activity and sport both within and beyond school.

Geneviève Rail is Professor of Critical Studies of Health at Concordia University's Simone de Beauvoir Institute. She is known as a feminist critic of body-related institutions and favours post-structuralist, de/post/colonial and queer approaches. With funding from the Canadian Institutes of Health Research, she is currently involved in projects investigating discourses and experiences related to human papillomavirus (HPV) vaccination, fatness and reproductive care, and breast and gynaecological cancer care for lesbian, bisexual, queer (LBQ) women and trans-persons.

Anthony Rossi is an Associate Professor with the School of Exercise and Nutrition Sciences at Queensland University of Technology, Brisbane, Australia. His research interests are in teachers' work as it relates to the health of young people, and he is the lead author on a recent book about workplace learning in physical education. He also conducts research on sport for development, specifically in Indigenous Australian communities. He is about to commence an international Sports for Development project with colleagues in Australia and Canada. Most of his work is funded by national and international competitive grant schemes.

Andy Smith is Professor of Sport and Physical Activity at Edge Hill University, UK, where he is also Programme Leader for the MSc Sport, Physical Activity and Mental course. His research interests and publications focus on sport, physical activity and health and on youth, sport policy and development. He is co-author of *Sport Policy and Development* (with Daniel Bloyce, 2010), *An Introduction to Drugs in Sport* (with Ivan Waddington, 2009) and *Disability, Sport and Society* (with Nigel Thomas, 2009), and co-editor of *Doing Real World Research in Sports Studies* (with Ivan Waddington, 2014). Andy's latest book, *The Routledge Handbook of Youth Sport* (co-edited with Ken Green), is published in 2016.

Julie Stirrup lectures in Physical Education and Sports Pedagogy at Loughborough University, England. Her research interests include issues relating to equity and identity, embodiment, and education within the early years and throughout the schooling process.

Matthew Vierimaa is a doctoral candidate in the Performance Lab for the Advancement of Youth in Sport, which is within the School of Kinesiology and Health Studies at Queen's University. His research broadly focuses on understanding how social relationships and contextual factors in the sport environment influence youth's performance, participation and personal development in sport.

Deborah Youdell is Professor of Sociology of Education in the School of Education, University of Birmingham. A concern with inequalities and modes of politics that can intervene in these are at the heart of Deborah's work, pursued through research into the connections between subjectivities, everyday practices, pedagogy, institutional processes, policy and inequalities, and spanning issues of race, ethnicity, gender, sexuality, religion, social class, ability and disability. Most recently Deborah has turned her attention to the possibilities offered to education by a synthesis of post-structural theories of the subject and epigenetic and nutrigenetic accounts of the influences of environment at a molecular level. Deborah is author of *School Trouble: Identity, Power and Politics in Education* and *Impossible Bodies, Impossible Selves: Exclusions and Student Subjectivities*. She is co-author of the award-winning book *Rationing Education: Policy, Practice, Reform and Equity*.

Acknowledgements

We want to thank our colleagues from around the world who have contributed chapters to this ambitious project. We would also like to extend our gratitude to the many families whose 'stories' are signified and shared in this book.

Symeon would like to extend his thanks to Professor David Coslett for his continuous support throughout this project.

Lisette would like to thank the School of Physical Education, Sport and Exercise Sciences at the University of Otago for the time and support needed to complete the book.

Finally, we would like to thank Routledge for supporting this project.

1 Family matters

An introduction

Symeon Dagkas and Lisette Burrows

Introduction

Families are the target of sport, health and physical activity initiatives locally, nationally and globally. Rendered variously responsible for the ill health of children and capable of ameliorating it, the interest in families as sites for health surveillance, monitoring, enhancement, sport participation, and as hubs for fostering physical fitness has burgeoned. Imperatives such as 'families need to …' and 'families should …' pepper healthy and physical activity policies (Burrows and Wright, 2007; Fullagar, 2009; Vander Schee, 2009; Dagkas and Quarmby, 2012), and, in many cases, the scientific literature (McCormack, 2013). This is hardly surprising. A recognition that schools are not the only institutions where learning occurs (Tinning, 2010), that boundaries between home and school are porous and that families do informal pedagogical work that matters (Rich and Evans, 2008; Leahy et al, 2016) has fuelled this focus on families. So, too, has the developmental investment in children as hopes for the future. When children can be removed from their homes and parents prosecuted because their child's weight is construed as a sign of neglect (Herndon, 2010), the extent of professional interest in families as places where future lifestyle habits are inculcated is evident.

Drawing on social science scholars who embrace a variety of theoretical perspectives (e.g. Foucault, Bourdieu, Deleuze, Bernstein, Barad) this book takes as its focus families as sites of pedagogical work. In particular, the book explores, across a range of cultural and geographical contexts, the relations between education, health, sport and physical education imperatives and families. Chapters address questions about how active living messages are taken up in diverse families, how parents perceive the role of education, physical activity, sport, health pedagogy and healthy living practices in their own and their children's lives; the ways in which culture, gender, religion and social class and family identities shape engagement in sport, physical activity and health initiatives; the constraints, facilitators and enablers families experience in relation to health and physical education (PE), and the impacts family pedagogies may yield for health education, sport and physical activity now and in the future.

When inviting contributions to the book, we did not prescribe how authors should think about or define families in their work. As a result, there are chapters which construe family as a biological entity, others that push for a more expansive notion of what constitutes family, and still others who challenge the ways in which family is envisaged in policy and practices related to health and physicality. As editors we want to maintain that family structures or formations and family relationships are in a state of *flux* paving the way for the development of a host of different families, parental styles, physical activity and health habits and sporting participation. In our minds, the standard biological definition of the family restricts the family unit to persons related by birth, marriage, adoption or those living in the same residence. This definition of family excludes various other families, including those living apart and/or in multiple homes and those not blood related.

Despite the diversity of theoretical perspectives, methodological orientations and subject matters embraced by contributors, there are several themes that reappear across the chapters, provoking fresh and enduring questions about what constitutes family, the affects and effects of family-focused health and physical activity interventions, and the ethical and pedagogical implications of academic and professional work in this sphere. It is through the hearing and telling of the stories within each of the chapters that we can begin to appreciate the range of positionalities and experiences on issues of family, pedagogy and health, PE youth sport and physical activity. Understanding difference, and respecting the interests of children and young people whoever they are, and whatever their needs, are first steps towards developing advanced pedagogies of inclusion in physical education and youth sport. We have divided the book into three sections: family, practice and pedagogy; family's health and physical activity; and family physical education and youth sport yet on reading the entire volume, we recognise the division as somewhat spurious. The theoretical, practical and philosophical conundrums the Health and Physical Education field grapples with are evident across and between each of the sections. While not wishing to impose a particular 'reading' of the chapters, or to prescribe how one should think about the relation between family, health and health pedagogy, and physical culture, we offer the following thoughts by way of a preamble.

Readers will notice the repeated appearance of 'matters' in each of the subheadings that shape this chapter. We use this word as a verb and a noun. That is, we think that each of the things we refer to below matter, yet there are also questions, conundrums, dilemmas, conversations to be had about each of them.

Childhood matters

Several chapters in this book disrupt widely held presumptions about the nature of young people's health and physical activity experience in relation to family. The narratives of young Muslim women in Allen's work (see Chapter 3), for example, fracture dominant understandings of youth being caught between two worlds, negotiating 'conflicting sexual ideologies from home and school'. Instead, she shows how dispositions and actions that at first glance seem contrary to familial or cultural norms, are, for at least some young people, in keeping with values they hold dear. Allen's chapter illustrates, albeit for one young woman, how young people can and do make sense of the borders between school and family life and sexual moralities across the two, in unexpected ways – ways that do not necessarily reflect everyday presumptions (i.e. stereotypes) about what life is like for young Muslim women in New Zealand. The tension between home and public pedagogy culture was documented also in Dagkas's (see Chapter 10) chapter using an intersectionality approach to uncover physical culture positionalities of young people in Asian families. Specifically Dagkas proposes that Asian family's enactment of physical culture is a result of a complex interplay of markers of habitus and capital. McMahon and colleagues (see Chapter 4) similarly disrupt common beliefs about the realities of so-called 'disengaged' young people's family life and dispositions. The testimonies from young people in their study point to the largely positive pedagogical work their families engage in. While assumptions that disengaged youth hail from families who don't support them prevail, McMahon and colleagues found that such deficit understandings of young people's worlds were unsubstantiated. Parents, siblings, aunties were pivotal in young people's decisions to re-engage with education and often served as inspirations driving future aspirations. Dowling's young people too (see Chapter 16) talk candidly about what constrains and enables their access to dominant sporting practices, and whether or not they care about these. They are acutely aware of how family priorities shape their engagement in sports and school-based physical education, yet their responses to family influence are varied and unpredictable. Similarly, Smith and Haycock (see Chapter 14) discuss extra-curricular sporting activities and the disparities experienced between families based on their economic capital. More specifically, they unpack issues of social class as both enablers and barriers to engagement with sport. The voices of three young disabled boys are foregrounded in Fitzgerald's Chapter 17. Each provide vivid descriptions of the ways in which family dispositions (and, in particular, parental values) shape their sporting life and, in turn, how their own sporting passions (e.g. wheelchair basketball) can inform what their families value.

As Quarmby (see Chapter 12) and Fitzgerald (Chapter 17) suggest, the voices of young people in care and those regarded as disabled are glaringly missing in most scholarship that examines family engagement in physical activity. Each of the aforementioned chapters urge a centring of young people's voices, attention to the nuances of individual and family experiences, and a recognition that everyday truths about young people, families and well-being are just that – everyday, common (perhaps), yet not necessarily reflective of the messy, located and unique experiences of persons engaging (or not) with health and physical activity messages from multiple places and positions.

Ethics matters

In terms of research engaging families, what we do, how we do it, and what we do with what we research matters. Several authors raise ethical and educational questions about not only policy work, interventions and health and physical activity measures, but about our own research investments, rationales and processes for doing work around families. For example, contributors point to the ways in which health and physical activity is diluted, repackaged and distributed for family consumption. They point to the ironing out of complexity, the problematic assignment of causal links between what families do and what children become, the convenient, yet unwarranted swing to emotive language in otherwise 'scientific accounts' (e.g. Pluim and Gard in Chapter 6; Petherick and colleagues in Chapter 8; and Babakus Curry in Chapter 9) that position and persuade parents to be morally culpable for the well-being of their young. When, as is often the case, academic work is recruited to justify, rationalize and/or support courses of action in relation to health, physical activity or sport, it would seem crucial to ensure that the evidence garnered is sound and any repackaging of it portrays the whole picture, rather than selective bits that service interests of specific health/physical activity promotion agendas. The role researchers themselves play in the pedagogization of families warrants further attention.

The spread of governmental technologies (Rose, 1999) into the domain of family life is an enduring theme across the chapters in this collection. While some authors regard governmental endeavours to ensure the well-being of children via family pedagogies quite favourably, others find the extent and repetitiveness of intrusions into family life deeply troubling. It is somewhat paradoxical that at a time when neo-conservative and neo-liberal forces (see Macdonald, 2011) are on the rise, the government of life (Dean, 2015) appears more intense and widespread than ever. As most of the contributors to this book contend, the neoliberal, individualistic and healthist intonations of most policies and interventions designed and enacted in the name of family health bear little relation to how families who are South Asian, comprised of young people in care, new immigrants, or youth who are disengaged from education think about who they are or their relation to others in their worlds.

Unsurprisingly, it would seem that families, however they may be conceived, have not escaped the imperative toward monitoring, assessing, reporting and measuring so endemic in education more broadly (Ball, Maguire and Braun, 2012). Justifications for funding of health and fitness products (Pluim and Gard, Chapter 6), introduction of family-focused physical activity policies (Burrows, Chapter 5) and health and physical activity scholarly research (Lindley and Youdell, Chapter 2) are more often than not premised on their likelihood to procure measurable outcomes. This requirement to illustrate 'impact' is difficult to achieve when dealing with something as multidimensional as 'health'. As several authors in this volume evidence, the fall-back indicator of programme or policy success tends to be Body Mass Index, or fitness testing results, or success in sports activities that are highly valued in any particular context (see Dowling in Chapter 16; Smith and Haycock in Chapter 14). The wisdom of continuing to fund and found health and physical activity programmes with recourse to these brands of evidence is a conundrum worthy of consideration. If, and the chapters in this book would suggest it is the case, the practice is problematic, then what, if anything, could public health or sports agencies consider as an alternative mode of gauging the value their interventions accrue?

Digital matters

Pluim and Gard (Chapter 6) deal directly with the ways digital technologies (in their case, *Fitnessgram*) can be and are used to reach and engage families in surveillance and monitoring of their children's behaviours. While digital pedagogies are rarely mentioned in other chapters, clearly the spread of online modes of engagement rates further investigation. Understanding how families negotiate health and physical activity promoting and monitoring devices, how engagement with these is embedded (or not) in family life, and with what effects and affects for their sense of selves as healthy or well would seem a fruitful ethnographic task for the field.

Efficacy matters

Much of the collection raises questions about the efficacy of family-focused fitness and health interventions. While millions of dollars and substantial human capital are expended on large-scale fitness, physical activity and health initiatives by governments, empirical work throughout this volume complicates any claims to the efficacy of these. While none of the chapters directly address whether or not such interventions work, they each problematize the notion that all families will necessarily respond to the government of life (Dean 2015) in predictable ways. Dowling's (Chapter 16) narratives of Norwegian immigrants' lives points to the complexities of doing life in an adopted country. Her narrating of Sohail's tale illustrates that assuming a desire to engage in sports dominant in Norway is misplaced. Ludvall and Barker (Chapter 15) show that despite the egalitarian declarations of government sport agencies, the Swedish sportive family is overwhelmingly comprised of middle-class people. The Swedish model may 'reach' one kind of family, but not others. Babakus Curry (Chapter 9) accepts the proposition that chronic disease is higher amongst ethnic minority populations and is keen to advance understandings of how physical activity proponents may better serve the needs/interests of these populations. Nonetheless, she acknowledges the limited success of interventions with ethnic minority groups to date, and provides fascinating insights as to how and why this might be the case. In particular, the ways in which some of her Bangladesh and Pakistani participants understand sedentariness as simply resting after a busy day, or physical activity as 'keeping busy or just moving around a lot' speak volumes when read alongside health promotion imaginings of what these two terms mean. Gard and Pluim (2014) argue that despite a prolific investment (both in terms of finance and personnel) in school-based physical activity and health initiatives, there is little evidence that these interventions actually work. There is nothing in this volume to suggest the scenario is any different in relation to family-focused initiatives.

Parents matter

The relationship between parents and educators and how each envisage their roles, responsibilities and modes of engagement across home and school contexts is a matter that surfaces across several chapters. Evans and colleagues (Chapter 18) hone their attention specifically on how parents shape young people's engagement in sport. They posit a developmental account of the parenting role across stages of a child's development, suggesting that the extent and nature of parents' involvement with their young ones' sport morphs as they age.

Stirrup and Evans (see Chapter 11) afford a glimpse into how early childhood educators think about the parents of the children they work with, and Enright and colleagues (Chapter 13) convey a nuanced understanding about how teachers doing health work regard parents. From helicopter varieties to recalcitrant parents and those whom teachers envisage as simply ill-equipped to provide children with the resources they need to develop healthy habits, it is clear that how parents are thought about, what they are assumed to bring (or not) to their off springs' well-being matters. It shapes how family pedagogues think about their students/clients/recipients of health messages and it informs how they envisage their role in health and/or physical activity promotion.

Further, the ways in which resources and interventions cultivate, are premised on and indeed rely on parental anxiety, fear, risk, guilt and 'love' are compellingly illustrated across chapters that analyse health and/or physical activity policy. As Pluim and Gard (Chapter 6) suggest, parents, their investments in their children, their anxieties about what they may become and their guilt if failing to provide the requisite resources to fulfil their potential are needed to 'make things work'. On the one hand, as signalled above, parents are oft-times regarded as obstacles to health and physical activity work; on the other, their commitment to the products and services conveyed is seemingly pivotal to the success of health and physical activity initiatives. Further work that explores the nuances of parents' day-to-day engagements with professionals and the embodied experience of trying to raise children in contexts where information on how to do this proliferates would seem worthwhile – that is, ethnographic work that endeavours to understand not only what parents do, but how they feel about what they do, who and what drives their willingness to embrace health, physical activity and sport agendas.

Theory matters

There is much to be gleaned from the theoretical challenges posed in several of the chapters in this volume. Indeed, one of the things that excites us about this collection is the unanticipated variety of social theory drawn on to think through and frame accounts of family–health–physical activity nexuses. Lindley and Youdell (Chapter 2) suggest that a richer, more nuanced encounter with the young, active body can be secured by looking both to the substantial ethnographic work that already exists in education more broadly and to bio-molecular work that considers molecules, chemicals, senses, mechanics – that is, the workings of the body itself. They advance an argument for a bio-social approach to understanding young people's physicality, health and subjectivity – one that addresses the relative absence of the corporeal body in much physical activity scholarship to date. In a similar vein, Allen (Chapter 3) explores the potential that Barad's materialist work offers scholars in our field. Like Lindley and Youdell, her chapter urges attention to the ethnographic detail of young people's everyday lives, the nuances of their experience, including the affective dimensions of these. It is these nuances that are relentlessly absent in much scholarship about young people, families, health and physicality. Dagkas (Chapter 10) considers markers of habitus, engaging with intersectionality as a framework and theoretical perspective. He engages with critical race theory and social theory of habitus and capital to examine the positionalities of the racialized bodies within the field of family and in various other (often overlapping) fields. Dowling (Chapter 16) points to the ways in which narrative enquiry can yield poignant and detailed understandings of how families and the young people within them experience and negotiate health and physical activity scapes. Ludvall and Barker (Chapter 15) engage Lamont and Molnars' notion of boundaries to frame their analysis of the Swedish Sport family and McMahon et al (Chapter 4) draw on Cambourne's (1995) Conditions of Learning to think through family engagement in explicit and implicit pedagogies related to young people's disengagement in education. In Pike and Leahy's chapter (Chapter 7), governmentality perspectives inform our understanding of how 'family meal' imperatives shape healthy conduct. They point to a range of pedagogies deployed in schools that are premised on the notion that a family who eats together stays together. Drawing on Foucauldian resources they subject taken-for-granted truths about the 'family meal' to critical scrutiny, raising questions about both the particular kind of family assumed to be sitting down together and the particular functions a 'family meal' is presumed to serve. Evans and colleagues (Chapter 18) use Côte et al's assets framework to understand parents' involvement in their children's sporting practices. The rich array of perspectives drawn on provoke multiple avenues for further research in relation to families, health and physical culture. They also remind us that theoretical resources drawn on to make sense of family engagement in health and physical culture inevitably shape the 'stories' that are told.

Dualisms matters

Across all of the chapters in this collection dichotomies appear to prevail in the minds of academics, teachers, parents, policy-makers and children alike. The spectre of 'good' versus 'bad' families (Chapters 2, 5, 6, 7), 'black' versus 'white' (Chapters 9, 10), 'informed' versus 'ignorant' (Chapters 9, 10), 'caring' versus 'negligent' (Chapters 13, 12) families runs through each of the chapters, whether policy analyses or reporting on ethnographic work with parents, teachers and children. Dagkas (Chapter 10) and Allen (Chapter 3) seek to challenge binaries that tend to position ethnic minority families as 'this' or 'that. Allen's (Chapter 3) analysis complicates the idea that we can ever bracket off the dispositions or commitments of young people (or families) by virtue of their ethnicity. Lindley and Youdell (Chapter 2) urge a reconsideration of the bio-social split so pervasive in health and physical activity research. They encourage a kind of social science that takes seriously the body material and at once socializes that body. As signalled earlier, they also offer theoretical resources to enable contemplation of such an approach. Interrogating these binaries, examining their usefulness and illustrating the ways in which simplistic dualisms work to position families as marginal or 'less than' would seem important.

Practical matters

One of the things that strikes reading across the chapters in this book is the relative absence of discussions about what doing and thinking family differently might look like in terms of on the ground practices. As is often the case with a critically orientated collection there is much brow beating about what is currently the case, and relatively less about what, if anything, a different scenario might entail. While clearly a premise, at least theoretically, of most of the chapters in this book is that there can never be a catch-all remedial response to situations that are not ideal, we do think that there is something to be said about futures, and not simply admonitions to do differently. As Enright et al (2014) attest, there is something unsettling about a relentless critique of existing practices. They argue for a less deficit-focused scholarship in our field. While clearly this is easier said than done, we hope some of the analyses contained within this book will fuel projects that address the 'what then?' question that springs from critique of orthodoxies.

Relationships matters

When considering the variety of theoretical approaches, contexts and subject matters engaged with by our contributors to this volume, the most consistent theme that presents itself across these is the way in which relationships matter. Whether considering the family–school–health/physical activity nexus (Chapters 13, 16, 10), the relationships between parents and their children (Chapters 17,

18), how family members relate to each other, the opportunities for social engagement sport and/or health activities afford, the ways in which children in care relate to their care givers, the relations between disengaged youth and their families, the intricacies of parent–child relationships in immigrant families or the links between parents and young people envisaged in policy documents, the quality of relationships between and across members of families seems to make the world of difference to how and if young people receive and engage with health and physical activity imperatives. As Quarmby (Chapter 12) puts it, when family is reconceived as "a way of thinking and talking", a matter of "doing" versus "being", our focus settles firmly on relational matters. No matter which policies, curricula, interventions or programmes are enacted in the name of securing children's well-being, what seems to matter most is the relationship established between key partners in the enterprise.

Concluding thoughts

Finally, the collection of chapters in this book provokes our thinking about what constitutes family. Burrows (Chapter 5), Quarmby (Chapter 12) and Pluim and Gard (Chapter 6) ask questions about how family is framed and defined in health policies/interventions and what parents are called on to do in the name of enhancing their children's well-being. Their analyses together with Stirrup and Evans (Chapter 11), Petherick and colleagues (Chapter 8), Pike and Leahy (Chapter 7) illustrates how seemingly benign products, like health policies, fitness grams, HPC vaccines, and Early Years programmes and admonitions for families to 'eat together' can and do yield consequences for families that are not necessarily healthful. Quarmby (Chapter 12), in particular, points to the mobile sense of family that characterizes the lives of children in care. Different notions of family are required to contemplate and engage children who do not live with so-called biological families. So, too, are broader understandings of what families are like, and what they value, when considering the South Asian families (see Babakus Curry, Chapter 9; Dagkas, Chapter 10; and Dowling, Chapter 16).

Across much of the policy aired, teacher testimony shared and ethnographic observations noted, there are signs that family is construed by some as if it was a monolithic thing, a universally understood unit to which health, health pedagogy, sport and physical activity agendas can be aligned. Our reading of this collection is that what counts as family, how 'family' is thought about and engaged with could benefit from a rethink. As each of the contributions to this book illustrate, albeit in different ways, family is a tricky customer. Recruiting families to state and profession-sponsored health and physical activity agendas is no simple matter, nor necessarily a desirable or realizable hope.

If nothing else, together the chapters in this volume remind us of the complexity of family life, the futility of one-size-fits-all models of health prevention or physical activity promotion, and the importance of ongoing research that progresses our understanding of what and how families do their lives in relation to and distinct from health, physical activity and/or sporting agendas that seek to reach and inevitably change them.

References

Ball, S. J., Maguire, M. and Braun, A. (2012) *How schools do policy: Policy enactments in secondary schools.* London: Routledge.

Burrows, L. and Wright, J. (2007) Prescribing practices: Shaping healthy children in schools. *International Journal of Children's Rights*, 15, 83–98.

Cambourne, B. (1995) Toward an educationally relevant theory of literacy learning, *The Reading Teacher*, 49, 3, 182–190.

Dagkas, S. and Quarmby, T. (2012) Children's embodiment of health and physical capital: The role of the 'pedagogised' family, *Sociology of Sport Journal*, 29: 210–226.

Dean, M. (2015) The Malthus Effect: Population and the liberal governance of life, *Economy and Society*, 44(1), February, 18–39.

Enright, E., Hill, J., Sandrod, R. and Gard, M. (2014) Looking beyond what's broken: towards an appreciative research agenda for physical education and sport pedagogy, *Sport, Education and Society*, 19(7), 912–926.

Fullagar, S. (2009) Governing Healthy Family Lifestyles. In J. Wright and V. Harwood (eds), *Biopolitics and the 'Obesity Epidemic' Governing Bodies.* New York/London: Routledge (pp108–126).

Gard, M. and Pluim, C. (2014) *Schools and public health: Past, present, future.* Maryland, US: Lexington Books.

Herndon, A. (2010) Mommy made me do it: Mothering fat children in the midst of the obesity epidemic, *Food, Culture and Society*, 13(3), 331–344.

Leahy, D., Burrows, L., McCuaig, L., Wright, J. and Penney, D. (2016) *School Health Education in Changing Times: Curriculum, pedagogies and partnerships.* Routledge: New York.

Macdonald, D. (2011) Like a fish in water: Physical education policy and practice in the era of neoliberal globalization. *Quest*, *63*(1), 36–45.

McCormack, J. (2013) *Obesity, parents and me.* PhD thesis, University of Otago, Dunedin.

Rich, E. and Evans, J. (2008) Performative health in schools: Welfare policy, neoliberalism and social regulation? In: Wright, J. and Harwood, V., eds. *Biopolitics and the Obesity Epidemic: Governing Bodies.* Oxon: Routledge, pp157–171.

Rose, N. (1999) *Governing the soul: The shaping of the private self*, 2nd edn. London: Free Association Books.

Tinning, R. (2010) *Pedagogy and human movement.* London: Routledge.

Vincent, C. and Ball, S. (2007) 'Making Up' the Middle-Class Child: Families, Activities and Class Dispositions, *Sociology*, 41(6), 1061–1077.

Vander Schee, C. (2009) Fruit, vegetables, fatness, and Foucault: Governing students and their families through school health policy, *Journal of Education Policy*, 24, 5: 557–574.

Part 1
Family, practice and pedagogy

2 The absent body

Bio-social encounters with the effects of physical activity on the well-being of children and young people

Martin R. Lindley and Deborah Youdell

Introduction

The physical activity of young bodies is currently the subject of massive policy activity and guidance for practice across service domains and sectors (DoH, 2011; PHE, 2013). Likewise, it is the subject of significant advocacy from lobby groups and third-sector associations (Sport and Recreation Alliance, 2012). Across these we see agreement over the importance of physical activity, with it linked to health (DoH, 2011); well-being (PHE, 2013); educational achievement and cognitive outcomes (PHE, 2013); and the amelioration or even prevention of social exclusion, anti-social behaviour and criminality (Sport and Recreation Alliance, 2012). Alongside this policy, guidance and advocacy there is a strong seam of sociological scholarship that approaches critically the ways in which physical activity comes to be connected to young people's health, well-being, achievements, and social behaviours (Evans, 2014; Leahy, 2009; Rich and Evans, 2013; Harwood, 2009). This chapter is located in the latter scholarship, aiming to extend it by making what the body feels and does central, and by beginning to identify a way of working across critical and post-structural sociological analyses *and* new biological insights into the functioning of bodies, as called for by Nikolas Rose (2013) and Celia Roberts (2014). This call seems to us compelling when popular and policy accounts are all but certain that lack of exercise and bad diets cause poor health, education and social outcomes, but when our own strands of social and biological science are uncertain that any mechanisms for these claims have been demonstrated. In particular, we suggest that the body of evidence – molecules, chemicals, sinews, mechanics, movements, affects, practices, sociality – is conspicuously absent.

In this chapter we illustrate current public health messages surrounding physical activity and young bodies and explore some of the research evidence that this calls up, demonstrating the gap between the certainties of public health guidance and the uncertainties in the evidence. We highlight the particular disciplinary and methodological locations of the studies we look at, and the particular ways of knowing and kinds of data that this brings. Throughout, we note a recurring absence in policy and research – *a rich encounter with the young, active body*. We respond to this absence from two directions: the ethnographic and the bio-molecular. We conclude by setting out our agenda for an experiment in bio-social critique that seeks to encounter this body, and consider positive moves that we might be able to make with bio-social thinking.

Making and managing healthy young bodies

There is a significant history of government reaching into the lives and bodies of children and young people, in particular through public institutions such as schools and health services, with a concern for maximizing health and productivity and minimizing behaviours deemed to be unhealthy or deviant (Foucault, 1991; Rose, 2000; Harwood and Allan, 2014). Such efforts have been effectively interrogated using the Foucauldian lens of governmentality and understood in terms of the practices of anatamo-power and bio-power – that is, the simultaneous government of individual bodies and of populations (Harwood, 2009; Leahy, 2009; Rose, 2000; Wright and Halse, 2014). Critical sociological studies of children and young people's health, health education and sport have provided powerful analyses of how these constitute and constrain the embodied subjectivities of children and young people (De Pian et al, 2014; Leahy, 2009; Saltmarsh and Youdell, 2004). The healthy body, then, becomes the object of a subjectivated subject who is at once divided from her/his body and inexorably tethered to and weighed down by it (Youdell, 2006, 2011). The embodied subject is governed and made recognizable as a *particular sort* of subject (healthy, unhealthy, obese, malnourished) through orientation to/as this body *and* enticed into these embodied and embodying practices as a form of self-care (Burrows and Wright, 2007; Butler, 1993, 1997; Foucault, 1990; Harwood, 2012; Leahy, 2009; Rich et al, 2011). Yet these powerful sociological critiques can at times seem to have a significant absence – the workings of the body itself. In molecular biology much is still being learned about the mechanisms of action of the body at a cellular level. While the relationships between human genetics and disease state are continually being interrogated (Mastana et al, 2013), more recent developments are within nutrigenomics (within-generation interaction between the diet and the body's genetic code), metabolomics (the intermediate chemical processes involved in metabolism) and the influence of diet, nutrition and exercise at a molecular level. Epigenetics suggests enduring inter- and even intra-generational interactions between the environment and the body's DNA (Belsey et al, 1991, cited in Roberts, 2014), while recent innovations in biological science are suggesting that exercise does not have a universally positive impact upon health and disease (Bouchard et al, 2012) and that there is a significant per cent of the population (estimated 8–13 per cent) that show a negative impact of exercise upon disease risk factors. One of the challenges therefore of 'systems biology' and 'functional genomics' is to integrate proteomic, transcriptomic, and metabolomic information to provide a better understanding of cellular biology. That is, in accord with sociology but through vastly different methods, molecular biology demonstrates the complexity of the processes that 'make' human subjects, the significant impact of environment and experience on the body, and the mutability of the body and self.

The promise of physical activity

Governmental concern with the 'healthy' body of children and young people is transnational, spanning the developed as well as the developing world and attending to the simultaneous incidence (including in single national contexts) of obesity, under-nourishment, sedentary lifestyles, and child mortality and poor health (International Food Policy Research Institute, 2014; World Health Organisation, 2013). The central importance of particular forms of physical activity is foregrounded in these accounts – regular sustained cardiovascular effort and resistance exercise, often in the form of participation in sport. A further transnational development has been the turn to 'well-being' which ties together a whole range of domains of life – from economy, education and the environment to community cohesion, personal finance and personal life satisfaction and health – and is measurable. Here, then, physical activity is tied not just to health, but to the bigger category of well-being.

The UK National Health Service website 'NHS Choices' offers the public a factsheet on *Physical Activity Guidelines for Children and Young People (5–18 Years)* (DoH, 2011), which sediments the connection between well-being, health and physical activity and parent/caregivers' responsibility for producing these healthy young subjects. It makes a series of assertions concerning the correct duration, regularity and intensity of physical activity and the need to avoid being sedentary:

1   All children and young people should engage in moderate to vigorous intensity physical activity for at least 60 minutes and up to several hours every day.
2   Vigorous intensity activities, including those that strengthen muscle and bone, should be incorporated at least three days a week.
3   All children and young people should minimize the amount of time spent being sedentary (sitting) for extended periods (DoH, 2011, p1).

The proposition that physical activity is causally related to all kinds of well-being is firmly established in policy and practice. As the factsheet illustrates, the causal connection is so widely accepted by policy-makers, professionals and the public that it can be said to have passed into common sense. The factsheet enlivens, in a very limited way, those activities being called up for children and young people. 'Moderate' activity includes 'bike riding' and 'playground activities'; 'vigorous' activity includes 'fast running' and 'sports such as swimming or football'; and activities that 'strengthen muscle and bone' include 'swinging on playground equipment', 'hopping and skipping' and 'sports such as gymnastics or tennis'. Here we get what seems to be a rare glimpse in the policy literature of young bodies engaging in sporting activities or simply in motion. In contrast, 'sedentary' behaviours include 'watching TV', 'using the computer', 'playing video games' and 'long bus or car journey[s]' (DoH, 2011).

An additional emergent feature of at least the UK government's orientations to the 'problem' of the (un-)healthy body has been a turn to 'social investment' where institutions and individuals are called on to make 'investments' in health and well-being now that will see some 'return' in the future (McGimpsey, in review). This claim to the long-term benefits of young people's engagement in physical activity is well illustrated by *Game of Life: How Sport and Recreation Can Make Us Healthier, Happier and Richer* (Sport and Recreation Alliance 2012) which claims '[s]port and recreation programmes can prevent boredom, teach important life skills, divert young people from crime and foster social inclusion' (Sport and Recreation Alliance 2012, p110). Physical activity, then, has much to deliver.

Public Health England's *How Healthy Behaviour Supports Children's Wellbeing* (Public Health England 2013) sets out the effects on well-being of 'screen time', 'physical activity' and 'healthy eating and diet'. While the report opens by acknowledging the primary influence of poverty on well-being, its focus is a series of claims about the relationship between 'healthy behaviours' and well-being. 'Physical activity' is one such healthy behaviour. The report associates it with a variety of bodily, affective, psychological and social phenomena: 'improved concentration levels'; 'more positive social behavior, such as being kind to classmates and attempting to resolve disputes'; 'feeling liked by peers and that they have enough friends'; 'lower levels of anxiety and depression'; 'being happier with their appearance'; and 'higher levels of self-esteem, happiness and satisfaction with their lives' (PHE, 2013, p7). It is important to note that what is being claimed technically is a series of associations, yet in the way that the report boldly states these repeatedly and proceeds to make strong recommendations for professionals, parents and caregivers based on them, it reads as though well-evidenced causal relationships have been established.

The evidence

The Public Health England report is supported throughout by endnotes that refer the reader to a range of material. A proportion of this material is reports, guidance and policy documents produced by other UK agencies and regions and by other such agencies internationally. This citing of guidance and policy *by* guidance and policy creates a tautological loop in which the causal relationship between physical activity and well-being is increasingly sedimented. In the main the supporting material is academic research published in refereed journals. We have selected a small set of examples of this academic research in order to examine the sorts of evidence that are cited, its disciplinary locations and methodological orientation, the sorts of data it presents and the sorts of claims it can make; to test whether the research base is being well used by the guidance in term of accuracy of attribution and interpretation; and to highlight the *absences* that run through both the guidance and the academic literature it draws on.

We focus here on four studies (Fedewa and Ahn 2011; Holder et al, 2009; Parfitt et al, 2009; and Sebire et al, 2013) located in sports and exercise science and sport and exercise psychology and published in reputable journals. Measures of both physical activity and well-being that are particular to these disciplinary locations recur across the studies. Physical activity is measured either as reported hours per day of physical activity over a given time period or as recorded by accelerometer and converted into counts per minute (CPM). Well-being is measured using a range of established psychological inventories that use self-reported statement agreement, usually on Likert scale.

The intensity of physical activity

As we have noted, policy and guidance is clear that children and young people should engage in physical activity of *moderate to vigorous* intensity. Parfitt et al (2009, p1040) report on the relationship between 'physical activity and psychological health' in nine- to ten-year-olds offering evidence in relation to the various intensities of these activities via accelerometry. Little used with children, these are widely employed with adults in the field of sport science and claimed to enable 'objective measurement'. Psychological health is measured using a series of inventories for anxiety, depression and physical self-perception on which children self-report. These are widely used and accepted in the field of child psychology.

The headline findings of the paper pertain to 'physical and global self-worth' and the *absence of correlation* with overall physical activity. What the paper does show is the significance of the intensity, or otherwise, of physical activity suggesting 'the opposing ends of the intensity spectrum may play a vital role in the relationship with psychological health' (Parfitt et al, 2009, p1041). For instance, 'children in the middle tertile group of very light activity had a more positive psychological profile than those spending a little time in very light activity'. This runs counter to the prevailing popular understanding that the more time spent in 'very light activity' – that is, sedentary behaviours – the worse it is for well-being. To further complicate the findings, the psychological health scores of this middle tertile very light activity group were *as good* as those for the group who spent the most time in vigorous activity. Ultimately the findings from the study suggest that 'up to 4 hours in very light intensity activity along with 30 minutes or more in vigorous intensity activity are associated with the most positive psychological profiles' (Parfitt et al, 2009, pp1041–42). That is, it's ok for children to sit or stand for up to 4 hours a day, as long as they also do 30 minutes or more of vigorous activity. This contradicts any straightforward 'TV is bad' claim, as made by the PHE report, and suggests that the DoH's demands for more than 60 minutes of moderate to vigorous intensity activity each day may be asking more of children than is necessary.

Physical activity and friendship

Sebire et al (2013) emphasize the social context of children and young people's physical activity (PA) and so start from the premise that 'how children get on with their friends and their functioning in friendship groups may be important in understanding how friendship dynamics influence their PA' (Sebire et al, 2013 p2). The research uses accelerometers to 'measure' physical activity among 10- to 11-year-olds, with a focus on the period directly after school, while forms of well-being are measured through young people's responses to questionnaire inventories designed to access 'social functioning' and 'acceptance' measuring 'conduct problems (e.g., aggression and dishonesty), peer problems (e.g., being isolated from friends) and prosocial behaviour (e.g., positive social actions)' (Sebire et al, 2013).[1] The findings are reported in terms of associations and variability taking account of the Index of Multiple Deprivation (IDM); gender; engagement in moderate to vigorous physical activity (MVPA); and 'counts per minute' (CPM) on the accelerometer.

The findings suggest that, irrespective of levels of deprivation, for boys, 'conduct problems were positively associated with MVPA, CPM, while 'peer problems were negatively associated with all PA variables' and 'prosocial behaviour was not associated with PA among boys' (Sebire et al, 2013, pp 4–5). That is, boys who report feeling angry show higher levels of physical activity, while boys who report not having friends show lower levels of physical activity, and boys who report being nice to people show no greater or lesser physical activity than boys who do not. For girls in the study, none of these reported behaviours showed a correlation to physical activity. Biological mechanisms or social or psychic processes that might contribute to explaining these potential relationships are absent.

Choosing leisure

The work of Holder et al (2009) is interested in the contribution to wellbeing of 'passive' and 'active' leisure, and specifically those activities that children choose for themselves. In both regards the research departs from the underpinning premises of the PHE's report, the DoH's guidelines and popular understanding. Based on child and parent self-reports of leisure activities and their importance, alongside children's scores on self-concept and happiness scales, Holder and colleagues suggest that the positive contribution of leisure activities may be 'because they involve autonomous and self-determined behavior', a feature absent from activities chosen for children by their parents or schools. This possibility leads the authors to offer that 'leisure may not be positively correlated with children's well-being' (Holder et al, 2009, p379). Yet, as they report their analysis the emphasis of the paper is on the 'link' between participation in physical activity and happiness, where measures of self-reported happiness act as proxies for wellbeing.

Holder et al (2009) foreground the 'association' between hours of participation in physical activity and 'well-being' as indicated by placement on a series of 5 'happiness' scales. Yet the evidence they offer shows that parents' and children's rating of *ability* and the *importance* of physical activity have *twice* the correlation value with hours of participation than does happiness. That is, how good at sport children are seen to be by themselves or parents and how important they believe sport to be is notably more strongly related to participation in physical activity than the happiness that is at the centre of the author's research question and the physical activity and well-being agenda it addresses. Holder et al (2009) do speak to perceived athletic ability, but relate this to well-being, not participation: 'We found that children's athletic ability, as assessed by either parents or children, is positively associated with well-being' (Holder et al, 2009, p384). With this emphasis, the finding is not that being good at sport and thinking it important is related to spending more time doing it. Rather, the finding becomes that children who are thought to be good at sport are happier.[2]

Physical activity and cognition

Fedewa and Ahn (2011) provide a systematic review of 59 studies of the relationship between physical activity and cognitive achievement. Starting from the claim that the health and psychological benefits of physical activity are 'common knowledge' (Fedewa and Ahn 2011, p521), the authors move to explore the cognitive benefits of physical activity. They do this in the context of the squeeze on physical education in US schools dominated by high stakes tests and in order to raise the possibility that physical activity in school may contribute to *academic* performance in these tests. Through their review they assert that 'all physical activity programs had a positive and significant impact on children's cognitive outcomes and academic achievement' (Fedewa and Ahn 2011, p527).

The review suggests a number of specificities to this relationship: the effect of physical activity on cognitive achievement was greatest in measures of maths performance, followed by measures of IQ, then by measures of reading; there was no effect on measures of creativity; there was a stronger effect when physical activity was engaged in three times a week 3, as opposed to twice a week; the effect was stronger when physical activity took place in mixed gender groups and when group size was small (<10 children); and the effect was stronger in elementary (primary) school than middle and high school.

The evidence in policy and guidance

The connection between the assertions made by Public Health England and the evidence they cite is not clear, and at times the evidence does not support the claims made.

Fedewa and Ahn (2011) is used by Public Health England to support their assertion that physical activity is associated with 'improved concentration levels' (PHE, 2013, p7). Yet, Fedewa and Ahn (2011) do not offer evidence of improved concentration, but claim an effect on performance in particular subject-specific assessment. PHE cite Sebire et al (2013) in the claim that physical activity is 'associated with children's reports of feeling liked by peers and having enough friends' (PHE, 2013, p7). Yet, as discussed, Sebire et al (2013) present a complex picture of association, including no association for girls and varied positive and negative associations amongst boys. Furthermore, the framing of the research by notions of conduct problems, peer problems and prosocial behaviour means it is not straightforward to move from its findings to the claim made by PHE. PHE also cite Parfitt et al (2009) to support the claimed association between physical activity and children feeling liked by their peers and having enough friends (PHE, 2013, p7). Yet, Parfitt et al (2009) use measures from self-report psychological inventories to show relationships between increased vigorous physical activity and children's assessments of their scholastic competence and social acceptance. PHE also cite Parfitt et al (2009) to support their claim that physical activity is associated with lower levels of anxiety and depression (PHE, 2013, p7) yet this is not a finding from Parfitt et al (2009). Rather, Parfitt et al (2009) frame their study of children by asserting that this association has been found in adults, using Biddle and Mutrie (2007), a chapter in an undergraduate textbook, as their own supporting material. PHE cite Parfitt et al (2009) to support their claim that increased TV is associated with lower self-worth and esteem. Yet Parfitt et al (2009) stress that youth sedentary behaviours are complex. In their discussion Parfitt et al (2009) state 'television viewing and physical activity are un-associated and separate constructs' referencing Gorely et al (2007). This is obverse to PHE's claim. PHE also cite Holder et al (2009) to support the claim that increased TV viewing is associated with lower reported self-worth, self-esteem and happiness. Holder et al's (2009) five measures include a child and parent report of children's happiness, a child report of happiness with their appearance, and a child report of being satisfied with their lives. Holder et al do not show an association between time spent watching TV and reduced well-being, but they do claim online social networking and multi-player online games are associated with lower levels of well-being. This may be taken as support for PHE's wider claim, although it is noteworthy that only two of Holder et al's (2009) five measures support this, and one of these is parent's report of children's happiness.[3]

Unknown mechanisms

In contrast to the certainty over the positive connection between physical activity and well-being found in policy, guidance and advocacy, what is striking across the research that we have looked at is the uncertainty and indeed silence over the potential factors or mechanisms underpinning the relationship between physical activity and particular aspects of well-being. This is well illustrated by Fedewa and Ahn's consideration of the relationship between physical activity and cognition:

> One proposed reason for this is that increased activity may enhance arousal and minimize fatigue and boredom (Shephard, 1996). An alternative explanation by Shephard (1996) proposes that increased physical activity leads to higher levels of self-esteem, optimizing students' academic achievement. Other, more neurological, theories tout that changes in brain structure, function, and neurotransmitter concentrations occur in individuals who are more physically active (Hillman et al., 2004; Hillman et al., 2006; see Trudeau and Shephard, 2010). All of these hypotheses could serve as possible explanations for the current findings, but more research is needed to investigate the complex relationship between physical activity dosage and cognitive outcomes in children (Fedewa and Ahn, 2011, p531).

Notable here is that the potential mechanisms that Fedewa and Ahn draw from other publications are themselves characterized as hypotheses, not evidence. Postulating on more specific associations, Fedewa and Ahn suggest that a small group size effect might suggest peer motivation, and that the greater effect in elementary school might be because physical activity is play-based in these settings. They also state that 'children who are more physically fit also tend to have higher cognitive functions and academic achievement' and offer that 'a myriad of potential moderators may affect this relationship' (Fedewa and Ahn, 2011, p530). Recognition of the likely complexity of these relationships is welcome, but they are left unexplored.

A null finding in Fedewa and Ahn that raises particular questions about mechanisms is that 'individualised physical activity interventions showed no significant impact upon children's cognitive outcomes or academic achievement' (Fedewa, 2011, p230). The suggestion is that physical activity does not confer the same 'benefit' when carried out individually as it does when carried out within a group setting. Not only does this mean that the recommended physical activity tasks of 'running, cycling etc.' would seem to be suboptimal (according to Fedewa and colleagues this should be conducted as a group or not at all?), but in addition it would appear to suggest that the benefits accrued from exercise are derived (at least in part) by the social interaction of the group setting. As such, this would seem to indicate that the group interaction is the driving factor and therefore similar benefits might be expected from social interactions without a physical activity component. There is also no supporting evidence or biological hypothesis presented to explain the physiological changes that may occur from group exercise and how they are distinct from either individual physical activity or group based non-physical activity.

Holder et al (2009, p384) are also equivocal about the sort of relationship their research uncovers:

> Though we report a relation between leisure and children's well-being, the direction of this relation is unclear. Past research suggested that happiness contributes to perceived health [...] Alternatively, active leisure may lead to more positive social interactions (e.g., interacting with teammates), which are related to children's happiness.

In this account from Holder et al, physical activity has receded, with social relations and interaction – being in a team – posited as drivers of well-being. Could this just as easily be a sedentary spelling team as a football team?

Yet, in apparent contradiction, Holder et al also report that 'children's athletic ability, as assessed by either parents or children, is positively associated with well-being' (p384). Thinking at the physiological level of the body, a child's current capacity to succeed in a physical activity (e.g., being good at football) should not influence the health benefit of the activity. That is, the players who 'lost the game' still spent 90 minutes running/jumping, etc. so that individuals who exercise at a certain percentage of their maximal aerobic capacity will derive similar physiological responses/benefits. However, if the emphasis shifts from the physiological – the bodily benefits of physical activity – to the social or psychological, then it is recognized as being competent (i.e., being good at football, and being on the winning team) that matters. And this shifts well-being out of the physical activity domain and into the biological–psychology and/or social arena. Ultimately, the authors make no attempt to claim cause or mechanism for the connections they offer – while they say they have 'investigated the relation between children's leisure and their wellbeing' what they present are mathematical 'correlations' between these.

Parfitt et al (2009) are similarly unable to account for the *nature or direction* of the association between accelerometer-measured physical activity and its intensity and psychological health as measured by self-report inventories, or the mechanisms underlying these. Referring to other research, the authors say:

> Potential mechanisms that could account for these effects include exercise induced stimulation of brain monoamine (5), neurotrophins (6) or improved self-esteem, which has been shown to be predictive of depression risk in obese adolescents (7) (Parfitt et al, 2009, p1037).

Parfitt et al (2009) are notable amongst the Public Health England source material examined because they specify the potential brain chemistry that might be at play in the connection between physical activity and well-being, namely, 'feel good' hormones monoamine and neurotrophin that may be released through the stimulation of physical activity. Notes 4 and 5, which Parfitt et al (2009) use to support this potential link, are both from the same author (Dishman et al, 1997, 2000) and both are studies of female rats that have had their ovaries removed. The human health application of the Dishman research is in understanding depression amongst older females (hence ovariectomy). The study used an 'escape deficit model of uncontrollable foot shock' (Dishman et al, 1997, p339) – that is, the rats were exposed to electric shock and the research measured the time the rats took to press a bar to make the shock stop. Ethics aside, the research method and subject in Dishman et al (1997, 2000) is so distant from the human children riding their bikes and feeling good as to make this a wholly inappropriate supporting source. These rat studies appear to be Parfitt et al's (2009) only supporting evidence for a suggested mechanism between children's participation in physical activity and the brain chemistry that may be related to the alleviation of depression.

What is a body doing?

Striking in the policy as well as the research evidence is the absence of the bodies of children and young people. What they are doing – running, jumping, leaping – and how they feel – the surge, the rush, the pain, the stitch, the sweat – seem peculiarly distant, even erased.

As we have seen, policy and guidance illustrates its recommendations by naming a small number of physical activities. In the research we find lists of activities which serve to illustrate classifications of intensity: 'very light' is sitting or standing; 'light' is playing catch; 'moderate' is walking and 'vigorous' is running (Parfitt et al, 2009) or the body comes into view through reference to the accelerometer and the hip to which it is taped. What the body does – run, jump, cycle – is erased and replaced with the proxy CPM (counts per minute). We find one exception in Sebire et al (2013) where the emphasis on the sociality of physical activity demands that we pause momentarily to imagine children's actual bodies in motion: 'children play active games with their friends, take part in team sports/games both formally and informally in and out of school and just hang out with friends which may offer opportunities to be active (such as walking around town, going out on bikes)' (Sebire et al, 2013, p1). This brings into relief a gap that accelerometres and inventories of 'well-being' are unable to speak to – the detail and nuances of young people's everyday lives. The study's focus period between 3.00 pm and 6.00 pm is the time between end of the school day and the end of the working day and shaped for children and young people by a range of factors. For instance, are their parent/guardian(s) at work; are they expected to go straight home from school; do they spend this period with an adult; are they free to go to friends' houses, the park, the shops; do they attend an afterschool facility and is this homework, recreation or sport focused; do they have responsibilities of their own during this time (e.g., helping in a family business or caring for a family member)? All of these have potential structural, social, discursive, subjective, psychic and affective dimensions. Sebire et al's (2013) study took place over a large part of the school year with different sub-samples moving in and out of the research. While the possibility of this having an impact is acknowledged, what these temporal flows might mean and 'do' is not approached. As these 10- to 11-year-olds grow older and as dark winter nights turn to spring and summer, it may well be that, for some, their autonomy shifts.[4]

Across the policy, guidance and the evidence it calls up, the nuances of these bodies' movements, the feelings that flow through them, the meanings that children and young people attach to them, and the social contexts and practices that make certain bodily practices possible for some and foreclose these for others are wholly absent. The policy and research terrain is devoid of the ethnographic detail of the everyday lives of the children and young people in whose bodies and wellbeing it is interested. This is the nuance and rich detail that characterizes ethnographic sociological research. There is a rich body of ethnographic work in the sociology of education that is deeply connected with the embodied practices, meanings and effects of children's and young people's engagement in a physical activity. This work offers detailed accounts of children and young people's everyday lives and the affects and effects in these of a whole range of physical activities: football in the primary school playground (Clark and Paechter, 2007); visceral arts practices in education (Allan, 2009; Hickey-Moody, 2009); embodied play in pre-school settings (Blaise, 2013) young people's physicality in 'special' education (Youdell, 2011) as well as in health education interventions (Evans et al, 2011; et al, 2010).

Likewise, the biochemical mechanisms within these bodies are absent – we see fleeting references to monoamine, neurotrophins and neurotransmitter concentrations but the detailed consideration of these that we find in molecular biology and neuroscience is not engaged. What goes unacknowledged is the fact that the mechanisms of cellular interaction (how brain cells [neurons] interact) and molecular action within metabolic signalling pathways (where proteins are made within the cell in response to messages sent to the cell as stimulated by exercise or indeed social interactions) are inherently difficult to demonstrate in detail. In molecular biology this means that animal models and/or isolated cell culture work is often used in order to investigate these phenomena. Despite the worthiness of interrogating these molecular actions more fully the process becomes impeded in that once the investigation has devolved down to the isolated atomic structure the interpretation of data with reference to whole body activities (in vitro up to in vivo) becomes virtually impossible. The additional complexity of neurobiological and psychological factors involved in human behaviour means that patterns/actions/trends of population behaviour become virtually impossible to predict based upon molecular changes alone.

The bio-social

This research evidence can say much less about the biomolecular and social mechanism at play than policy and pedagogic interventions seem to suggest. This means that professionals as well as parents/caregivers and children and young people might push back against the governmental reach into their practices, ways of living and bodies. It may also suggest a continued openness to well-being that might offer generative potentialities.

We want to pursue a social-biological science that engages the body and is able to encounter its molecular, affective and social flows, bringing together what the body does and can do and recognising how these processes are constitutive of a biological *and* social subject. In *Re-considering the Turn to Biology in Feminist Theory*, Samantha Frost (2014) foregrounds the need to escape a bio/cultural binary to consider '[t]he body engaging the world as an organism' (Frost, 2014, p316) and 'what it means to say that we, as biological organisms, are alive' (p316). This suggests that we recognize the body as simultaneously social and biological and engage their 'infoldings' (Roberts, 2014, p300), We advocate, then, an agenda for empirical research that captures the fine-grained ethnographic detail of children and young people's engagement in physical activity – how and where it takes place, the discursive and material flows that frame and constrain it, what bodies do, what children and young people say it means, how they say it feels, what it looks like and feels like (panting, laughing, scowling, blowing, sweating) – and the molecular and biochemical effects of these activities – the changes that can be measured from the exhaled breath and circulating blood. This opens up a new line of empirical research that has the potential to transform our understanding of how bodies are made and move as they live, and specifically our understanding of how physical activity, health and wellbeing *may and may not* be mutually implicated through a range of bio-social processes.

Note

1 Sebire et al (2013) aim to examine constructs such as 'social functioning', 'acceptance', 'conduct' and 'peer' 'problems' and 'prosocial' behaviour. To give a flavour of the research tools: 'The prosocial scale consists of 5 items assessing positive social actions (e.g., I am kind to younger children). The peer problems scale consists of 5 items assessing the degree to which the child experiences difficulties with their peers (e.g., I am usually on my own. I generally play alone or keep to myself). The conduct problems scale consists of 5 items assessing anger, aggression and dishonesty (e.g., I get very angry and often lose my temper)' (Sebire et al, 2013, p2).
2 These findings start to point towards the sample's limited capacity to speak to a general population – of the 1630 children invited to participate, just over 500 chose to do so, potentially a sample of children from families in which physical activity is considered important and in which the children are considered to have sporting ability.
3 A similar pattern is evident for a number of the authors' findings, with inconsistency between claims made in the main text of Holder et al (2009) and their Table 1 of results, which presents data showing associations between hours of participation in physical activity and some but not all measures of happiness, esteem and satisfaction.
4 Winter samples cannot be easily compared to summer samples, and there is evidence of seasonal variability in young people's recreational amenity use and physical activity.

References

Allan, J. (2009) *Rethinking Inclusion: the philosophers of difference in practice.* Dordrecht: Springer.

Belsky, J., Steinberg, L. and Draper, P. (1991) Childhood Experience, Interpersonal Development and Reproductive Strategy: An Evolutionary Theory of Socialization, *Childhood Development*, 62(4), 647–670, in Roberts, C. (2014) Evolutionary psychology, feminism, and early sexual development, *Feminist Theory*, 14(3), 295–304.

Biddle, S. J. H. and Mutrie, N. (2007) Chapter 9: The relationship between physical activity and anxiety and depression: Can physical activity beat the blues and help with your nerves. In *Psychology of Physical Activity*. 2nd ed. London: Routledge, pp99–242. In Parfitt, G., Pavey, T. and Rowlands, A. V. (2009) Children's physical activity and psychological health: The relevance of intensity, *Acta Paediatrica*, 98, 1038–1043.

Blaise, M. (2013) Charting new territories: Reassembling childhood sexuality in the early years classroom, *Gender and Education*, 27(5), 801–817.

Bouchard, C., Blair, S. N., Church, T. S., Earnest, C. P., Hagberg, J. M. et al (2012) Adverse Metabolic Response to Regular Exercise: Is It a Rare or Common Occurrence?, *PLoS ONE* 7(5), e37887.

Burrows, L. and Wright, J. (2007). Prescribing practices: Shaping healthy children in schools, *International Journal of Children's Rights*, 15, 1–16.

Cabinet Office (2010). PM Speech on Wellbeing. Retrieved 18 February 2015 from https://www.gov.uk/government/speeches/pm-speech-on-wellbeing.

Clark, S. and Paechter, C. (2007) 'Why can't girls play football?': Gender dynamics in the playground, *Sport, Education and Society*, 12(3), 261–276.

Butler, J. (1993) *Bodies that Matter: On the discursive limits of 'sex'*. New York: Routledge.

Butler, J. (1997) *Excitable Speech: A politics of the performative*. London: Routledge.

DoH (Department of Health) (2011) *Physical activity guidelines for children and young people aged 5–18: factsheet 3*, web-resource downloaded 18 February 2015 from http://www.nhs.uk/Livewell/fitness/Documents/children-and-young-people-5-18-years.pdf.

De Pian, L., Evans, J. and Rich, E. (2014). Mediating biopower: Health education, social class and subjectivity. In K. Fitzpatrick and R. Tinning (Eds.), *Health Education: Critical perspectives* (pp129–141). London: Routledge.

Dishman, R. K., Renner, K. J., Youngstedt, S. D., Reigle, T. G., Bunnell, B. N., Burke, K. A. et al (1997) Activity wheel running reduces escape latency and alters brain monamine levels after footshock, *Brain Research Bulletin*, 42, 399–406. In Parfitt, G., Pavey, T. and Rowlands, A. V. (2009). Children's physical activity and psychological health: The relevance of intensity, *Acta Paediatrica*, 98, 1038–1043.

Dishman, R. K., Renner, K. J., White-Welkley, J. E., Burke, K. A. and Bunnell, B. N. (2000) Treadmill exercise training augments brain norepinephrine response to familiar novel stress, *Brain Research Bulletin*, 52, 337–342. In Parfitt, G., Pavey, T. and Rowlands, A. V. (2009) Children's physical activity and psychological health: The relevance of intensity, *Acta Paediatrica*, 98, 1038–1043.

Evans, J., De Pian, L., Rich, E. and Davies, B. (2011) Health Imperatives, Policy and the Corporeal Device: Schools, subjectivity and children's health, *Policy Futures in Education*, 9(3), 328–340.

Evans, J. (2014) Neoliberalism and the future for a socio-educative physical education. *Physical Education and Sports Pedagogy*, 19(5), 545–558.

Fedewa, A. L. and Ahn, S. (2011) The effects of physical activity and physical fitness on children's achievement and cognitive outcomes, *Research Quarterly for Exercise and Sport*, 82(3), 521–534.

Foucault, M. (1990) *The Care of the Self: The History of Sexuality, volume three.* London: Penguin.

Foucault, M. (1991) *Discipline and Punish: The birth of the prison.* London: Penguin.

Fraser, S. M., Maher, J. and Wright, J. (2010) Between bodies and collectivities: Articulating the action of emotion in obesity epidemic discourse, *Social Theory and Health*, 8(2), 192–209.

Frost, S. (2014) Re-considering the turn to biology on feminist theory, *Feminist Theory*, 15(3), 307–326.

Gorely, T., Marshall, S. J., Biddle, S. J. H. (2007) Patterns of sedentary behaviour and physical activity among adolescents in the United Kingdom: Project STIL, *Journal of Behaviour Medicine*, 30, 521–531.

Harwood, V. and Allan, J. (2014) *Psychopathology at School: Theorising mental disorders in education.* London: Routledge.

Harwood, V. (2012) Neither good nor useful: Looking ad vivum in children's assessments of fat and healthy bodies, *Discourse*, 33(5), 693–711.

Harwood, V. (2009) Theorising Biopedagogies. In V. Wright and V. Harwood (Eds.), *Biopolitics and the 'Obesity Epidemic': Governing Bodies* (pp15–30). London: Routledge.

Hickey-Moody, A. (2009) *Unimaginable Bodies: Intellectual disablity, performance and becomings.* Rotterdam: Sense.

Holder, M. D., Coleman, B. and Sehn, Z. L. (2009) The Contribution of Active and Passive Leisure to Children's Well-being, *Journal of Health Psychology*, 14, 378–386.

International Food Policy Research Institute (2014) *Global Nutrition Report 2014: Actions and Accountability to Accelerate the World's Progress on Nutrition.* Washington, DC: International Food Policy Research Institute. Downloaded 18 February 2015 from http://www.ifpri.org/sites/default/files/publications/gnr14.pdf.

Leahy, D. (2009) Disgusting Pedagogies. In V. Wright and V. Harwood (Eds.), *Biopolitics and the 'Obesity Epidemic': Governing Bodies* (pp172–182). London: Routledge.

Mastana, S. S., Kumar, A. and Lindley, M. R. (2013) Influence of glutathione S-transferase polymorphisms (GSTT1, GSTM1, GSTP1) on type 2 diabetes mellitus (T2D) risk in an endogenous population from North India, *Molecular Biology Reports*, 40, 7103–7110.

McGimpsey, I. (in review) Post-neoliberalism and social investment: Diagnosing a new phasing of education policy making, *Journal of Education Policy.*

Parfitt, G., Pavey, T. and Rowlands, A. V. (2009) Children's physical activity and psychological health: the relevance of intensity, *Acta Paediatrica*, 98, 1038–1043.

PHE (Public Health England) (2013) *How Healthy Behaviour Supports Children's Wellbeing.* London: Public Health England. Downloaded 18 February 2015 from https://www.gov.uk/government/uploads/system/uploads/attachment_data/file/232978/Smart_Restart_280813_web.pdf.

Rich, E. and Evans, J. (2013) Changing times, future bodies? The significance of health in young women's imagined futures, *Pedagogy, Culture, and Society*, 21(1), 5–22.

Rich, E., Evans, J. and De Pian, L. (2011) Children's bodies, surveillance and the obesity crisis. In E. Rich, L. F. Monaghan and L. Aphramore (Eds.), *Debating Obesity: Critical Perspectives* (pp139–163). Basingstoke: Palgrave Macmillan.

Roberts, C. (2014) Evolutionary psychology, feminism, and early sexual development, *Feminist Theory*, 14(3), 295–304.

Rose, N. (2000) Government and Control, *British Journal of Criminology*, 40, 321–339.

Rose, N. (2013) The Human Sciences in a Biological Age, *Theory, Culture and Society*, 30(3), 3–34.

Saltmarsh, S. and Youdell, D. (2004). 'Special Sport' for misfits and losers: educational triage and the constitution of schooled subjectivities, *International Journal of Inclusive Education*, 8(4), 353–371.

Sebire, S. J., Jago, R., Fox, K. R., Page, A. S., Brockman, R. and Thompson, J. L. (2013) Associates between children's social functioning and physical activity are not mediated by social acceptance: a cross-sectional study, *International Journal of Behavioural Nutrition and Physical Activity*, 8, 106.

Sport and Recreation Alliance (2012) *Game of Life: How sport and recreation can help make us healthier, happier and richer*. Sport and Recreation Alliance. Downloaded 18 February 2015 from http://www.sportandrecreation.org.uk/sites/sportandrecreation.org.uk/files/web/Game_of_Life/3310_SRA_literary%20review_v9%20WITH%20HYPERLINK.pdf.

World Health Organisation (2013) *Guidelines on Maternal, Newborn, Child and Adolescent Health approved by the WHO Guideline Review Committee: Recommendations on child health* (31 pages). Geneva: World Health Organisation. Downloaded 18 February 2015 from http://www.who.int/maternal_child_adolescent/documents/guidelines-recommendations-child-health.pdf?ua=1.

Wright, J. and Halse, C. (2014) The healthy child citizen: Biopedagogies and web-based health promotion, *British Journal of Sociology of Education*, 35(6), 837–855.

Youdell, D. (2006) *Impossible Bodies, Impossible Selves: Exclusions and Student Subjectivities*. Dordrecht: Springer.

Youdell, D. (2011) *School Trouble: identity, power and politics in education*. London: Routledge.

3 Learning about sexuality 'between' home and school

A new materialist reading

Louisa Allen

Introduction

This chapter is concerned with understanding how young people live religion, culture and sexuality between home and school. Specifically, I seek to understand how Chana, a 16-year-old Muslim woman makes sense of meanings about sexuality gleaned from her African family and sexuality education in her New Zealand state secondary school. The chapter aims to rethink dominant framings of this experience, in which youth from religious and cultural minorities are portrayed as caught between conflicting sexual ideologies from home and school. In these depictions youth are conceptualized as needing to navigate these diverse environments while gravitating towards the teachings of one. Instead of re-inscribing this scene, this discussion attempts to shift its terms of reference by understanding it in an ontologically different way. To do this, I employ a methodological strategy Lenz Taguchi (2010) characterizes as 'exorbitant deconstruction'. This process involves a 'turning, bending and twisting' of a conventional analysis, 'to try and displace the meanings of it; in order to identify....what other analysis might be possible' (Lenz Taguchi, 2010, p41). The purpose, is to imagine what *newness* might be incited by such a process in terms of conceptualising the intersections of religion, culture, sexuality and schooling for young people (Lenz Taguchi, 2012).

This reworking emerges from a desire to escape the binaries a more common interpretive approach to this issue might invoke, where home and school are set in opposition. The existing literature characterizes learning about sexuality in mainstream schools as predominantly problematic for Muslim students (Smerecnik et al, 2010). Writing of Muslim adolescents' perceptions of sex education in Canada, Zain Al-Dien (2010) describes three aspects Muslim families might oppose. 'Firstly, some sex education material offends the Islamic principle of decency and modesty. Secondly, sex education tends to present certain behaviours as acceptable which Muslims consider sinful. Thirdly, sex education may be perceived as undermining the Islamic concept of family life' (p392). Within the secularized space of mainstream Western schooling, this perspective is typically constituted as 'conservative' and 'backward' leading to a perception these youth are less well informed about sexuality than the majority population (Hendrickx et al, 2002). A Westernized secular paradigm also casts Muslim families as holding 'restrictive' and 'traditional' views. 'Evidence' of these is often touted in relation to the roles of women and girls whose chastity holds family significance and value (Imtoual and Hussein, 2009). School-based sexuality education via adherence to secular 'logic' that is not invested in faith-based principles is, by contrast, constituted positively as 'liberal' and 'progressive' (Rasmussen, 2012). As Yip and Page (2013, p5) argue, such dichotomous depictions are highly problematic in that, 'By holding up religion as an intolerant space, dominant discourses position secular spaces as having an exclusive claim to progressive ethics'.

Generally within the existing literature, the values of sexuality education in western countries are presumed to conflict with Muslim teachings on sexuality. Subsequently, Muslim students are faced with the dilemma of which to follow (see Sanjakdar, 2014, as an exception). This situation characterizes them as 'caught' between opposing worlds of home and school which they must learn to navigate. Within this balancing act, families can play an important role in counteracting information from sexuality education that contravenes the moral values of home (Orgocka, 2004; Zain Al-Dien, 2010). In some accounts, families are attributed with strong powers of persuasion;

> Although African youth are constantly exposed to western values, their interpretations of these values are often based on their interactions with, and their relationships with their families, and family relationships are often characterised by experiences that are based on traditional culture (Airhihenbuwa cited in Hendrickx et al, 2002, p89).

In other accounts, schools are seen to irreparably contaminate Muslim students, challenging their existing views on sexuality to the point of their abandonment (for examples see Yip and Page, 2013). The school's mobilization of 'permissive' and 'individualized' discourses of sexuality are deemed responsible for this phenomenon. Greater attention to cultural and religious diversity of students in sexuality education is subsequently called for by some Muslim groups:

> [T]he permissive sexual ideology, which endorses many forms of non-procreative sexuality including masturbation, oral sex and homosexuality, is the driving force shaping the nature and scope of sex education today. The dominant influence of one sexual ideology can be both damaging and destructive to Muslim students and those young people who do not identify with it. Consequently, school-based-sex education in Canada and Western countries need to recognize and respect the reality, diversity and cultural specificity of student experiences in the classroom, including the needs of appropriate sex education for Muslim students (Zain al-Dien, 2010, p398).

Opposition and conflict frame existing understandings of this issue which manifests as a contest in which ultimately home or school must prevail, or where students must live duplicitously. This approach establishes restrictive views of both ethnic minority youth and their families, as well as possibilities for sexuality education to engage with cultural and religious diversity in secular schools.

This chapter seeks to understand what *more can we think* (Blaise, 2013) about this scene in ways that endeavour to escape binaries which constitute (an)other which is always denigrated. This 'other' is either, the home and its strict cultural and religious values as backward, or school as irreverent of religious perspectives and morally lax. To undertake this work, I draw on ideas from 'new'[1] feminist materialist thought, specifically Barad's (2007, 2003, 1999) concept of intra-activity (explained below) for its capacity to recast the ontological foundations of this debate. The effect of this theoretical interference is to reframe this issue not as a debate about whether culture and religion from home trump the secular values of schooling. Rather, via a new materialist reading, this is an exploration of how students' negotiation of sexuality *becomes* via culture/religion/sexuality/family/school *intra*-relations. Within a new materialist account this is no longer recognisable as a contest, but instead an enfolding of understandings of how students' negotiation of sexual meanings *come into being*.

Given the conceptual density of these ideas, the next section outlines the key theoretical concepts underpinning this discussion. This is followed by a brief account of details of the overarching project orienting the reader to fieldwork observations and narrative excerpts offered. To illuminate how new materialist thought reconfigures this issue, first a representational (interpretive) reading of these 'data' occurs. Next, a new materialist understanding is invoked to imagine a new ontological scene and its possibilities for understanding students' negotiation of 'conflicting' sexual ideologies at home and school.

New materialist thought

To recast the ontological foundations of the empirical scene in which Chana is found, it is helpful first to outline a more conventional theoretical approach to its ontology. Falling within the 'linguistic turn', one such approach is interpretivism (MacLure, 2013). Within an interpretivist framework the scene before us is understood as accessible via linguistic systems which can represent it or (as in post-structuralism) discursively produce it. Chana is understood as a subject who acts in a material world which she is part of, but ontologically a distinct entity within. It is the researcher's separation as a distinct ontological entity herself that enables her to stand back and interpret what Chana does and says using language and discourse. The ontology of this empirical scene is one that the researcher can represent via interpretations of Chana's words and home/school worlds, positing these as reflecting a reality that materially exists (or within post-structuralism is discursively constituted).

For researchers like Jackson and Mazzei (2012) there are several problems with this linguistic-reliant approach. The first is the assumption that a researcher can 'know' what Chana was attempting to convey by her words. That is, that the researcher's interpretation of what Chana said, was actually what Chana meant. As Jackson and Mazzei (2012, pviii) write:

> Interpretation thus falls into the representation trap of trying to figure out what the interviewee really means. It is a process of sense-making and positioning the subject of research as the source of meaning that enables the researcher to construct a coherent and interesting narrative, bound by themes and patterns understood to emerge from the data.

The ability to know or even correctly 'hear' those from cultural 'categories' (or other social groups) different to one's own has been an enduring concern within feminist theory (Ellsworth, 1989). Given that I do not share the same cultural or religious background as Chana my ability to 'hear' what she says, as she intends it, is limited. Secondly, there are several hierarchies apparent in this framing of the research scene. As the person who interprets its meaning the researcher sits higher in the empirical hierarchy than the research subject. Even if the researcher was to take a reflective and critical approach to the situatedness of their knowledge, 'the researcher nevertheless produces his/her self-reflexive interpretations (ontologically speaking) as separate from the data' and the materiality of the research context (Lenz Taguchi, 2012, p269). Further, it is human actors who preside over data and human participants who are perceived to hold a prominent and active position in the material world. The ontological foundations of this empirical scene establish a number of hierarchical dyads where one side is necessarily diminished; researcher/participant, researcher/data, human actors/material world. While the side perceived most agentic can vacillate, one is thought to exert more power in any one moment and each side is understood as ontologically separate from the other. How then might we move beyond these regulatory dualisms that require the relegation of one side in order to make sense of the other, in a way that enables a different way of thinking Chana and the home/school relation?

The work of new materialist feminisms offers an alternative way of conceiving this empirical scene. While new materialisms have many proliferations (Alaimo, 2011), they are 'united in ... [their] ... insistence on the significance of materiality in social and cultural practices' (Hird, 2009). In a move often critical of the 'linguistic turn', this means taking matter seriously by recognising it as having its own intensities and force (Bennett, 2010). As MacLure (2013) writes, 'In place of the hierarchy of representation, therefore materialist ontologies prefer a 'flattened' logic (Hultman and Lenz Taguchi, 2010) where 'discourse and matter are mutually implicated in the unfolding emergence of the world' (p659). In order to explain these ideas and indicate their relevance for thinking through the empirical scene involving Chana, I utilize the concept of intra-activity from feminist philosopher and physicist Karen Barad (2007).

The concept of intra-activity derives from quantum physics and establishes an ontological understanding whereby the conventional divide between the material/discursive (or nature/culture) is dissolved. In the current research scene, material elements include the geographical and architectural features of home and school, the physical bodies of Chana, other students and myself as researcher. Discursive features refer to the discourses, social, cultural and language-based meanings which represent and constitute how all of these material features are understood. In the process of intra-activity these discursive and material features are no longer separate entities but *come into being via their relation*. Barad (2007, p152) explains the process of intra-activity this way:

> Discursive practices and material phenomena do not stand in a relationship of externality to each other; rather, *the material and the discursive are mutually implicated in the dynamics of intra-activity*. The relationship between the material and the discursive is one of mutual entailment. Neither discursive practices nor material phenomena are ontologically or epistemologically prior. Neither can be explained in terms of the other. Neither is reducible to the other. Neither has privileged status in determining the other. Neither is articulated or articulable in the absence of the other; matter and meaning are mutually articulated.

Intra-activity differs from the more familiar concept of inter-activity as the latter, 'refers to a relationship between bodies that are taken to be separate entities, including an interpersonal relationship between two humans' (Lenz Taguchi, 2012, p271). Within an inter-active paradigm the empirical scene would be understood as one in which Chana and myself (as humans bestowed with agency) exist ontologically separately from the material worlds of home and school which provide the backdrop to our actions.

Intra-activity invokes an ontological reconfiguration of this scene in which hierarchies between researcher/research subject, researcher/data, human actors/material world are 'flattened' (Hultman and Lenz Taguchi, 2010). Instead, the research scene becomes an (unending) entanglement of discourse and material elements that include sexuality, home, school, Chana, researcher. None of these elements is ontologically prior to the other, but all are instead produced intra-actively in the *becoming* of sexuality, religion and culture as lived by Chana at school/home. Within this rendition, there is no separation *between* home *and* school (or myself and Chana) because these spaces and materialities are not ontologically separate. Rather, what home and school are, comes into being in the moment of their *intra*-relation. To speak of home and school as separate geographical/discursive entities between which Chana is caught, becomes an ontological impossibility. This is because, as Barad (2007) outlines above 'Neither has privileged status in determining the other. Neither is articulated or articulable in the absence of the other'; instead, they are mutually articulated in the moment of their *intra*-relation. Before exploring how these theoretical ideas might open up new ways of thinking the home versus school debate, some brief methodological details are offered to orient the reader to Chana's story.

Methodology

The context for this discussion comprises fieldwork observations and interview narratives from a project concerned with understanding the sexual cultures of schooling (see Allen, 2009). This research was concerned with the way in which meanings about sexuality are produced unofficially in schooling spaces where formal learning is not perceived to occur (e.g., gym locker rooms, sports fields, desk top graffiti, peer groups). It was a small-scale exploratory study involving two schools and 22 students in the last two years of secondary education (aged 16 to 17). In New Zealand, 'decile rankings' indicate the extent to which a school draws its students from low socio-economic communities, with decile 1 schools containing the highest proportion of these students and decile 10 the lowest (verbatim Ministry of Education, 2004). Chana came from Kowhai College, allocated a low decile rating (i.e. 2–3) by the Ministry of Education. In total, 12 participants self-identified as European, six Maori, two Pasifika and two were from African countries. All participants were volunteers and the research was granted ethics approval from the University of Auckland Human Subjects Ethics Committee (see Allen, 2009). Although the project employed visual research methods, including photo-diaries, only photo-elicitation interviews and field work observations are included here. As empirical data is not employed in a conventional way for this discussion, the study's methodological details are delineated elsewhere (see Allen, 2011).

Concentrating on one participant exclusively is a deliberate ploy for working with data in a non-normative way. In accordance with new materialist thought, this approach exercises a rejection of what MacLure (2013, p658) names above as 'the hierarchical logic of representation'. Fieldwork observations and interview narratives are not understood as representing something about how Chana negotiates sexual meanings between home and school. Instead, this discussion is offered as *a way into thinking* about understanding this issue in an ontologically different manner. Chana's narratives do not provide evidence of rethinking the ontology of this problem; rather, her story provides *a point of entry* for accessing this conceptual shift. The objective is not to offer Chana as exemplary of meanings, themes or categories enabling an understanding of negotiation of sexuality between home and school. In the flattened logic (Hultman and Lenz Taguchi, 2010) of new feminist materialisms instead, 'discourse and matter are mutually implicated in the unfolding emergence of the world' (pp659–660). As explored next, this unfolding emergence occurs in relation to how we conceptualize Chana's negotiation of sexual meanings between home and school. As this is not an investigation in the conventional empirical sense that seeks to provide evidence, the number of participants included is extraneous.

Chana in the empirical scene

There were several moments in my interactions with Chana where competing values of home and school appeared to emerge. First, Chana's physical presence embodied what is characterized as 'conflicting' values between home and school. She stood out amongst a classroom of Maori and Pacific Island faces because she was the only one wearing the hijab and because she bore African features. Chana's hijab referenced a familial set of Muslim values she carried to school. These stood in contrast to her school's secular foundations and a classroom of peers for whom Muslim immigrants from Africa were a relatively recent phenomenon. Chana explained how being a new arrival to Aotearoa-New Zealand commonly meant facing misconceptions of her cultural and religious beliefs.

> Louisa: What faith would you say you are?
> Chana: Islam. Muslim.
> Louisa: Family are strongly Muslim as well?
> Chana: Yeah. Religious background, I would say. Not terrorist background. You see the stereotypical, Muslim equals terrorist. There's a huge difference. Because usually you know how you've got that conflict in the Middle East, people usually interpret that … as what people see you are. But it's like, I was having this huge argument with these guys. …
> Louisa: It's ignorant, isn't it?
> Chana: It's annoying, but you can't really blame them in a way. Stereotypes are always stereotypes.

Here Chana presents herself and her family as committed Muslims carefully dissociating this identity from its conflation with 'terrorism' in Western perception. This presentation of self as a Muslim different from stereotypical perceptions of this identity constitutes another tension she faces between home and school.

Other instances of a home/school divide surfaced when interviewing Chana about her experiences of learning about sexuality.

> Louisa: Where would you get most of your information about sexuality from?
> Chana: People you hang out with outside of school. They influence you more because you are out there more often and because you're only here [at school] like six hours a day.
> Louisa: What sort of stuff do you learn from outside of school?
> Chana: I'm Muslim so it's not accepted to be lesbian or gay … they don't like lesbians and gays in Muslim countries.
>   [Later in the discussion.]
> Louisa: What are the main things that you've learned about sexuality from school?

> Chana: You can be straight, bi or gay and you can be happy. Nothing else. I haven't learned anything from sexuality education at school.

Chana articulates a disparity here between what she learns from home about being gay and lesbian and what school teaches about sexual diversity. What then does Chana do with these seemingly diametrically opposed sets of meanings?

A further interview moment offers insight into her negotiation of these conflicting ideas. Chana explained that at school she hung out with a group where there was an 'out' lesbian couple who were her friends. These young women had been subject to ongoing verbal and physical abuse for being lesbian and this had culminated in a confrontation where Chana was punched. Explaining how she tried to intervene during this fight Chana says, 'They [the perpetrator] was like just swearing and I went to break up like try to push my mate out of the way and she [the perpetrator] took a swing at me and got me.' Seizing on what I presumed as a conflict between Chana's actions in defending her friends and the Muslim community's opposition to lesbianism I say:

> Louisa: So how does that work, hanging out with these guys at school and then being part of the Muslim community where it's not accepted?
> Chana: I have my own religious views but it doesn't mean I approve of people hitting other people. I'm not going to be like ooh you shouldn't be a lesbian, it's their personal thing. ...
> Louisa: So it's not a tension for you?
> Chana: I just don't care. I'm not going to change someone because that's what they are and I accept that, but I don't necessarily have to take on what they believe.

Having introduced these empirical moments where presumed conflict between home and school and Chana's management of these occurs, I now provide an interpretive reading against which to situate a new materialist approach. Undertaking these readings 'is not about uncovering the essence or truth of these data. This is an uncovering of *a* reality that already exists among the multiple realities being enacted in an event, but which has not been previously disclosed' (Lenz Taguchi, 2012, p274).

One interpretive account

An interpretive reading might understand Chana as skilfully negotiating discordant meanings about sexuality between family and school. One way of understanding her defence of her lesbian friends is that she instigates a conscious separation between her life at school and home. Elsewhere in her interview Chana divulges that outside school she doesn't 'normally hang out with people from school', reinforcing a sense of this divide. Subsequently, school offers a discrete space in which Chana can temporarily cast off specific elements of her Muslim being (e.g., the unacceptability of lesbianism) and partake in relationships normally shunned at home. Page and Yip (2012) document a version of this position in their research around experiences of schooling with young adults of diverse religious faiths in the UK. In their study, some young people 'endorsed the sexualised culture of school and used it as a site of experimentation, which contrasted sharply with the religious and home context, engaging in activities that were expressly disallowed, such as drinking, smoking and sexual activity' (Page and Yip, 2012, p411). In this interpretation, Chana can be seen to lead two lives, in which her actions at school diverge from those at home. This duplicity may be constituted as necessary for her survival in a contemporary world of conflicting sexual ideologies.

Another way of analysing Chana's experiences is to reconcile her actions as commensurate with Islamic tenets. Such an interpretation can be drawn from her words, 'I have my own religious views but it doesn't mean I approve of people hitting other people.' As Halstead (2005) writes, 'Contemporary Muslim writers on sex and sex education take pains to point out that the bullying or persecution of homosexuals is, like all bullying, unacceptable' (p40). In fact, it is patronizing to assume, 'tolerance, understanding, and respect for human dignity and personal integrity are exclusively liberal virtues, and that it is surprising when they are shown by Muslims' (Halstead, 2005, p40). Here Halstead carves a distinction between faith-based expressions of disproval over a particular identity or activity and tolerance for these, rendering disproval and tolerance compatible. Chana may convey similar sentiment when she says, 'I'm not going to change someone because that's what they are and I accept that, but I don't necessarily have to take on what they believe.' In this reading, the strength of Chana's faith triumphs against school values. Chana keeps her faith via a disproval of lesbianism, while exhibiting tolerance in defending her friends' humanity. In the previous interpretation above, the school wins Chana's allegiance via her violation of Muslim principles of home, even if this violation is school-bound. Both readings frame this issue dualistically, representing home and school as holding opposing views where one must prevail and the winner is determined by Chana's actions (agency).

(Not a) conclusion: A new materialist account

Approaching these data via a new materialist account necessitates a shift from understanding Chana's words as 'interpersonal discursive subject positionings' (Lenz Taguchi, 2012, p277). Chana is therefore not seen as discursively positioned within the divergent sexual discourses of home and school which she must navigate. In a 'flattening' (Hultman and Lenz Taguchi, 2010) of this research scene, Chana is no longer its central actor capable of exercising individual agency as to which path (home or school) she will follow. Neither are home or school distinct and divided dominant players, exerting power over Chana through discursive and material means. Instead, Chana, home, school and disparate discourses of religion, culture and sexuality operate on the same ontological plain, so that none claim foundational status (Taylor and Ivinson, 2013). Boundaries of school, home, Chana and diverse discourses of religion and sexuality are now understood as porous each enfolding into the other making it impossible to see where they begin and end, rendering their separateness unintelligible.

For the research scene this means that what 'has been considered passive and minor is now perceived as active and forceful in its intra-activities with other bodies' (Lenz Taguchi, 2012, p278). For example, Chana's hijab is no longer viewed as a symbol which she mobilizes as a marker of her faith or which others recognise as such. As a material object, the hijab plays a forceful role (Bennett, 2010) *in the becoming* of Chana's religious and cultural identity. The materiality of the hijab *intra*-acts with Chana's physicality, spatial arrangements of home and school and attendant discourses of religion, culture and sexuality. These phenomena do not exist as separate entities, ontologically distinct from each other. Rather, their boundaries are porous invoking an endless enfolding of material-non-material entanglements.

Negotiating differing ideas about sexuality from home and school are no longer Chana's preserve because within a new materialist understanding human status does not confer agency. It is not that Chana chooses how she will manage the home/school divide because as Barad (2007) conceptualizes it, agency is produced *intra*-relation. In this empirical scene, agency is a material-discursive intra-activity, involving the force of various performative agents (Lenz Taguchi, 2012). Power is not held by the family at home, or the school – instead, agency is produced via their *intra*-relation, so these elements *become* differently, contingent upon the phenomena relating. The idea Chana is caught between home and school is rendered just one more intra-active enfolding in the becoming of this research.

This reading exorbitantly de-constructs (Lenz Taguchi, 2010) a conventional interpretive account of the empirical scene. In so doing, it seeks to displace dominant discourses that might render Chana 'caught between home and school'. It attempts this by reorienting the ontological foundations of an interpretive reading by suggesting there is no home and school, or, even Chana, as separate entities exercising attendant powers. This thinking attempts to unravel the idea that meanings from home and school are necessarily oppositional and therefore something Chana must reconcile/negotiate. Viewing the relationship of these elements intra-actively relies on different ontological presumptions so that there is nothing to reconcile (in the conventional interpretive sense). The point of undertaking such exorbitant deconstruction is to open up spaces for 'newness' to be generated. Within a new materialist framing however this 'newness' is not nameable because that would once again cast the researcher back into the ontological strictures of representational thought – as the 'birds-eye' figure who sees, and then explains what all this now means. As Lenz Taguchi (2012) writes, 'More than offering just another point of view, *or* the point(s) of view of those with epistemic privilege, material feminist readings aspire to invoke other possible material realities that can have political and material consequences' (p278). What then are the political and material consequences of displacing the ontological foundations of home and school as separate and conflicting entities in a contest for the ideological allegiance of students like Chana? What *becomes* of this issue when the research scene is flattened and conceptualized as intra-active material-non-material entanglements?

Note

1   That these ideas from new materialist thought are 'new' is contested. As Taylor and Ivinson (2013, p 666) note, Hoskins and Jones (2013) argue perceptions of the world as an entangled continuity of the human–natural have always been part of traditional Maori thought in Aotearoa-New Zealand.

References

Alaimo, S. (2011) New materialisms, old humanisms, or, following the submersible, *NORA Nordic Journal of Feminist and Gender Research*, 19(4), 280–284.

Allen, L. (2009) 'Snapped': Researching the Sexual Culture of Schools Using Visual Methods, *International Journal of Qualitative Studies in Education*, 22(5), 549–561.

Allen, L. (2011) 'Picture this': Using photo-methods in research on sexualities and schooling, *Qualitative Research*, 5(11), 487–504.

Barad, K. (1999) Agential realism: Feminist interventions in understanding scientific practices, in: M. Biagioli (Ed.) *The science studies reader*. New York: Routledge, pp1–11.

Barad, K. (2003) Posthumanist performativity: Toward an understanding of how matter comes to matter, *Signs: Journal of Women in Culture and Society*, 28(3), 801–831.

Barad, K. (2007) *Meeting the universe halfway: Quantum physics and the entanglement of matter and meaning*. Durham, NC: Duke University Press.

Bennett, J. (2010) *Vibrant matter: A political ecology of things*. Durham, NC: Duke University Press.

Blaise, M. (2013) Activating Micropolitical Practices in the Early Years: (Re)assembling Bodies and Participant Observations. In R. Coleman and J. Ringrose (Eds.), *Deleuze and Research Methodologies* (pp184–200). Edinburgh: Edinburgh University Press.

Ellsworth, E. (1989) Why doesn't this feel empowering? Working through the repressive myths of critical pedagogy, *Harvard Educational Review*, 59(3), 297–325.

Halstead, M. (2005) Islam, homophobia and education: A reply to Michael Merry, *Journal of Moral Education*, 34(1), 37–42.

Hendrickx, K., Van Lodewijckx, E., Royen, P. and Denekens, J. (2002) Sexual behaviour of second generation Moroccan immigrants balancing between traditional attitudes and safe sex, *Patient Education and Counseling*, 47, 89–94.

Hird, M. (2009) Feminist engagements with matter, *Feminist Studies*, 35, 329–346.

Hoskins, T. and Jones, A. (2013) Object Lessons: 'Vital Materiality', methodology and indigenous studies in education, Te Puna Wānanga Research Seminar 2013, Thursday, 31 October. Faculty of Education, University of Auckland. Epsom Campus.

Hultman, K. and Lenz Taguchi, H. (2010) Challenging anthropocentric analysis of visual data: A relational materialist methodological approach to educational research, *International Journal of Qualitative Studies in Education*, 23(5), 525–542.

Imtoual, A. and Hussein, S. (2009) Challenging the myth of the happy celibate: Muslim women negotiating contemporary relationships, *Contemporary Islam*, 3, 25–39.

Jackson, A. and Mazzei, L. (2012) *Thinking with theory in qualitative research: Viewing data across multiple perspectives.* Abingdon, Oxon: Routledge.

Lenz Taguchi, H. (2012) A diffractive and Deleuzian approach to analysing interview data, *Feminist Theory*, 13(3), 265–281.

Lenz Taguchi, H. (2010) Doing collaborative deconstruction as an 'exhorbitant' strategy in qualitative research, *Reconceptualizing Educational Research Methodology*, 1 (1), 41–53.

MacLure, M. (2013) Researching without representation? Language and materiality in post-qualitative methodology, *International Journal of Qualitative Studies in Education*, 26(6), 658–667.

Ministry of Education (2004) *Ministry of education.* Available online at http://www.minedu.govt.nz/print_doc.cfm (accessed 2 April 2004).

Orgocka, A. (2004) Perceptions of communication and education about sexuality among Muslim immigrant girls in the US, *Sex Education*, 4(3), 255–271.

Page, S. and Yip, A. (2012) Religious young adults recounting the past: Narrating sexual and religious cultures in school, *Journal of Beliefs and Values*, 33(3), 405–415.

Rasmussen, M. (2012) Pleasure/Desire, sexularism and sexuality education, *Sex Education*, 12(4), 469–481.

Sanjakdar, F. (2014) Sacred pleasure: Exploring dimensions of sexual pleasure and desire from an Islamic perspective, in: L. Allen, M. Rasmussen and K. Quinlivan (Eds) *The politics of pleasure in sexuality education: Pleasure bound.* New York: Routledge, pp95–114.

Smerecnik, C., Schaalma, H., Gerjo, K., Meijer, S. and Poleman, J. (2010) An exploratory study of Muslim adolescents' views on sexuality: Implications for sex education and prevention, *BMC Public Health*, 10(533), 1–10.

Taylor, C. and Ivinson, G. (2013) Material feminisms: New directions for education, *Gender and Education*, 25(6), 665–670.

Yip, A. and Page, S. (2013) *Religious and sexual identities: A multi-faith exploration of young adults.* Surrey, UK: Ashgate.

Zain Al-Dien, M. (2010) Perceptions of sex education among Muslim adolescents in Canada, *Journal of Muslim Minority Affairs*, 30(3), 391–407.

4 Challenging the myth that 'the parents don't care'

Family teachings about education for 'educationally disengaged' young people

Samantha McMahon, Anna Hickey-Moody and Valerie Harwood

Introduction

This chapter focuses on families as sites of pedagogical work. We take up a focus on the pedagogical work of families in relation to formal education and educational exclusion. When describing families' pedagogical work in relation to formal education, we pay particular attention to their teachings about the school and university. Family pedagogies that impact upon educational participation and exclusion are important to consider in parallel with this book's focus on family pedagogies in relation to health. This is because there is a close relationship between levels of educational attainment and health; the more years of formal education that a person experiences, the better their health outcomes (ABS, 2013; Cutler and Lleras-Muney, 2010; Egerter et al, 2006). Our aim is to demonstrate that family pedagogies of formal education are key to practices of educational inclusion and exclusion and as such they are important to understand, and to reconsider in educational theory. It is simply not the case that all young people who are disengaged from education (either not attending at all or attending sporadically) have a background lacking in family pedagogies connected with education.

Young people who are educationally disengaged or at the margins of formal education are rarely consulted in educational literature and policy-making (Bland, 2012; Duffy and Elwood, 2013; Harwood and Allan, 2014; Morgan et al, 2008). It is not surprising, therefore, to find that while there is a rich literature on families' pedagogical work on young people's position in education (Brooks, 2003; Lucey et al, 2006), less literature is available on pedagogical work of families of young people not engaged in education (Stein, 2006). This lack of attention is gradually being redressed. Yet there are assumptions we encounter anecdotally in our experience with teacher education students (in the UK and Australia), that these parents 'don't care' or they set 'bad examples'. Such anecdotes echo literature that describes teachers' deficit understandings of socioeconomically disadvantaged and 'disengaged' children and young people (Comber and Kamler, 2004; D'Addio, 2007; Machin, 1999).

This chapter seeks to contribute an understanding of the pedagogical work of families of young people who are currently disengaged from or at the margins of formal education. The young people in our study are, hereafter, summarily described as 'disengaged' from education because they all experienced precarious relationships with mandatory schooling, further and higher education. The school-aged participants were not attending school or attending sporadically, they were excluded from schools, or they were pursuing alternative education programmes. Those participants who were legally old enough not to attend school were also not participating in further or higher education. Whilst we are not claiming that post-school pursuits other than further or higher education lack value, we can state that participants were not involved in post-school formal education options and so may still be described as not educationally engaged.

We discuss how these educationally disengaged participants' family pedagogies relating to education are not homogenously negative. We will argue that their pedagogical work is varied, complex and often positive. Following a brief description of the study, the chapter is structured into three sections that reflect the findings from our data: families as sites of pedagogy and learning about 'education'; families' *implicit* teaching about education; and lastly, families' *explicit* teaching about education. Theoretically, we use Cambourne's (1995) Conditions of Learning to think through the family's explicit and implicit teachings.

The study

Our purpose in this study was to understand how university was imagined by educationally disengaged young people from disadvantaged communities.[1] The research project was funded by the Australian Research Council (DP110104704) and involved in-depth semi-structured interviews with two hundred and fifty young people in five Australian states (New South Wales – NSW; Victoria – VIC; Queensland – QLD; Tasmania – TAS; South Australia – SA), over the years 2012–2013.[2] All of the young people interviewed lived in socio-economically disadvantaged communities and experienced problematic relationships with education. The disadvantaged community settings included urban, suburban and regional communities. These communities were chosen because: they were identified as low socioeconomic status (ABS, 2013; Vinson, 2007); had high rates of school behavioural problems, school non-attendance and non-completion to year 12 and featured attendance and absenteeism intervention programs (DECS, 2010; NSWDET, 2009; Stehlik, 2006); and experienced disadvantage in terms of health, community safety, economic and education factors (Vinson, 2007). Here health is conceptualized in terms of seven indicators: 'low birth-weight, childhood injuries, immunisation, disability / sickness support, life expectancy, psychiatric patients: hospital / community, suicide' (Equity and Diversity, UWS, 2015, citing Vinson, 2007). Youth settings such as youth centres in these communities became the sites for the interviews. Participants

Table 4.1 Search words for coding family data (* indicates truncation)

Famil*	Father*	Pa	Sibling*
Mum	Brother*	Pop	Daughter*
Mother*	Sister*	Aunt*	Son*
Dad	Gran*	Uncle*	Parent*

were recruited via these youth centres, with youth professionals often joining the interviews.

Families' pedagogies regarding education and exclusion were discernible in our interview transcripts. In these transcripts the young people's feelings and stories of their families stood out to us, prompting us to conduct a closer analysis. Analysis of the transcripts was computer assisted using NVivo software. The word 'family' was one of the top fifty most frequent words in the NVivo dataset. This was surprising to us because the only direct question about families in our interview schedule was: 'tell me a bit about your family's education'. This question was designed to collect simple demographic information, not to generate detailed discussion about family. In order to capture and analyse this extensive 'family' data, we purposively searched our transcripts for terms that would indicate references to family (these terms are listed in Table 4.1).

Excerpts featuring these terms then underwent logico-inductive analysis (Kervin et al, 2006). The emergent themes featured discernible family pedagogies. These themes were then further analysed in terms of their relationship to an existing theory of pedagogy, Cambourne's (1995) Conditions of Learning.

Families as sites of pedagogy and learning about 'education'

When talking about family pedagogies, we are leaning on definitions of pedagogy as 'the art, occupation or practice of teaching' (Oxford University Press 2015) to conceptualize families as sites of 'teaching and learning' about education. Despite their own, troubled relationships with education, our dataset repeatedly showed how the participants valued learning about education from their families. For example:

> I: You've already mentioned TAFE – is that where you go after high school to get an education?
> J: Go to your parents. They know enough.
> I: They might teach you some stuff?
> J: They taught me a lot.
>
> (Janis, 16 years old, outer city NSW)

Here, Janis clearly identified his parents as connections to and providers of further education. Extended family, especially uncles and aunts, were also identified as valuable sources of education (e.g., group interview, 13-year-olds, outer city NSW). In this sense family is construed by the young people as a valued site of *explicit* learning about education.

The perceived importance of families' teaching and learning about 'education', was described by some of the young people who were already in parenting roles. Two examples of this strong belief in education are included below, examples that reveal an *implicit* approach to family education. Teah, a young woman who lives in a suburb that is statistically considered one of the most disadvantaged places in Australia,[3] states her firm belief in the importance of school selection because of the 'area' in which she lives:

> I don't want to encourage that unemployment that's in the area so I'm looking at the opportunity to send her [my daughter] to a private school so the people she's friends with have working parents that understand if you want to get somewhere you need to work hard ... all the feedback I'm getting from people that I explain it to is that the education starts at home.
>
> (Teah, 21 years old, outer-city SA)

Here Teah demonstrates not only her beliefs about the family and education, but also her awareness of the importance of social capital (Winkworth et al, 2010), namely the school and the friends and family with whom her daughter interacts.

Teah was not alone in holding strong views about education and the role of family. Perhaps the most poignant story of education and family shared with us during our interviews occurred with Krissie, an Indigenous young woman who had two very young children and was also involved in caring for her partner's 16-year-old younger brother. Krissie spelled out to one of the authors just how crucial family is, and as has been discussed with South Australian colleagues, Faye Blanch and Simone Tur,[4] the failure of schools to recognise and build on this valuable family network of support (Harwood et al, in press):

> K: Me and my partner – he's 17 in a couple of weeks – we've been looking after Jye, his little younger brother for the last three years because his mother moved away to Queensland in the outback, in the bush, where they didn't even have a house to live in. They were in caravans with no running electricity and Jye has difficulties when he goes into a classroom, with trying to settle in with students and teachers.
> I: How old is he?
> K: Jye's 16 now and we thought it would be best to have him down here with us where we could slowly get him back into schooling.
> I: So you're being a teacher?
> K: Yes. Just slowly getting there because Jye's had a lot of trouble since he was a young boy. Since primary school – since the age of eight – Jye's been in and out of programmes – not actually mainstream. Schools for kids that have troubles being in classrooms where they might be really

disruptive, get into trouble a lot or just didn't attend; he's been put into a lot of them and they've never worked out, sometimes because of other students – he doesn't get along – and he might get banned from there or he just might not attend.

Jye doesn't have a lot of confidence in himself; he thinks he can't read and write but he can. I've seen him – he can write fine on Facebook. That's when I say: 'You can read and write fine on Facebook; that means you can write and read a piece of paper.' It's the same words, it's just not on a computer screen and it doesn't have Facebook written in the corner – it's just on a piece of paper.

(Krissie, 18 years old, outer city SA)

Again, we have an interview with a young person who became disengaged with schooling, and for whom family and education has retained a significant level of importance. As Krissie explains in the interview excerpt below, she connects with Jye in her role as his Aunty:

I: You're pretty young to be such a big mentor
K: A lot of people put him down.
YW (youth worker): That's because a lot of … just as another idea – throwing it out there. The importance of extended family [in] Indigenous culture because you are just expected to take on …
I: Oh because you're Aunty? Is that why?
K: Yes.

(Krissie, 18 years old, outer-city SA)

Because so few of the participants in our study were parents or caregivers, these interview transcripts are unique because they discuss participants' family pedagogies from the parental perspective. Unlike the first two quotes which made reference to families as sites of explicit teaching and learning, the above two interviews demonstrate how families can 'teach' *implicitly.* For Krissie and Teah, this meant enacting a certain ethos and values of 'getting Jye slowly back into education' and that 'education starts at home'. This also meant creating opportunities for children and young people to learn from immersion in certain types of experiences and observations, as well as 'clever pedagogies' that made literacy connections between activity on Facebook and the concept of 'writing'.

Thinking through this data on 'family as teachers', we suggest a useful way to consider the pedagogical work that families do regarding education is to think explicitly about the young people as 'learners'. To this end, our analysis is, in part, framed by 'Conditions of Learning', a naturalistic learning theory developed by Brian Cambourne (1995).

Although now widely used in primary and secondary teacher education as a theory and method for constructivist classroom teaching and learning, Cambourne's (1995) Conditions of Learning were originally derived from longitudinal ethnographic work with families that focused on trying to understand how very young children successfully learned to talk. In this sense, it is a theory of learning that directly theorises learning and meaning making with and from family, family environments and family interactions.

From his studies of young children learning to talk at home, Cambourne (1995) found that there are eight interrelated conditions for successful learning:

1 immersion;
2 demonstration;
3 engagement;
4 expectations;
5 responsibility;
6 employment;
7 approximation; and
8 response.

A brief description of these conditions is available at Table 4.2. We contend that the conditions that relate most closely to the implicit and explicit teaching and learning about education described in the data are 'immersion', 'demonstration', 'engagement' and 'expectations'. While the purpose of this chapter is not to use a learning theory to explain how young people learn

Table 4.2 Cambourne's Conditions of Learning (a summary)

Immersion	*The state of being saturated by or enveloped in that which is to be learned.*
Demonstration	The ability to observe (see, hear, witness, experience, feel, study, explore) actions and artefacts.
Engagement	Immersion and demonstration are necessary conditions for learning to occur but they are not sufficient (they must be engaged with). Principals of engagement include: the learners belief that they are capable, that the learning is valuable, the learner is free from anxiety and that they admire, respect and trust the person giving the demonstrations.
Expectations	Messages that significant others communicate to learners. They are also subtle and powerful coercers of behaviour.
Responsibility	Learners are permitted to exercise choice regarding what they engage with and what they ignore.
Approximations	'Having a go' (i.e., attempts to emulate what is being demonstrated).
Employment	The opportunities for use and practice of the content being learned.
Response	The feedback or information that the learner receives from the world about their learning.

Source: this table is synthesised from Cambourne (1995) and Harris et al (2001).

about education from their parents, Conditions of Learning can be used to provide a shared language for explaining the pedagogical role of the family in these educationally disadvantaged young people's meaning making, especially around notions of school, education and university.

We have established that the young people involved in our research tended to value their families as educators and position themselves as learners from their families, we have also gestured towards a theoretical lens that renders this as reasonable and offers a language for discussing it. *So, what are families teaching about education to these young people who experience difficult relationships with schooling, and to what effect?* The rest of the chapter will describe the explicit and implicit teaching and learning about education discernible in the young people's talk.

Families' implicit teaching about education

To understand the implicit teaching families do (or don't do), we will first consider Cambourne's condition of *immersion*. We do this by illustrating the 'educational worlds', or educational contexts of the participants' families. The young people in this study recounted facts and narratives regarding their family's experiences of education. The stories often featured descriptions of how much schooling and/or further and higher education family members had achieved. Statements about immediate family members' education levels varied greatly: few family members left school in primary school while many left before completing high school. Only a few completed high school and fewer still went on to further education.

Overwhelmingly, the participants' families' stories included accounts of not completing schooling. Not completing school was most often referred to as 'dropping out'. Reported reasons for 'dropping out' varied. For instance, there were stories of having to leave school due to illness, disability, financial hardship and immigration. However, these stories did not always imply a lack of agency. The 'dropping out' stories could infer an element of family members' reasoning and choice. For example, there were stories of family members' choices to leave school in order to pursue paid work, trade qualifications and to prioritize caring for family members.

Contrasting to stories regarding choice, the young people themselves spoke of being almost 'forced out' of schooling, especially by their teachers (McMahon et al, 2015). Likewise, there were stories that pointed to family members' systemic educational exclusion and being 'kicked out' or excluded from school:

> All four of my brothers got expelled so their education is shit.
> (Xavier, 17 years old, regional NSW)

> My dad got kicked out and then my mum left in year 10.
> (Sakara, 17 years old, outer-city NSW)

In many respects, education emerges from recounts of family members' educational experiences as something that is beyond their biographies and something that excludes them. These commonplace stories of family members leaving schooling early (whether seemingly by their own choice or via school exclusion) also point to a lack of cultural and social capital (Bourdieu, 1979) for these young people (for further examples of the role of social and cultural capital in schools and education, see DiGiorgio, 2009, and Smyth, 2004). As we noted above, despite participants such as Teah being aware of the value of her daughter mixing with children with 'working parents', in the main the participants in our study did not describe having connections with people who have had positive and uninterrupted experiences of education.

Within this broader context of *immersion* in the educational biographies of families, other implicit teaching about education occurs. This additional implicit pedagogy most clearly links to Cambourne's condition of *demonstration*. The young people report observing family members 'doing' things and listening to family members' talk that either supported or discouraged the young people's educational participation and engagement.

Positive messages

Without expressly stressing the importance of education, our data features stories of families *demonstrating* support for their children's current educational pursuits. For example, there was talk of parents making sure kids get ready for school in the morning (Bella, outer-city NSW) and parents turning up to parent information sessions at the school regarding university (Lexi, 15-year-old, regional TAS).

Families were also reported to connect young people with places of further study by accessing university campuses for leisure purposes. This may be interpreted as asserting the *expectation* that it was okay to go to a university campus. Examples of this included, one parent taking her son for a 'drive around' a university campus after a swimming competition there (Susan, 13 years old, regional NSW), another young man's dad taking him to a university that had a Marine Studies school and took his surfboard to check out the university boats and 'test out the water' (Ashton, 14 years old, regional TAS). In these cases there was no explicit message that universities should be attended for study, but there was a concerted effort from these parents to show their children what a university was like and that these could be positive spaces to be in.

Accounts of families implicitly promoting education also rested on notions of *engaging* with both families' shared interests and their success stories of education. There were stories of family members making explicit links between encouraged family-based hobbies and education. Examples of this include a young man noting how his sister encouraged him to study IT because of the family's shared enjoyment of computer gaming (Sebastian, 11-year-old, outer-city SA) and another young woman's wish to study mechanical engineering stemming from her family's shared interest in 'fixing cars' and their acknowledgement that she was talented at this (Kim, 15 years old, regional NSW). There were also instances where the young people looked to members of their family as inspiring role models for engaging in education:

> K: No. Haven't had that much luck with a lot of people actually completing school in my family; my mother did and that's probably about it because a lot of them have gone to maybe year 10 or 11 and just dropped out.
> I: Will you be one of the first to finish?
> K: Yes. I won't be the first because my mother completed it.
> I: Congratulations. You'll be the second. Like your mum.
> K: Yes, follow my mum. That would be nice.
>
> (Krissie, 18 years old, outer-city SA)

Here we see one of Cambourne's (1995) key principals of *engagement* at work. Krissy was directly linking her aspirations and responsibility to engage with education to the educational success of her family members (in this case, her mother) whom she respects and wishes to emulate.

Mixed messages

Family members' educational engagements were not always positive *demonstrations* for the young people. There were several instances where the young people described close family members' experiences of TAFE and university as non-ideal. There were multiple stories of family members getting into TAFE or university and then dropping out before completing their studies, which we argue compounds messages that education is 'not for them'. But, even for some family members who experienced success in these settings the young people sometimes read their success negatively:

> I don't know how my dad could have managed because he had to write thousands of words of essays and he's a very slow typer.
>
> (Group interview, 15-year-olds, outer-city SA)

> My mum does at-home uni; it's very stressful ... she's really stressed.
>
> (Tilly, 15 years old, outer-city SA)

> Well I know my sister went to Swinburne and did her language degree there ... and my brother did study to be a teacher through Deakin up in Burwood. I don't know. I don't really pay much attention to what they say because apparently all it was just lectures and assignments ... it just sounds like high school but the casual clothes so it's like [trails off].
>
> (Bronwyn, 15 years old, regional VIC)

Here we see young people garnering understandings of university as difficult, stressful and all too similar to the school education they had already disengaged from. These understandings were not explicitly taught by family members. Instead, these messages were implicit in the young people's observations or 'readings' of their families' *demonstrations* of successful educational engagement offered by their family.

Another 'grey area' of 'mixed messages' regarding families implicit pedagogies about education was family members' *demonstrations* of educational disengagement. Families' educational contexts of disengagement from formal education (e.g., not completing high school) served as both a potential example to follow and inspiration to do differently:

> If I do go to university, out of my whole, entire extended family, I'll be the first person in my family to go to university. ... my dad and one other uncle only went to year 12. My brother, out of us kids, was the only person to complete year 12 so far, which is another reason I want to do it. Mum dropped out in year 9 – pregnancy. My sister Tiyana, she dropped out in Year 8 for very bad reasons. And then me, but I left to do another education. A lot of people are leaving earlier now and having families that have left school earlier, you don't really have a goal to look up to. It's like 'Oh, you know, I want to do what you've done. I want to be like mum.' You can look at it and go 'I don't want to end up like that' and then you think 'Oh, if I try, what's the point, she couldn't do it – why should I be able to do it' and things like that.
>
> (Eileen, 18 years old, outer-city NSW)

The above quote is one of the few clear examples of contemplation whether or not to follow the families' *demonstrations* of educational disengagement. More often there were accounts, similar to this one, of determination to defy such *demonstrations* of educational disengagement and be the 'first in family' to complete year 12 and go on to further studies and employment. This quote and, indeed this entire subsection, is important: it shows how families' complex and implicit teachings about education are always complicated further as each message may be interpreted and felt differently by individual young people.

Families' explicit teaching about education

As demonstrated in the previous section on implicit teaching, explicit family pedagogies also generate messages that are positive, negative and confusing in regards to understanding education. Like the previous section on implicit teaching, families' explicit pedagogies regarding education can be understood in terms of Cambourne's conditions of *engagement* and *expectations*. The distinction between explicit and implicit family pedagogies rests in their different modes of Cambourne's condition of *demonstration*. Unlike the *demonstrations* describing implicit teaching that the young people observed and experienced, explicit *demonstrations* were heard, almost exclusively, as direct speech from family members.

Positive messages

The families in these interviews are often described as explicitly verbally encouraging young people to complete high school and further education (either in trades or at university):

> I wanted to study tourism after school and so I will and mum told me about this [course currently studying]. My aunty told me about the [course] too.
>
> (Edith, 17 years old, regional QLD)

> Well like my dad said, 'You always want something behind you', like at the end of the day once you know your trade you can do whatever else you want but you've got something to fall back on.
>
> (Jarren, 14 years old, inner-city TAS)

> B: You've got so many parents and adults telling you 'Stay at school.'
> …
> E: Like I've sat there for years and listened to my parents go 'Look I dropped out of school at this age; I want you to continue your education instead of ruining your life.'
> …
> I: So it's always been there has it – the idea of university?
> B: Yes, it's always been there.
>
> (Bethany and Eileen, 17 and 18 years old, outer-city NSW)

These interview excerpts directly challenge popular discourse that cast families from disadvantaged communities as 'not caring' enough to do the concerted work that middle-class families do to further their children's education. Indeed, beyond merely being 'told' to pursue school, trades and university, there was acknowledgement of a forcefulness to these messages:

> I always wanted to do music but my auntie's pushing me more towards speech pathology.
>
> (Kaye, 15 years old, regional NSW)

> Mum used to pressure me to try and go to uni but I used to go '*No.*'
>
> (Mara, 16 years old, outer-city SA, emphasis added)

This sense of feeling 'pushed' and 'pressured', we contend, points to the importance that families give to promoting education and university. Beyond such explicit promotions of educational engagement, the data also showed how parents' positive *expectations* positively influence educational aspirations.

> I just want to finish year 12 and prove my point.
>
> I: Your point about?
>
> My point about being a young mum and still being able to finish your education.
>
> I: Yes. Have you guys seen that *Plumpton Girls High*? There's like ...
>
> Yes, I've seen that.
>
> ...
>
> Yes, dad's got all of them for me. He brought them when we found out I was pregnant.
>
> I: What's that?
>
> *Plumpton High*.
>
> I: *Plumpton High*. It's a school that's in the suburbs of Sydney and ... a pretty cool principal set up a school and he said 'No ... girls that are pregnant don't have to leave; they can stay' and it was pretty radical.
>
> (Group interview, 14- to 25-year-olds, outer-city SA)

> I: Yeah. Can you imagine yourself at uni?
>
> C: I can, 'cause both my parents really want me to go.
>
> (Cameron, 15 years old, regional NSW)

> I don't know what I'm set for [in my career] and my dad thinks I'm smart enough so I'm going [to university].
>
> (Group interview, 16-year-olds, outer-city NSW)

These statements clearly show how parental belief, support and encouragement, as opposed to 'bossing' or 'instructing' a child to attend university, actually work to instil beliefs that young people can achieve post compulsory education.

Negative messages

For the most part this article has focused on the positive pedagogical work of families of educationally disengaged young people in socioeconomically disadvantaged communities. We did find rare data that aligned with popular discourses of families that 'don't care' about their children's education. This data may be understood in terms of Cambourne's (1995) condition of *expectation*. Family members reportedly articulated low *expectations* of young people's educational engagement and success. For example, there were reports of family members explicitly telling young people not to go to school or supporting their non-attendance. Low *expectations* also manifested in reports of family members telling young people they were not capable of engaging in the educational pursuits they were contemplating:

I did [know what I wanted to study] too but then my aunty told me it's hard so I said, 'No.'

(Group interview, 15 years old, regional TAS)

B: It is very hard being a returnee at 18, going back into school because it's a lot more discriminating because a lot of the students look at it and go 'Oh you're stupid, you can't do it' and things like that which makes it even harder for you. And you're trying to push yourself through to prove yourself while being told you can't.

...

E: You get not only your parents say it but some of your close friends say it.

(Bethany and Eileen, 17 and 18 years old, outer-city NSW)

While there are clearly less instances of active discouragement, we are very aware that the barriers to higher education facing the young people in our study are large. Even those who are actively encouraged by their families do not have a huge amount of financial support and practical support with their homework. As such, the impact of the negative talk performed by parents and peers is potentially very big.

Conclusion

Our research into the family pedagogies of higher education for disadvantaged and low socioeconomic status students shows that there is no one 'true' situation characterising the pedagogical work undertaken in and by families. There are many messages transmitted about University education and these range in kind. This said, it is clear that families really matter in terms of teaching young people about higher education and shaping the possibility of educational achievement for youth. The father who bought his daughter the DVD about pregnant girls succeeding at school had clearly instilled in her the belief that she could complete her high school study. Our fieldwork also shows that the positive educational pedagogies which occur in family settings are not limited to parent–child relationships. Siblings, aunties, uncles and extended family members all have power to positively impact on young people's education. What is clear is that, while there is no 'best way' or 'right' way to encourage young people to explore university options, positive discourse about Higher Education and belief in young people's capacity to achieve are powerful educational tools.

Notes

1 This research focus of 'imagining university' generated interview discussions centred mostly on educational contexts such as compulsory schooling and university. The analysis in this article thus tends to mostly feature data regarding school and university attendance. There is no intention to frame the university, particularly, as the most appropriate, desirable or only means of engaging with education post-school. The

absence of data about other post-school educational and non-educational options, in this chapter, is mostly because this was not the topic of the semi-structured interviews.

2   The CI for the ARC Discovery Project is Professor Valerie Harwood (UOW). The semi-structured interviews were conducted by the second and third authors of this chapter and also by five research assistants. For information regarding semi-structured interview methods, Galletta (2013) offers a comprehensive description of the method, albeit within a psychology discipline focus.

3   The location is not specified in order to protect anonymity

4   Colleagues Faye Blanch and Simone Tur from the Yungorrendi First Nations Centre, Flinders University, collaborated with Harwood and Allan to analyse Krissie's transcript. As they explain:

> In the process of responding to Krissie's narrative around her relationship with Jye, there is a greater need for other interpretations and analysis that privilege the worldview of Indigenous participation and engagement within the schooling sectors. Therefore sections of this paper occur through a collaborative analysis through the lens of an Indigenous pedagogical praxis that speaks to family, community, and Indigenous ways of being and doing. Our scholarly engagement is contextualized within an intellectual space that signifies education as key to empowerment, agency, success and the possibility of transformative lives for Indigenous students. Working within the higher educational sector, as teachers, academics and community members we teach mainly non-Indigenous student teachers, to understand Indigenous students in the schooling context.
>
> (Blanch and Tur, cited in Harwood et al, in press)

References

ABS (Australian Bureau of Statistics) (2013a) *Census of population and housing: Socio-economic indexes for areas (SIFA)*, Australia, 2011, cat. No. 2033.0.55.001, viewed 12 July 2011, <http://www.abs.gov.au/websitedbs/censushome.nsf/home/seifa2011?op endocumentandnavpos=260>.

ABS (Australian Bureau of Statistics) (2013b) *Education and Health: Links between education and health*, ABS, viewed 14 April 2015, <http://www.abs.gov.au/AUS STATS/abs@.nsf/lookup/4704.0Chapter365Oct+2010>.

Bland, D. (2012) Imagination for re-engagement from the margins of education, *The Australian Educational Researcher*, 39, 1, 75–89.

Bourdieu, P. (1979) *Distinction: A Social Critique of the Judgement of Taste*. Boston, MA: Harvard University Press.

Brooks, R. (2003) Young People's Higher Education Choices: The role of family and friends, *British Journal of Sociology of Education*, 24, 3, 283–297.

Cambourne, B. (1995) Toward an educationally relevant theory of literacy learning, *The Reading Teacher*, 49, 3, 182–190.

Comber, B. and Kamler, B. (2004) Getting out of deficit: Pedagogies of reconnection, *Teaching Education*, 15, 3, 293–310.

Cutler, D. M. and Lleras-Muney, A. (2010) Understanding differences in health behaviours by education, *Journal of Health Economics*, 29, 1, 1–28.

D'Addio, A. (2007) *Intergenerational Transmission of Disadvantage: Mobility or Immobility across Generations?* OECD, France. 29 March 2007, No. 52, p115. DOI 10.1787/217730505550.

DECS (Department for Education and Children's Services) (2010) *ICAN: Innovative community action networks*, Department for Education and Children's Services, viewed 15 January 2010, <http://www.ican.sa.edu.au/pages/aboutus/>.

DiGiorgio, C. (2009) Application of Bourdieuian theory to the inclusion of students with learning/physical challenges in multicultural school settings, *International Journal of Inclusive Education*, 13, 2, 179–194.

Duffy, G. and Elwood, J. (2013) The perspectives of 'disengaged' students in the 14–19 Phase on motivations and barriers to learning within the contexts of institutions and classrooms, *London Review of Education*, 11, 2, 112–126.

Egerter, S., Braveman, P., Sadegh-Nobari, T., Grossman-Kahn, R. and Dekker, M. (2006) *Education Matters for Health*, Robert Wood Johnson Foundation, viewed 14 April 2015, <http://www.commissiononhealth.org/PDF/c270deb3-ba42-4fbd-baeb-2cd65956f00e/Issue%20Brief%206%20Sept%2009%20-%20Education%20and%20Health.pdf>.

Equity and Diversity, University of Western Sydney (2015) *Dropping off the Edge: Mapping Disadvantage in Australia*, viewed April 15 2015, <http://www.uws.edu.au/equity_diversity/equity_and_diversity/open_fora/dropping_off_the_edge_mapping_disadvantage_in_australia>.

Furlong, A. and Cartmel, F. (1997) *Young People and Social Change*. Berkshire, UK: Open University Press.

Galletta, A. (2013) *Mastering the Semi-Structured Interview and Beyond*. New York and London: New York University Press.

Harris, P., Turbill, J., Fitzsimmons, P. and McKenzie, B. (2001) *Reading in the Primary Years*. Katoomba: NSW Social Science Press.

Harwood, V. and Allan, J. (2014) *Psychopathology at School: Theorizing mental disorders in education*. Oxford: Routledge.

Kervin, L., Vialle, W., Herrington, J. and Okely, T. (2006) *Research for Educators*. South Melbourne, Victoria: Thomson Social Science Press.

Lucey, H., Melody, J. and Walkerdine, V. (2006) Uneasy hybrids: Psychosocial aspects of becoming educationally successful for working class young women, in M. Arnot and M. Mac An Ghaill (eds.), *The RoutledgeFalmer Reader in Gender and Education*. London: RoutledgeFalmer, pp238–252.

Machin, S. J. (1999) Childhood disadvantage and intergenerational transmissions of economic status, in *Persistent Poverty and Lifetime Inequality: The Evidence: Proceedings from a workshop held at HM Treasury*, pp17–21. London: CASE, LSE / HM Treasury.

McMahon, S., Harwood, V. and Hickey-Moody, A. (2015) Students that just hate school wouldn't go: Educationally disengaged and disadvantaged young people's talk about university education, *British Journal of Sociology of Education*, DOI: 10.1080/01425692.2015.1014546.

Morgan, T., Morgan, P. and O'Kelly, B. (2008) Youth Work in Schools: An Investigation of Youth Work, as a Process of Informal Learning, *Formal Settings*, 48, Department of Education Northern Ireland online, reviewed 9 January 2015, <http://www.deni.gov.uk/no_48-3.pdf>.

NSWDET (New South Wales Department of Education and Training) (2009) *Enforcement of Compulsory School Attendance*. Sydney, NSW: NSWDET.

Oxford University Press (2015) pedagogy, n., in *OED Online*, viewed 14 April 2015, <http://www.oed.com/view/Entry/139520?redirectedFrom=pedagogy>.

Smyth, J. (2004) Social capital and the socially just school, *British Journal of Sociology of Education*, 25, 1, 19–33.

Stehlik, T. P. (2006) *Levels of Engagement: Report of findings of the School Retention Action Plan action research project*. Adelaide: University of South Australia.

Stein, M. (2006) Research Review: Young people leaving care, *Child and Family Social Work*, 11, 3, 273–279.

Vinson, T. (2007) *Dropping Off the Edge: The distribution of disadvantage in Australia*. Richmond, Victoria: Jesuit Social Services/Catholic Social Services.

Walkerdine, V., Melody, J. and Lucey, H. (2003) Uneasy hybrids: Psychosocial aspects of becoming educationally successful for working-class young women, *Gender and Education*, 15, 3, 285–299.

Winkworth, G., McArthur, M., Layton, M. and Thompson, L. (2010) Someone to check in on me: Social capital, social support and vulnerable parents with very young children in the Australian Capital Territory, *Child and Family Social Work*, 15, 206–215.

Wright, C., Standen, P. and Patel, T. (2010) *Black Youth Matters: Transitions from School to Success*. London and New York: Routledge.

5 Close to home

What kind of family should we become?

Lisette Burrows

Introduction

'No obese child is an island' declares Director of Yale Prevention Research Center, David Katz in a 2011 blog (http://www.huffingtonpost.com/david-ka tz-md/no-obese-child-is-_b_841382.html). In the opening paragraphs the rationale for this declaration is unveiled. As he puts it, 'In my view, children and adults will control their weight and get to health together, or almost certainly will not do so at all.' At first glance, there are both troubling and exciting possibilities emerging from this simply, yet definitely expressed statement. On the one hand, the claim generates unhelpful and simplistic cor-relations between weight and health that have been roundly critiqued (Campos et al, 2006; Gard and Wright, 2005). On the other hand, the notion that children are not necessarily solely responsible for their own health, however this may be conceived, is refreshingly apposite. A more nuanced reading of the above statement, however, raises issues that are the impetus for this chapter. What is it that families, and parents, in particular, are being called on to do in the name of their children's health currently? How are families hailed to engage in health enhancing (or fat-busting) projects, and what notion of family is imagined when family-focused health messages are imparted?

In an effort to address the aforementioned questions, I draw on media, professional and scholarly commentary on families as health-enhancing sites and empirical material derived from ethnographic studies with young children. Theoretically, analysis is informed by post-structural resources that hone attention to the ways public health discourses, and obesity discourses in particular, generate notions about how families are expected to function and what work they are required to do (Burrows, 2009). I am interested in not only what messages are conveyed to families about health, through government missives, health interventions, and family-focused programmes, but also what these resources *do* to and for families. That is, how do the instructions on 'how to live' (Foucault, 1977) transmitted to families produce family rela-tionships, dispositions towards bodies and shape who parents and children can 'be'? Furthermore, I am interested in the kinds of families who are imagined in health discourse. What comprises a 'family', and what assumptions about 'family' drive the intensification of family-focused health policies currently? To begin I briefly discuss the burgeoning interest in families as sites for remedial and/or preventative health work, charting the key messages expressed in scholarly and health promotion narratives and the justifications advanced for an escalating concern to 'reach' families wherever they may be located. Next, I trace the techniques advanced for reaching families – that is, the pedagogical projects initiated by government and health promotion agencies *and* the pedagogical work families are hailed to do. To conclude, I draw some, albeit tentative arguments about what undergirds the contemporary obsession with targeting families in health work, and what other ways of thinking about families could usefully be drawn on.

What should families do?

Any cursory scan of media commentary on obesity currently points to a proliferating interest in families as pedagogical sites for health work (Burrows, 2009; Fullagar, 2009). Weight Watchers US declares 'Fighting fat isn't a one person job – it's a family responsibility that can directly affect overweight children' (http://www.thestar.com/life/health_wellness/2010/05/05/parents_of_ overweight_children_need_to_fight_fat_too.html). Harvard's School of Public Health claims 'Healthy Eating and Active Lifestyles Begin at Home' (http:// www.hsph.harvard.edu/obesity-prevention-source/obesity-prevention/families/) and *The Atlantic* reporter Olga Khuzan asks 'Can your Family Make you Obese?' (http://www.theatlantic.com/health/archive/2014/02/can-your-family-ma ke-you-obese/283757/). These are just three of a burgeoning number of family-focused headlines gracing news media currently. These, and thousands like them, leave one in little doubt that families are not only sites where health imperatives can be enacted, but also that families are responsible *and* culpable for what children may become.

Biomedical treatises on obesity in reputable journals tell a similar story. As McCormack (2012) compellingly demonstrates in her analysis of a selection of New Zealand empirical studies on obesity, even when researchers' findings do not explicitly examine familial trends, nor roles that families may play in fostering childhood obesity, researchers leap readily to recommendations that produce what she calls a 'parent effect'. That is, despite no evidence to support the notion, parents (and mothers, in particular) are regularly cast as not only culpable for any accumulating fat on their children's bodies, but also capable of fixing this given the right instructions. Grounded in developmental arguments and explanations of family that emphasize parents' role in socializing their young, the parent effect tangles 'parents up in a causative relationship with fat on children's bodies that begins before their child is conceived' (McCormack, 2012, p147).

In terms of health promotion campaigns and government imperatives, across nation state, continent and context, the positioning of families as vitally involved in procuring good health outcomes for their young is a shared motif. New Zealand's launch of a Healthy Families New Zealand campaign in May 2015, for example, focuses on 'Encouraging families to live healthy lives by making good food choices, being physically active, sustaining a healthy weight, not smoking and drinking alcohol only in moderation' (http://www. health.govt.nz/our-work/preventative-health-wellness/healthy-families-nz). In Australia, the Be Active Eat Well and Healthy Together Victoria projects are both designed to build community capacity to promote health eating, physical activity and healthy weight in children and families (Office of the Minister of Health, 2013). In Scotland, the National Health Service, Lothian, has launched Get Going, 'a new family-based healthy lifestyle programme that offers support to help your child get active, eat well and work towards a healthy weight' (http://www.nhslothian.scot.nhs.uk/getgoing/) and throughout the rest of the United Kingdom, Canada and the United States, there are similar programmes, all focused on bringing health enhancing resources to families and communities (see Gard and Pluim, 2014). In a nutshell the message seems to be that eating better and exercising more are the keys to unlocking a slimmer, and therefore, a healthier future.

This intent is further elucidated when the anticipated 'results' of programs like those signalled above are considered. As with any generously funded governmental scheme, evidence of 'results' is a precursor to a program's on-going sustainability. The Healthy Families NZ initiative (Office of the Minister of Health, 2013) portrays desired programme impact in years two to four in the following way: 'Years 2–4: Intermediate indicators of progress e.g. health literacy, daily serves of fruit and vegetables, participation in moderate physical activity, waist circumference in children' (p6). Year four onwards is described in terms of population outcomes – 'e.g., body-mass index, reduction in tobacco smoking, proportion of children and adults at unhealthy weight' (p6). The other programmes mentioned above inevitably use weight loss, body mass index (BMI) or some other measure of body size as a marker of success. For example, aspirations for Australia's Be Active Eat Well pilot (Colac, Australia) were realized with 'a number of measurable improvements … in the first three years of the Colac pilot, children had significantly lower weight (about 1kg), smaller waist (about 3dm) and had a lower body mass index (BMI) score compared with children in a nearby control area' (Office of the Minister of Health, 2013, p1). Thus, even when programs are ostensibly not 'top-down', but rather premised on the needs, interests of specific families and their communities, the broader agenda is clear. Families, as sites where impressionable and trainable youngsters reside, and parents, as guardians of their futures, are best positioned to assist with reducing their waistlines, and thereby improving their health.

For families to 'work' as health enhancing units, tools for evaluating current wellbeing, monitoring one's progress and effecting change in families are needed. In the next section, I examine how these projects for change are enacted, the kinds of pedagogies deployed and the ways in which families are constituted in pedagogical work conducted within and on families in the name of health.

Pedagogizing families

The practice of regarding families as key pedagogic sites for transmission and retention of health messages is nothing new. Postman (2011) drawing on Aries's history of childhood, points to the ways families became endowed with educational functions back in the 18th century. Arguably, what is relatively new is the volume and diversity of technologies harnessed to govern the actions of families in contemporary times, and particularly in relation to obesity. As Wright and Harwood (2009) in their text *Biopolitics and the 'Obesity Epidemic'* suggest, individuals are being 'offered a number of ways to under-stand themselves, change themselves and take action to change others and their environments' (p2). Families are currently being drawn into this change project in droves. In this section I canvass some of the deliberate and more subtle pedagogical practices being deployed within, across and on families.

Re-contextualization of scientific knowledge

As Petherick et al (see Chapter 8 in this volume) suggest, persuading families to act in specific ways requires a manufacturing of consent. Key to producing families as willing workers in the name of their own and their off-springs' health is legitimating the need for some kind of transformation in the first place. The translation of expert knowledge from the primary field (epidemiology in this case) into manageable and consumable chunks for an audience in a secondary field (i.e., parents) is crucial in this legitimation. In effect, complex and oft-times uncertain findings yielded from empirical studies are simplified, their uncertainty erased and messages packaged for distribution. For example, developmental psychological findings that what happens in the early years of a person's life matters considerably for what happens later, are applied to specific health issues (Mayall, 1994). So, in the case of obesity, a re-contextualization of developmental psychological knowledge to the health field results in the message, fat kids turn into fat adults. Parents, as producers of fat children are drawn in to the pedagogical project to trim the fat off children's bodies (McCormack, 2012) to alleviate intergenerational fatness. Sociological work exploring societal influences on eating patterns points to families as key sites where habits and dispositions around food are formed (Boutelle et al, 2006; Caplan, 1997). This, in turn, fuels calls for families to 'eat together'. As Pike and Leahy (see Chapter 7) suggest, the rhetoric is that a 'family who eats together stays together'. Although the processes of re-contextualization are of course a little more nuanced than the ways I have described them here, in essence, scientific expertise, whether this be sociological, psychological or epidemiological (or any other variety) is drawn on to validate health messages, to give them currency and legitimacy in the public eye.

The affect effect

An imprint of expertise is not always enough to ensure potentially recalcitrant populations and individuals enact health messages. As Fullagar (2009) and Leahy (2012) convincingly convey, affect is routinely mobilized in the ways in which health messages are delivered to families. Risk discourses, in particular, infuse and work in tandem with health discourses generating emotions of fear at what will happen to self or family if healthy practices are not engaged in, guilt at unwillingness to enact health missives, and shame in relation to having or rearing a body that falls outside of normative ideals conveyed in health messages (e.g., BMI). Furthermore, often there is an urgency attached to the messages imparted that suggests unless preventative action is taken immediately it will be too late (Burrows, 2010).

Work in New Zealand schools that has sought to understand health from the perspectives of young people illustrates the ways affect surfaces in even very young people's commentary on their own and their families' health-related dispositions and behaviours. Burrows (2010), for example, points to the ways children, particularly those from more privileged locations readily cast aspersions on families (or parents) who fail to put the right food in their children's lunch boxes or understand what constitutes healthy food in the first place. 'Cause some silly parents ... the children ring up and say that they haven't got any lunch so the parents bring them fish and chips or MacDonald's' (p247) declares one child in the study. 'I feel sad for them (kids) because their parents might not be taking action to try and at least feed them vegies or trying new things that have vegies in them' (p247) suggests another. In both of these excerpts parents are positioned as miscreant, failing to provide their children with the requisite nutrients. Other children speak of their fears for their families' well-being, should healthy eating and exercise messages not be adhered to. Still others talk about the guilt they and their parents experience when knowingly reaching out for foods that are regarded as unhealthy (e.g., ice creams, pies and chips).

In many ways the aforementioned apparent folding in (Ellsworth, 1997) of health knowledge for children can be regarded as heralding the success of pedagogical strategies geared toward recruiting children as agents of change. Notions of young people as social actors, as beings who can and do make a difference by helping their families and communities understand the importance of good nutrition and physical activity, certainly prevail currently. The fact that for some children at least, these messages have 'sunk in' and fuel emotive responses about others and their own families would for some, constitute a success. Alternatively, the fact that young children and in some cases very young children are worrying about their own and others' health, fretting about their families' prospects, and casting aspersions on the behaviours of others whose lives they presumably know little about, could be conceived as a cause for concern. Indeed, given the push, in many countries (e.g., New Zealand, Australia, Canada, United States) toward understanding health in more holistic ways, and envisaging well-being as something that signals something other than physical health only, the anxiety produced *en route* to learning about health, could well be conceived as producing outcomes contra to the desires of health promoters (Burrows and Sinkinson, 2014).

We're all in this together

One of the key understandings driving much family-focused pedagogy is the notion that 'context' matters. In the Australian and New Zealand initiatives signalled at the beginning of this chapter, the message is clear that making healthy lives requires input at the 'local' level, or where people 'live, learn, work and play' (Ministry of Health, 2014). Key to most of the approaches geared toward families (Healthy families NZ) is moving services 'closer to home', and particularly to the homes of those communities perceived to have 'higher-than-average' rates of preventable chronic diseases, rates of risk factors for these disease and/or high levels of deprivation (Ministry of Health, 2014). While principles of voluntary action and community-led health promotion are espoused, heralding a departure from the individualism of much health promotion work, the resources and activities promoted under these family-focused umbrellas and the ways these resources are delivered leaves one in little doubt that the old vintage has simply reappeared in new bottles, however.

First, the 'it's up to you' thrust of much health promotion effort seems simply to have been replaced by an 'it's all up to the family' ethos. While cloaked in a language of 'support' and 'encouragement' to do as one wills, the fine print clearly signals an emphasis on strengthening both the capacity and the necessity for families to play 'a role in creating better health outcomes for themselves and others through the choices that they make' (Office of the Minister of Health, 2013, p3).

Secondly, as Seedhouse (2004) and Fox (1993), have argued, reaching more people (e.g. families, neighbourhoods, communities) and considering health in more holistic ways does not necessarily dilute the individualism of the message. That is, extending the pedagogic regulation (Walkerdine, 1984) from individuals to families in one sense means there are simply more aspects of people's lives, and locations that become governable (albeit amiably). It is no longer what one eats and how much one exercises that is surveyed, but rather, the *ways* in which families function, the ways family is 'done' in different locales that is under scrutiny. Further, the expansion of visions of health as purely corporeal to an understanding that health has social, cultural, socio-economic dimensions, inevitably renders state intervention and assistance in procuring health more justifiable in the lives of indigenous and minority groups as well as those regarded as working-class. Families who do not engage with the tools provided them in positive ways are positioned as negligent, poorly educated and sometimes simply as mistakenly imagining they are alright as they are (see Fight the Obesity Epidemic, 2008; Taylor, 2007; Torbitt, 2006; TVNZ, 2006). In New Zealand, Māori are disproportionately the focus of health promotion efforts as are those perceived as lacking the economic and/or knowledge resources to make healthier choices. Health researchers, together with Māori 'role models' from the popular sphere (e.g., the All Blacks) are often enlisted to assist with the transmission of these healthy choice messages, essentially being recruited to convince their own families that Western health ideals and neo-liberal, individualistic practices are the keys to salvation (Burrows, 2011). Hokowhitu (2009) refers to this tendency for the tools of the colonisers to be deployed by the colonised to work on their own populations as a 'colonisation of the mind'. While best intentions no doubt motivate this health work, what Evans et al (2009) describe as 'socio-cultural hierarchies' remain entrenched, not only with respect to whose knowledge, values and bodies are celebrated in particular communities but also in relation to broader national health promotion efforts. That is, it is Western knowledge regarding what counts as healthy eating and exercise that is framed as the orthodoxy, while socio-cultural norms linked to non-Western populations are barely visible in contemporary healthscapes (Burrows, 2009).

At work here is a brand of topographical science where specific areas have been marked off as having a character and a population that breeds more risky and unhealthful behaviours than others. While cloaked in a language of 'support' and 'encouragement', the approach can more readily be apprehended as a brand of pedagogic regulation (Walkerdine, 1984), infused with neoliberal discourses emphasizing both the capacity and the necessity for families to play 'a role in creating better health outcomes for themselves and others through the choices that they make' (p3). Inevitably their current choices are regarded as problematic, yet there is seemingly little cognisance of the diverse ways in which people 'do family' nor the fact that risk is experienced differently within and across families and contexts. Fullagar's (2009) work with diverse families in Australia points to the ways risk (albeit not in the way health promoters may view it, is an everyday part of some families' lives. One of the families she interviewed 'described abductions, paedophiles living in the next street, indecent exposure on local bike paths and violence, which shaped the risk contours of public leisure spaces and directly affected what Dan allowed the children to do' (p121). She illustrates the constant calculation of risk (both moral and physical) families engage in, weighing the potential harm children may encounter with the benefits derived from participating in family leisure pursuits. Her analysis complicates the 'at risk' descriptors applied to particular families and ruptures the notion that families who play together stay together (a familiar trope in health promotion literature).

Thirdly, what is also striking about the pedagogical practices families are encouraged to undertake is the disconnect between what it is imagined young people and their parents/caregivers will do together and the realities of young people's lives. When carrying out research with young people in New Zealand schools (see Burrows, 2011), children were quick to point out the disjunctures between school-based and public health imperatives and the realities of their lives at home. One young girl, for example was chastised by her family for being 'stick thin', while public health discourse relentlessly pushed slim bodies as healthy ideals. Another young boy struggled with adhering to the healthy lunch box regime at his schools as his mum always put too much in his. Still others declared that they had no desire to eat like Palangi (i.e., non-Māori or Pasifika New Zealanders) anyway. Hokowhitu (2008) sheds light on why Māori families can appear resistant to the kinds of Western bio-pedagogical (Wright and Harwood, 2009) advances. He, and others (e.g., Sharples, 2007) reveal that notions of fatness, fitness and health have meanings in Māori culture that bear little relation to the versions expressed in health promotion initiatives. As he suggests, it is a startling exemplar of monoculturalism at play that is seen when so much energy is expended trying to get Māori families to do health in the ways Pakeha are urged to.

Ethnic affiliation, aside, a raft of work in the sociology of youth points to what shapes and informs young people's dispositions toward health messages and life in general (see Austen, 2009; France, 2000; Harrison, 2011; Mayall, 1994; Wyn and White, 1997). In much of this work, family does not necessarily feature strongly. Thing and Ottersen (2015), for example, in their research on young people's perspectives on health, risk and physical activity in Denmark, foreground the ways in which young people are 'maturing and negotiating friendships and relationships in schools' (p466). They write of the pleasurable dimensions of behaviours others find risky or health debilitating (e.g., drinking and partying) that young people experience. They talk of young people's interdependence with friends and the breathing spaces young people desire and find. Furthermore, their research suggests that many young people are not overly bothered by health messages. Rather, they engage with health directives with humour and irony, with an optimism and pleasure that belies the gloomy forecast for youth regularly unveiled in public health discourse.

Postman (2011) points to the declining authority of families, the loss of 'the intimacy, dependence, and loyalty that traditionally characterize the parent-child relationship' (p15). James and James (2004) elucidate the ways in which peers and 'the media have diminished the role of the family in shaping the values and sensibilities of the young' (p15). Others discuss the ways digital devices have superseded engagement with family members (Lupton, 2014). Understanding how young people view their selves in relation to families, what they care about and what shapes their inclinations and their worlds would seem a crucial precursor to investing heavily in family-focused health pedagogies. Rarely, however, are their views and experiences considered.

What kind of family should we become? Concluding thoughts

The above, albeit brief, exposition of some of the key messages being conveyed to families, their modes of transmission and the ways in which health promotion expertise is used to shape family life is, on its own, no surprise. Indeed the message – eat right, exercise and lose weight – is enduringly familiar to all, as is the idea that habits learned in childhood will be reproduced in adulthood. What is surprising, however, is the conviction that families should be or are the focus of such excessive attention in contemporary times. On the one hand, social commentators and researchers alike (granted they are often one and the same) suggest that parents, as heads of families, at least those conceptualised in the 'modern' sense, have 'lost much of its authority and aura, and the idea of deference to one who is older has become ridiculous' (Postman, 2011, p133), yet on the other hand in health promotion literature and increasingly in health promotion policy and multimillion dollar interventions the 'family' is rendered the crucial cornerstone in any community health initiative.

Embedded in each of the initiatives referred to in the body of this chapter, is a claim to presence (Fox, 1993), an underpinning assumption that it is possible to know what families are and what they are capable of. The starting point for family pedagogies is inevitably drawn from health discourses that have currency in biomedical and largely Western locales. The 'data', evidence and research re-contextualised in the public sphere is communicated to families by professionals who, for the most part, appear already committed to the notion that health is largely a matter of individual responsibility, that families work in particular ways, and that community is a 'thing' that can be identified, collated and worked with or on. The notion that some families may value a different kind of health currency, or indeed may think about and live health in completely contrasting ways barely seems to register. When it does, the desired approach seems to be helping these families to understand that the practices (and bodies) they are happy with should not be regarded as such.

As I have endeavoured to portray throughout this chapter, what family comprises, how family functions and the locales where family is found are diverse, even when families ostensibly share social class or ethnic affiliations. At the very least, a more complex notion of family, a more nuanced notion of difference seems important as a platform for family focused health work. What seems to be at play currently is a rhetoric of difference, of diversity and a recognition of the impact socioeconomic, cultural and geographical factors may have on families' willingness and capacity to engage with health imperatives. Yet there is still a particular notion of 'family' assumed – one that will be (or ought to be) thoroughly invested in the procurement of a healthy ideal largely derived from Westernised premises.

Further, it seems ironic that a time when it is widely acknowledged, at least in sociological scholarship, that family is a contested term, diffuse in its application and realized differently in different contexts, that efforts are accelerating to direct health interventions to a family that is at once considered universal and bounded, reachable by family-focused pedagogies. Perhaps it is the difficulty of imagining family any other way that gets in the way. If, as St Pierre (2011) would urge us, we were to dispense of metanarratives of family, what might a less comfortable, less certain notion of what family comprises permit?

To what would family-focused health interventions be directed and how? Barad (2003) urges a dissolution of the distinctions we (and I include myself here) so readily make between groups, classes, families. In her view, it would no longer make much sense to think of family per se as a unit, or home as a place distinct from the intra-relational messiness of life. Any boundaries health promoters or researchers for that matter establish are at best porous and in Barad's terms not necessarily helpful in thinking about social life nor negotiating it. For her, we are engaged in an ongoing process of assembling, enfolding, relating to and drawing from different material-discursive elements. To contemplate Barad's thesis in a family health context would mean refraining from considering the family as a 'thing', as a discrete entity that impacts young people or as an institution, or grouping that can be conveniently targeted as a site for health work. I have no idea what such a radical shift in how we imagine family might do to family focused health promotion, yet family as it is constituted currently seems to be a troubled concept. Anything that disrupts health promotion discourse from its claim to know family. Anything that jolts health promotion from its relentless march into the heart of homes and anything that provokes cognisance that family is found in many places, in many incarnations, and indeed may not even exist as a 'thing' can only be health-enhancing to my mind.

References

Austen, L. (2009) The social construction of risk by young people, *Health, risk & society*, 11(5), 451–470.

Barad, K. (2003) Posthumanist performativity: Toward an understanding of how matter comes to matter, *Signs: Journal of Women in Culture and Society*, 28(3), 801–831.

Boutelle, K., Fulkerso, J., Neumark-Sztainer, S. M. and French, S. (2006) Fast food for family meals: Relationships with parent and adolescent food intake, home food availability and weight status, *Public Health Nutrition*, 10(1), 16–23.

Burrows, L. (2011) 'I'm proud to be me': Health, Community and Schooling, *Policy Futures in Education*, 9(3), 341–352.

Burrows, L. (2010) Kiwi kids are Weetabix kids: Body matters in childhood, *Sport, Education and Society*, 15(2), 235–251.

Burrows, L. (2009) Pedagogizing families through obesity discourse. In J. Wright and V. Harwood (eds), *Biopolitics and the 'Obesity Epidemic' Governing Bodies*. New York/London: Routledge, pp127–140.

Burrows, L., and Sinkinson, M. (2014) Mental health in corporeal times. In K. Fitzpatrick, and R. Tinning (Eds.), *Health education: Critical perspectives* (pp156–170).

Campos, P., Saguy, A., Ernsberger, P., Oliver, E. and Gaesser, G. (2006) The epidemiology of overweight and obesity: Public health crisis or moral panic?, *International Journal of Epidemiology*, 35(1), 55–60.

Caplan, P. (1997) *Food, Health, & Identity*. New York: Routledge.

Ellsworth, E. (1997) *Teaching positions: Difference, pedagogy, and the power of address*. New York, NY: Teachers College Press.

Evans, J., Rich, E. and De Pian, L. (2009) Global Healthscapes, Education and Cultural Reproduction: The conceptual challenges for international, collaborative, comparative research. Paper presented at British Education Research Association, Manchester, 2–6 September.

Fight the Obesity Epidemic (2008) http://www.foe.org.nz/facts3.html (accessed 2 January 2008).

Fox, N. (1993) *Postmodernism, Sociology and Health*. Buckingham: Open University Press.

Foucault, M. (1977) *Discipline and Punish: The Birth of the Prison*. London: Penguin.

France, A. (2000) Towards a sociological understanding of young people and their risk-taking, *Journal of Youth Studies*, 3(3), 317–331.

Fullagar, S. (2009) Governing Healthy Family Lifestyles. In J. Wright and V. Harwood (eds), *Biopolitics and the 'Obesity Epidemic' Governing Bodies*. New York/London: Routledge (pp108–126).

Gard, M. and Pluim, C. (2014) *Schools and public health: Past, present, future*. Maryland, US: Lexington Books.

Gard, M. and Wright, J. (2005) *The 'Obesity epidemic': Science, ideology and morality*. London: Routledge.

Harrison, L. (2011) 'I don't know anyone that has two drinks a day': Young people, alcohol and the government of pleasure, *Health, Risk & Society*, 13(5), 469–486.

Hokowhitu, B. (2009) Foucault and Culture, Presentation to Humanities Foucault Symposium, University of Otago, 21 May.

Hokowhitu, B. (2008) Understanding the Maori and Pacific Body: Towards a critical physical education pedagogy, *Journal of Physical Education New Zealand*, 41(3), 81–91.

James, A. and James, A. L. (2004) *Constructing Childhood: Theory, Policy and Social Practice*. New York: Palgrave/MacMillan.

Leahy, D. (2012) *Assembling a Healthy [y] Subject*. PhD thesis, Melbourne: Deakin University.

Lupton, D. (2014) Critical Perspectives on Digital Health Technologies, *Sociology Compass*, 8(12), 1344–1359 (on-line edition).

Mayall, B. (1994) *Children's childhoods: Observed and experienced*. London, England: The Falmer Press.

McCormack, J. (2012) *Obesity, parents and me*. PhD thesis. Dunedin: University of Otago.

Ministry of Health (2014) *Healthy Families NZ*, http://www.health.govt.nz/our-work/preventative-health-wellness/healthy-families-nz.

Office of the Minister of Health (2013) *Healthy Families NZ*. Wellington: Cabinet Business Committee.

Pethrick, L., Norman, M. E. and Rail, G., (2016) Manufacturing (parental) consent, In Dagkas, S. and Burrows, L. (eds), *Families, Young People, Physical Activity and Health: Critical Perspectives*. London: Routledge.

Pike, J. and Leahy, D. (2016) 'The family that eats together stays together': Governing families, governing health, governing pedagogies, In Dagkas, S. and Burrows, L. (eds), *Families, Young People, Physical Activity and Health: Critical Perspectives*. London: Routledge.

Postman, N. (2011) *The Disappearance of Childhood*. New York: Knopf Doubleday Publishing Group.

Seedhouse, D. (2004) *Health Promotion: Philosophy Prejudice and Practice. (2nd ed)*. Chichester, Sussex: John Wiley & Sons.

Sharples, P. (2007) Tino Rangitiratanga: A key determinant for good health in Aotearoa, Keynote address delivered at New Zealand Health Teachers' Association Conference 'Our Health, Our Children, Our Future', Dunedin, 3 July.

St. Pierre, E. A. (2011) Post Qualitative Research. The Critique and the Coming After. In N. Denzin and Y. Lincoln (Ed.) *The SAGE Handbook of Qualitative Research*, Thousand Oaks, CA: Sage Publications, pp611–625.

Taylor, R. (2007) What's hot and what's not, Keynote address presented at New Zealand Health Teachers' Association Conference: 'Our Health, Our Children Our Future', Dunedin, 30 June–3 July.

Thing, L. and Ottersen, L. (2013) Young people's perspectives on health, risks and physical activity in a Danish secondary school, *Health, Risk & Society*, 15(5), 463–477.

Torbitt, T. (2006) Diabetes Could 'Wipe Out' Maori by End of Century, *The Dominion*, 14 November, 1.

TVNZ (2006) One Shows A to Z: Fighting fat, http://tvnz.co.nz/view/page/410965/ 945999 (accessed 20 December 2006).

Walkerdine, V. (1984) Developmental psychology and the child-centred pedagogy: The insertion of Piaget into early education. In W. Henriques, C. Hollway, C. Urwin, C. Vemi, and V. Walkerdine (Eds.), *Changing the subject: Psychology, social regulation and subjectivity* (pp153–202). London: Methuen.

Wright, J. and Harwood, V. (2009) (Eds.) *Biopolitics and the 'Obesity Epidemic' Governing Bodies*. New York/London: Routledge.

Wyn, J. and White, R. (1997) *Rethinking Youth*. St Leonards: Allen and Unwin.

Part 2

Family's health and physical activity

6 Parents as pawns in *Fitnessgram*'s war on obesity

Carolyn Pluim and Michael Gard

Introduction

In this chapter we interrogate the increasingly widespread use of *Fitnessgram* in physical education classes in the United States and, particularly, the ways in which children and their families are implicated in its use. Ultimately, we suggest that the implementation of *Fitnessgram* products in schools has the potential to influence the roles, responsibilities and obligations of parents and caregivers in problematic ways. We also discuss the way in which *Fitnessgram* encourages parents to adopt a range of health-related attitudes, behaviours, and subject positions designed to intensify parental surveillance in lives of children.

For readers who may be unfamiliar with this product, *Fitnessgram* is an American-made digital platform designed to assist physical education teachers test the fitness levels of their students. It also enables teachers to collect, record and disseminate the results of these tests to students, parents and the public in paper and electronic form. It has become the most popular digital platform of its kind and is used in a number of American states.

Given the famously fragmented governance over educational policy and practice in the United States, the rise and spread of *Fitnessgram* across jurisdictional boundaries is a remarkable achievement. An increasing number of state governments and departments of education have amended their legislation and school codes to specifically include *Fitnessgram*'s use by name, which has the effect of excluding any competitor for the foreseeable future. The large district implementations include New York City Public Schools, New York, Baltimore County Public School District, Maryland and Miami-Dade County Public Schools, Florida, as well as mandated state-wide implementations in Texas, Georgia, Delaware, California and Kansas.

Fitnessgram's apparent dominance in school physical education is a particularly striking development in a political context shaped by the rhetoric of free enterprise and the virtues of vigorous competition. The Cooper Institute's most recent statistic estimates that their product is used in approximately 68 per cent of schools nationwide (Plowman and Meredith, 2013). It is also being exported and is the most widely utilized fitness assessment software systems utilized across the globe (Plowman and Meredith, 2013). As such,

Fitnessgram represents a significant global development in how physical education is taught and assessed and experienced by educators, students and parents.

The story of *Fitnessgram*'s unfinished but apparently inexorable journey towards world domination is a mixture of other stories about public health policy, electoral politics, for-profit business, network building, educational reform and the national/global fixation with assessment and accountability. Our focus in what follows here is a small but important part of this larger narrative; the discursive positioning of parents within both The Cooper Institute's own manoeuvrings and the broader debate about *Fitnessgram*'s place in the war on childhood obesity. Our argument is that parents have been, and will continue to be an increasingly important discursive entity in justifying *Fitnessgram*'s implementation, deflecting criticisms and facilitating the Cooper Institute's marketing strategies. As we will show, it is difficult to know how much notice flesh-and-blood parents are taking of all this, although anecdotal evidence that we provide suggests that at least some parents are concerned. However, we conclude this chapter by arguing that there are pressing ethical and educational questions that the physical education research community has yet to grapple with. Above all, our interest here is in questioning the ways in which *Fitnessgram* presumes to insert itself in intimate family life and thereby seeks to impose new forms of scrutiny, surveillance and accountability on the interpersonal relationships between parents and children.

The *Fitnessgram* phenomenon

In 1981 Charles Sterling, formerly a Texas school system director of health and physical education, joined Kenneth H. Cooper's Dallas-based health research and education organisation, the Cooper Institute (Plowman et al, 2006). At this time Sterling had already developed *Fitnessgram* and implemented it in a small but growing number of schools. Following its 1982 pilot launch in 30 schools in the state of Oklahoma, Sterling used the Cooper Institute's infrastructure and resources, as well as sponsorship funds from the Campbell Soup Company®, to expand *Fitnessgram*'s reach and scope. Over subsequent years, various corporate sponsors have been involved in the promotion, distribution and sale of *Fitnessgram* products. These entities include the National Football League's *Play 60* program, Human Kinetics, and the Prudential Insurance Company. *Fitnessgram* has also been endorsed by the American Alliance for Health, Physical Education, Recreation and Dance (AAHPERD), now known as Society of Health and Physical Educators (SHAPE) America. SHAPE America has a membership of 20,000 individuals and is the leading professional association for practitioners, researchers and policy advocates in the area of physical and health education. SHAPE America's endorsement of *Fitnessgram* is a noteworthy accomplishment given the association recently created and approved the nation's first National Standards for K-12 Physical Education (Kun, 2013).

Recently, the Cooper Institute announced their decision to partner exclusively with US Games as opposed to their previous vender, Human Kinetics.[1] US Games is a for-profit company that distributes athletic and physical education equipment and a subsidiary of BSN Sports, the largest distributer of sports team apparel and equipment in the United States. This merger, which began on 1 July 2015, gives US Games exclusive rights to sell *Fitnessgram* software. More than this however, since US Games has acquired a 'large manufacturer government contract code', they are able to sell significant quantities of their products directly to schools, school districts or entire states with relative administrative ease.

Although the specific requirements of *Fitnessgram*'s tests have varied over time, their most recent edition, Version 10, assesses students in six physical fitness domains: aerobic capacity, abdominal strength and endurance, upper body strength and endurance, body composition, trunk extensor strength and endurance, and flexibility. Individual *Fitnessgram* test scores are then compared to criterion-based standards known as 'Healthy Fitness Zones'. Following the entry of a student's fitness score into a database, *Fitnessgram* software generates a personalized report for each student. Depending on the school, district or state policy, personalized reports are sent home with students and/or mailed to parents. In 2012, a Cooper Institute document claimed that more than 22 million fitness reports had been disseminated (Plowman and Meredith, 2013). In addition to publicizing scores in this way, schools also have the option of making student fitness data publically available in aggregate form. States like California and Illinois, for example, store their fitness data on a publically available website hosted by their respective Departments of Education. Other states such as Delaware and Georgia house and publicise their fitness scores directly through The Perot International Youth Data Center, which was donated to the Cooper Institute by Ross Perot Sr. and is described as a 'highly secure data center that houses international student information' (Cooper Institute, 2014).

Implicating parents

Our focus in the remainder of this chapter is on the information that the Cooper Institute directs at parents via its website, user handbook and the messages and recommendations contained in the *Fitnessgram Parental Report* – a computer-generated analysis of each child's individualized fitness test scores. While some schools, even where *Fitnessgram* is mandated, are not required to send these reports to parents, it is a practice that *Fitnessgram* strongly encourages. In fact, our analysis of these three primary data sources suggests that *Fitnessgram*'s creators have gone to great lengths to address parental concerns and to justify its use and appearance in official school policies.

It is clear from Cooper Institute documents that garnering parental approval for *Fitnessgram* is a strategic priority (Plowman and Meredith,

2013). This is also evidenced by the documents and sample letters schools implementing the product are encouraged to send home. Hosted by their distributor Human Kinetics at the time of this writing, the Fitnessgram.net website also goes into explicit detail enumerating to parents the merits of fitness testing generally, and the value and importance of *Fitnessgram* more specifically. These self-referential promotional tactics appear alongside bleak warnings about the current and future health of children, health risks that an unhealthy child is prone to develop, and the parental duty to ensure this fate does not befall one's own child. It is a discursive strategy that Evans (2010, p22) has described as 'pre-emptive politics'; a rhetorical device that positions bodies as significant because of what they are and what they may eventually become. In turn, the tactic 'intensifies affects such as guilt, shame, fear and hope to make dystopian futures felt as present realities' and has the effect of 'quick, knee-jerk' reactions and poorly constructed policies (Evans, 2010, pp22–23). Baez and Talburt's (2008) work on school family relations is also relevant here. Schools and school policies, they argue, wittingly or not motivate parental involvement through 'a mixture of love and fear: a love that guarantees parents act in the best interests of their children, and a fear that failing to act will lead to disastrous consequences for their children and society as a whole' (Baez and Talburt's, 2008, p35).

To illustrate this point, the first paragraph on a *Fitnessgram* webpage devoted to answering parents 'frequently asked questions' begins with the following admonition: 'No matter what your children grow up to become, they will live happier, more productive lives if they are healthy- and physical fitness is vital to overall health' (Fitnessgram, 2013). Parents are also then told that 'by having a complete report, you (and your child) will know more about their overall level of fitness and how it can be improved' (Fitnessgram, 2013). Fitness testing and reporting the results of fitness testing are described as necessary so that parents have information about their child's health 'in an easy to read format'. But, 'more importantly', they go on to say, 'the report provides personalized tips and suggestions that can help introduce goal setting and plan an individualized fitness plan ... [and] provides a way for teachers (and parents) to teach children the importance of being active and fit throughout a lifetime' (Fitnessgram, 2013).

Parents are then warned of the consequences for failing to attend to their child's physical fitness by referring to a 1996 report authored by the United States Department of Health and Human Services. According to this report:

> Physical activity reduces the risk of premature mortality in general, and of coronary artery disease, hypertension, colon cancer, and diabetes mellitus in particular. Physical activity also improves mental health and is important for the health of muscles, bones, and joints (Fitnessgram, 2013).

The Cooper Institute is certainly not alone in their apparent belief that parents should be actively engaged in their child's health and fitness. A number of research studies over the years including one authored by the National Committee on Prevention of Obesity in Children and Youth echo this sentiment:

> Parents play a fundamental role as household policy makers. They make daily decisions on recreational opportunities, food availability at home, and children's allowances; they determine the setting for foods eaten in the home; and they implement countless other rules and policies that influence the extent to which various members of the family engage in healthful eating and physical activity (Koplan et al, 2005, p137).

In much of the anti-obesity literature, then, parents are portrayed as critical allies in the prevention of obesity and 'permissive parenting' (i.e., allowing children to eat unhealthy food or not encouraging physical activity) is cited as a significant reason for the reported rise in obesity levels. Further, schools are almost always positioned as the conduit for communicating these imperatives to parents (see, for example, Lindsay et al, 2006; Kaphingst and French, 2006; Anderson and Butcher, 2006). Thus, the Cooper Institute's message regarding parent's role in solving the childhood obesity crisis is consistent with the directives parents receive from a range of institutions. What is striking about the way in which the Cooper Institute attempts to communicate with parents is the level of detail included in the *Parental Report*, and particularly the potentially disastrous health consequences for children if parents do not take appropriate action.

Our point is not to disregard or devalue the role and influence that parents and caregivers have when it comes to young people's health and well-being. What we are concerned with, however, is how very personal and private messages and imperatives around health and well-being are communicated, by whom and with what potential effects on children, parents and family dynamics and/or relationships. Empirical research, for example, suggests that when health-related messages are communicated, they are often imbued with guilt, blame and/or disgust (for example, see Leahy, 2014). When Power and his colleagues (2010) conducted focus groups with young people, their parents and teachers about young adolescent's eating habits, the researchers found that conversations often centred on who *should* be and who *was not* taking responsibility for ensuring appropriate consumption patterns. In fact, their focus group interviews suggested that significant emphasis was placed on individuals who were to blame for the unhealthy eating behaviours of young people. They write: 'group members rarely blamed themselves. Teachers were more likely to discuss how poor parenting contributes to unhealthy behaviours (e.g., parents not monitoring their children, parents being permissive or inconsistent, parents overscheduling their children's lives)' (Power et al, 2010, p16). Parents, on the other hand, tended to blame their children, 'making references to poor appetites, picky eating, preferences for junk and fast food, and resistance to parental attempts to encourage healthy behaviors' (Power et al, 2010) while young people often blamed their parents for not purchasing healthy foods or having too many unhealthy foods around the house that were difficult for them to resist. Whatever else may be true, these findings should at least give us pause to think about the rationale, wisdom and effect of the Cooper Institute's decision to communicate with parents or caregivers by way of a computer generated letter that, depending on a child's results, may suggest that the child's disease risk and life expectancy is being harmed by the child's home environment.

Early criticisms

The Cooper Institute's online publicity material for *Fitnessgram* appears particularly designed to address parental anxiety about the fitness testing process. For example, the website dedicated to product information, www.fitnessgram. net, includes a great deal of information about the Cooper Institute's product development process, their philosophy, various endorsements received, *Fitnessgram's* widespread use, efficacy and overall necessity. Perhaps understandably, significant attention is given to concerns about three issues: privacy; whether a child's fitness score contributes to their grade in physical education class; and the body composition component of the test.

While it is difficult to know how widespread objections to *Fitnessgram* are, a number of media reports have generated disquiet about its use. Not surprisingly, the weighing of female students – publically or not – has generated some of the most vocal opposition. Under the headline 'School 'fitness' reports unleash howls of complaints from parents, kids', online media reported on the apparent dismay of Staten Island fifth-grader Gina Rocco and her mother when Gina's *Fitnessgram* report classified her as overweight (Lore, 2014). A slight twist on this theme appeared later that year in a story about Ireland Hobert-Hoch, an Iowan junior high-school student who, with the support of her family, refused to submit to *Fitnessgram* weight and BMI tests (Warren, 2014). And when Cameron Watson, a fourth grader from Massachusetts, gave his assessment to his parents, they told the press that they believed the assessment was pointless, simply threw it in the trash and said that these kinds of assessment encourage individuals (both students and educators) to focus 'too much on a number rather than looking at a child's overall health.' Cameron's mother also voiced her concern that the assessments were costing the school districts money that could be allocated more appropriately ('School Sends Home Letter', 2013). Her misgivings about the policy prompted her to file a grievance with the state, requesting them to remove the body composition portion of the test from the assessment.

In response, the local department of public health issued the following statement justifying the process: 'Children with high BMI are more likely to become overweight or obese adults and be at a higher risk for diabetes, heart disease, and some cancers. Helping children maintain a healthy weight may prevent serious illness later in life. BMI screenings are intended to raise parents' awareness about the issue' ('School Sends Home Letter', 2013). Similar misgivings were voiced by 25 parents in Elmhurst, Illinois, when their school began linking students' composition scores to their overall grade in physical education. Although parents successfully lobbied to have body composition results decoupled from a student's grade, they were not able to overturn the district's policy of mandating routine testing of children. According the one school official, the district must 'continue the measurements because those statistics are needed when applying for fitness grants' (Branson-Potts et al, 2011). In other words, when schools apply for grants related to physical education, they often have to provide a rationalization as to why the intervention is needed. Body composition scores are frequently used as one such justifying statistic.

Apart from these media reports, there has been some research into the reaction to and effectiveness of *Fitnessgram*'s letters to parents (such as Madsen, 2011; Thompson and Card-Higginson, 2009). Madsen and Linchey's (2012) summary of the literature is probably the most authoritative account although it is important to mention that virtually all of the US-based research in this area has focused on BMI scores only. That is, there appears to have no scholarly or popular interest in or concern about the value of reporting to parents student scores on *Fitnessgram*'s other tests that measure cardiovascular fitness, muscular strength or flexibility.

Overall, Madsen and Linchey's (2012) report that parental opposition has declined over time in the various jurisdictions where parental letters have been used. It is hard to know why this happened although Madsen and Linchey speculate that more effort has gone into explaining the value of the letters, a point which is reflected in the Cooper Institute's publicity material for *Fitnessgram* described above. Another interpretation not considered by Madsen and Linchey is that many parents may decide that resistance is futile or simply that the shock or novelty of receiving the letters has worn off over time; *Fitnessgram* letters are, in other words, becoming an increasingly normal part of sending one's children to school.

What is abundantly clear from this work, however, is that clear evidence of the student health benefits of sending *Fitnessgram* results to parents is hard to find. This is perhaps not surprising given that a wide range of formats for parental letters are used in American schools and often include very little explanatory information. As Madsen says in an earlier publication:

> ... school-based BMI reporting fails one of the most salient aspects of a useful screening test: having an effective therapy if the disease (or condition) is detected. Lifestyle interventions to treat pediatric obesity are largely ineffective, and recommending individual behavior change is unlikely to meet with success, if the experience of multidisciplinary pediatric obesity clinics is any guide. Thus, expecting a single BMI report

to parents to have a meaningful effect on a child's weight status, in the absence of environmental changes, may be wishful thinking (Madsen 2011, p991).

Although Madsen herself appears to be generally sympathetic to the general idea of schools reporting children's BMI scores to parents, one way of interpreting her comments here is to wonder why anyone might have imagined these letters to be a promising public health measure in the first place. There is certainly no published research that we are aware of from which a successful precedent might be gleaned. In fact, while the media reports mentioned above provide somewhat sensational examples of vehement opposition to *Fitnessgram's* letters to parents, a less newsworthy but more obvious conclusion presents itself. That is, as Madsen herself concedes, many parents probably take little notice of the information contained in the letters, either because they do not understand the information or because they think their child's weight or health is not the business of schools in the first place. It is also clear enough that many parents never receive letters because children fail to pass them on, because they have changed address or because some school districts have simply decided not to send the letters. After all, the generation of letters is now a cost that many schools have to bear themselves and this is why a number of vendors have sprung up offering, for a fee, to create and send *Fitnessgram* letters on behalf of schools.

It is apparent that the *Fitnessgram* letters to parents have become a business opportunity for some and an important means by which the Cooper Institute has sought to deflect criticism of *Fitnessgram*. In passing, it is interesting that public opposition to *Fitnessgram* in general has come from children, parents/caregivers and the popular media while the physical education profession and the research community have been almost uniformly silent or supportive. Nonetheless, the broader point is that it is hard to see the Cooper Institute's decision to involve parents in the *Fitnessgram* regime as anything other than a *strategic* move. After all, there are few if any signs that parental letters were conceived or have acted as a public health measure.

Surveillance and the governing of family life

Fitnessgram is a noteworthy example of how the presumed need to develop and implement new forms of surveillance are aligned with for profit interests and motivations, which intersect and become imbedded in school policies and practices. This happens on multiple levels. Most obvious is the issue of money; states and school districts mandated to use *Fitnessgram* must find the funds and resources to purchase the equipment and train personnel who will administer the testing regime. And while some states and districts have been provided grants to help them comply with these policies, others are left to find the necessary resources to meet the requirements of these largely unfunded mandates. Even schools fortunate enough to secure funding are often required to complete tedious grant applications and commit to sharing the results of their school's fitness testing. For example, the Presidential Youth Fitness Program (PYFP), a major sponsor of *Fitnessgram*, oversees one of the largest grant programs. In their application, each educator requesting funds must agree to the following on an annual basis: to participate in training and professional development, conduct the *Fitnessgram* Assessment, record and submit student achievements and submit an end of year report. For many schools, compliance also requires teachers to send student results to their respective local or state boards of education. In places where these data are required, they are also often posted online for the public to see. In some cases it is used as a way to compare individual school or district fitness scores or the aggregate fitness scores of students by race, ethnicity, gender or socio-economic status. While this level of reporting is relatively new to the field of physical education, it only mimics recent federal and state mandates that seem preoccupied with measuring student achievement, teacher performance and the most banal minutia of school life. According to the Center for American Progress, students in the United States take as many as 20 standardized assessments annually requiring teachers to report on everything from their progress in academic, dispositional and physical fitness domains (Hefling, 2015). It is also now commonplace in the United States for state boards of education to implement various performance and incentive schemes that connect student progress in these domains to teacher salaries.

Returning to the focus of this paper, however, families too are now caught up in these assessment regimes and projects of surveillance and are further positioned as critical partners and necessary 'helpers' when it comes to their child's physical fitness (Cooper Institute, 2005). Parents are explicitly encouraged to perform certain tasks out of their commitment to and concern for their child's health and well-being. In the most recent version of the *Fitnessgram* user handbook – a document designed to give instruction on the proper implementation of the product – educators are told that stressing to parents the benefit of regular fitness testing 'provides a powerful message that the *Fitnessgram* results are important and that it is possible for individuals to change their level of fitness by assessing where they are, setting appropriate goals, and creating and enacting plans that work toward the chosen goals' (Plowman and Meredith, 2013, pp2–3). By referencing a 2003 study published in the *Archives of Pediatrics and Adolescent Medicine*, the Cooper Institute claims that parental reports constitute an important way to 'motivate' parents so they are involved in their child's physical activity regime. The report goes on to say that 'parents should be encouraged to use the messages on the *Fitnessgram* parental report to help their children 'plan personal physical activity programs,' or what they refer to as 'family activity plans' (Cooper Institute, 2005, p28). According to the Cooper Institute, schools should be actively involved in 'alerting parents that they are responsible for helping their children with the other half of their daily physical activity' Cooper Institute, 2005, p5.3).

In the example *Parental Report* posted on their website that is meant to be illustrative of the kinds of messages contained in a typical report, parents are advised that 'Long periods of inactivity are inappropriate for children' (Cooper Institute, 2005). Physical activities are then further designated into three levels. For each level, parents are provided tips on how much activity children need at each level, when in their life it is appropriate for children to participate in that activity level and how they should encourage activity at that level. Level 1, for example, is described as 'lifestyle activities.' For this level parents are encouraged to suggest that children walk, bicycle, skateboard, and participate in housework or yard work. Level 2 includes aerobic sports and other aerobic activities like field sports such as baseball, football or soccer and court sports such as basketball, volleyball, hockey, and soccer. Finally, Level 3 is designated as flexibility and muscular fitness activities. Appropriate activities in this level include martial arts (tai chi), stretching, yoga, ballet, weight lifting, wrestling and cheer, dance and/or drill teams.

In many ways, the concerns we are raising about the ways in which schools are complicit in the enlistment of parents and caregivers to assist, accomplish – or at the very least – quietly acquiesce to certain imperatives and/or priorities are not a new. As Baez and Talburt (2008, p26) point out, the history of schooling is marked by a series of shifts in the management of relationships between families and educators, the state and the economy. Consistent with Baez and Talburt's ideas, the Cooper Institute positions the responsible parent as wanting to raise healthy children who are physical active on a regular basis, both for the sake of childhood health and happiness and the nation. In this way, products like *Fitnessgram* represent a 'pedagogising' of parenting whereby the imperatives, systems of accountability and forms of surveillance that are assumed at school, make their way into the private sphere of family life – from the (re)structuring of conversations that parents have with children around their health and physical activity to the actual activities that they should participate in to remain 'healthy.' In this case, it is the Cooper Institute's *expert* knowledge that is of most value, as opposed to parents own knowledge and intuition about their own child's needs and desires (Pike and Leahy, 2012). These kinds of admonitions may have the effect of creating new roles and responsibilities for parents as, again according to Baez and Talburt (2008, p27), they constitute imperatives that are reliant on 'the logic of empowerment': 'parents are given the tools and knowledge for helping themselves to help their own children' (Baez and Talburt, 2008). At the same time, the messages the Cooper Institute directs at parents can also be seen as a strategy to get parents, not just children, to value particular notions of health and, by extension, the fitness testing product it sells.

This last point brings us to a final concern about the widespread use of *Fitnessgram* and its insertion into family life. Soliciting parental approval seems an obvious marketing strategy; parents are the individuals who vote for school board members and policy makers who serve on committees that make decisions about whether or not to purchase the product. By extension, having a monopoly over communication with the individuals who purchase or, at the very least, advise on decisions about the purchase of sport and physical activity equipment for schools yield significant financial benefits, particularly for the Cooper Institute, BNS Sports and US Games. What we are suggesting is that, rather than important elements in a significant public health initiative, perhaps parents have simply become pawns in the Cooper Institute's overall business plan to expand the reach of *Fitnessgram* paraphernalia.

It is also not beyond the scope of possibility that US Games may use student and parental reports as a venue to promote their brand and its products. Given that the Cooper Institute has estimated that 22 million reports have already been sent home, and more schools are adopting their products each year, the reports represent an inexpensive and convenient way to market products. Apart from direct marketing tactics (i.e., putting their logo directly on the reports), we envision more subtle forms of self-promotion. Consider, for example, that US Games (via of its parent company BSN Sports) is the largest manufacturer of sport and physical education equipment in the United States. It is not difficult to imagine how the parental interventions and activities recommended by *Fitnessgram* letters to parents might align with the products that US Games sell. At the same time, however, given these expanding commercial networks, we might also wonder about potential use or misuse of the data generated by *Fitnessgram*? While the Cooper Institute assures schools that neither the Cooper Institute, *FitnessGram*, its technical support staff nor US Games will have access to individual student data, this disclaimer does not stop them or others from benefiting from the collection and dissemination of aggregate data describing student fitness levels. After all, in the age of 'Big Data', data is money and new ways to commercially exploit large data sets will always be tempting to entities with the computing power to do so.

Conclusion: Towards a critical academic response to *Fitnessgram*

For the purposes of this chapter our attention has centred on the knowledge claims and imperatives *Fitnessgram* reports direct at parents and guardians and the implications that these messages may have on parenting practices and families. At this point in our analysis of *Fitnessgram*, however, a degree of circumspection is necessary. It is unclear, for example, in what ways or to what extent parents take up these messages. Do the ideas included in these reports resonate with parents' understandings of what it means to embody a 'good' parent. After all, the idea of the parent explicitly acting as a child's body weight counsellor may strike at least some parents as new or unwelcome. Particularly because parenting is (or at least was) an inherently personal and private sphere of life, we also wonder about the affective dimension of parenting; how might the dissemination of these data influence parental self-efficacy beliefs about 'responsible' caregiving. Very little is known about how *Fitnessgram* reports to parents change parental behaviour and the possible effect they might have on familial relations, the pace and rhythm of family life and a child's response to these potentially shifting dynamics.

At present, there exists a dearth of critical scholarship examining the influence and use of digital technologies such as *Fitnessgram* as these interface and influence students, their families, teachers and physical education pedagogy. Future research could examine the information and imperatives contained in the *Fitnessgram*-generated student and parental reports and the ways both students and their families take up these health-related messages. This is a particularly necessary line of research given the widespread implementation of *Fitnessgram* in addition to the fact that a number of scholars have issued concerns regarding the implications and ramifications of administering these types of body-centric assessments. While we have provided anecdotal evidence to suggest that not all parents and teachers are convinced of the benefits of regular fitness testing because of its potential to embarrass students, create unnecessary body image anxiety and/or encourage disordered or problematic food and exercise behaviours, empirical work that examines these issues would be a valuable addition to this debate. Finally, there is a need for scholarship that interrogates the effect publishing fitness scores online may have for students, teachers and schools. In particular, there is a pressing but as yet unanswered questions about issues of privacy and how *Fitnessgram* data might be exploited for financial profit or used as a mechanism to reward or punish students, teachers and schools.

Note

1   Human Kinetics will continue to be permitted to sell the test manuals for Fitnessgram products but will no longer sell the software.

References

Anderson, P. M. and Butcher, K. F. (2006) Childhood obesity: Trends and potential causes, *The Future of children*, 16(1), 19–45.

Baez, B. and Talburt, S. (2008) Governing for responsibility and with love: parents and children between home and school, *Educational Theory*, 58(1), 25–43.

Branson-Potts, H., Meyer, E. and Rhodes, D. (2011) Physical fitness grade linked to body fat: After parents protest, Elmhurst school says BMI data will no longer affect report card, *Chicago Tribune* [online]. Available from http://articles.chicagotribune. com/2011-01-18/news/ct-met-body-mass-20110118_1_physical-fitness-bmi-progress-report [accessed 10 April 2015].

Cooper Institute (2005) *Fitnessgram: Report for parents* [online]. Available from file:/// Users/A135665/Downloads/FGparent%20(2).pdf [accessed 15 April 2015].

Cooper Institute (2014) *Fitnessgram* [online]. Available from https://www.cooper institute.org/youth/fitnessgram [accessed 29 June 2015].

Evans, B. (2010) Anticipating fatness: childhood, affect and the preemptive 'war on obesity', *Transactions of the Institute of British Geographers*, 35(1), 21–38.

Fitnessgram (2013) Parents FAQ: English Fitnessgram [online]. Available from www. fitnessgram.net/faqs/parents-faqenglish [accessed 15 May 2015].

Hefling, K. (2015). Do students take too many tests? Congress to weigh question [online]. Available from http://www.pbs.org/newshour/rundown/congress-decide-testing-schools/ accessed 3 June 2015.

Kaphingst, K. M. and French, S. (2006) The role of schools in obesity prevention, *The Future of Children*, 16(1), 109–142.

Koplan, J. P., Liverman, C. T. and Kraak, V .I. (2005) Preventing childhood obesity: Health in the balance: executive summary, *Journal of the American Dietetic Association*, 105(1), 131–138.

Kun, P. (2013) Press release: AAHPERD becomes SHAPE America [online]. Available from http://www.shapeamerica.org/pressroom/2013/aahperd-becomes-shape-am erica.cfm [accessed 24 June 2015].

Leahy, D. (2014). Assembling a health [y] subject: Risky and shameful pedagogies in health education, *Critical Public Health*, 24(2), 171–181.

Lindsay, A. C., Sussner, K. M., Kim, J. and Gortmaker, S. L. (2006) The role of parents in preventing childhood obesity, *The Future of Children*, 16(1), 169–186.

Lore, D. C. (2014) School 'fitness' reports unleash howls of complaints from parents/ kids [online]. Available from http://www.silive.com/news/index.ssf/2014/05/school_fit ness_reports_unleash.html accessed 4 October 2015.

Madsen, K. A. (2011) School-based body mass index screening and parent notification: a statewide natural experiment, *Archives of Pediatrics and Adolescent Medicine*, 165(11): 987–992.

Madsen, K. A. and Linchey, J. (2012) School-based BMI and body composition screening and parent notification in California: methods and messages, *Journal of School Health*, 82(6), 294–300.

Pike, J. and Leahy, D. (2012) School food and the pedagogies of parenting, *Australian Journal of Adult Learning*, 52(3), 434.

Plowman, S. A. and Meredith, M. D. (eds.) (2013) *Fitnessgram/Activitygram reference guide (4th Edition)*. Dallas, TX: Cooper Institute.

Plowman, S. A., Sterling, C. L., Corbin, C. B. et al (2006) The history of FITNESS- GRAM, *Journal of Physical Activity and Health*, 3, S5–S20.

Power, T. G., Bindler, R. C. and Goetz, S. et al (2010) Obesity prevention in early adolescence: Student, parent, and teacher views, *Journal of School Health*, 80(1), 13–19.

'School sends home letter calling some students obese' (2013) [online]. Available from http://www.myfoxboston.com/story/21348194/2013/02/25/school-sends-home-letter- calling-some-students-obese [accessed 20 May 2015].

Thompson, J. W. and Card-Higginson, P. (2009) Arkansas' experience: Statewide surveillance and parental information on the child obesity epidemic, *Pediatrics*, 124 (supplement 1), S73–S82.

Warren, L. (2014) Student, 13, is sent to the principal's office after refusing to be weighed in front of her classmates during gym class [online]. Available from http://www.dailymail. co.uk/news/article-2841084/Student-13-sent-principal-s-office-refusing-weighed-classma tes-gym-class.html [accessed 4 October 2015].

7 'The family who eats together stays together'

Governing families, governing health, governing pedagogies

Jo Pike and Deana Leahy

Introduction

In this chapter we consider how families are targeted by a myriad of initiatives that seek to cultivate and shape health[y] conduct. In considering the various initiatives at play, we explicitly focus our discussion on school programmes that operate as key mediating spaces that permit governmental imperatives to reach into the lives of families. Our discussion will interrogate the mechanisms by which families are incited to be healthy with a particular emphasis on the moral aspects of governmental work.

In the play *August, Osage County* (2008), Tracy Letts provides a powerful and confronting portrayal of a family meal. Following the funeral of the family patriarch, Beverly Weston, extended family members gather around the family dinner table to mark his passing with the sharing of a communal meal. Dishes are prepared and brought to the table, grace is said, multiple conversations commence and run along simultaneously as Letts captures something of the dynamism, the spontaneity and vibrancy generated through everyday, mundane relational family mealtime encounters. This scene represents a pivotal point in the play where the audience recognizes a shift in the balance of power which transfers from the bitterly acerbic Violet to her daughter Barbara. After heated discussions covering vegetarianism, marriage breakdown, infidelity, domestic abuse, alcoholism and substance misuse where every character's particular proclivities, frailties and vulnerability are laid bare, probed and dissected, the scene culminates in a display of physical violence – a full-on wrestling match between daughter and mother:

VIOLET: You can't do this! This is *my* house! This is *my* house!
BARBARA: You don't get it, do you? (*With a burst of adrenaline, she strides to Violet, towers over her*) I'M RUNNING THINGS NOW!

Part of the power that Letts generates through this scene as it builds to its violent conclusion emerges through contrasting what the audience might imagine could and perhaps *should* happen as families come together around the dining table to share memories and experiences of grief, and what unfolds in these exchanges. This juxtaposition relies on the audience's shared under-standings and assumptions about the nature and function of the family meal; while it might be imagined in an idealized form as a cohesive, supporting and nurturing experience bringing families together around the table, it is often experienced as highly problematic, fraught with tension, anxiety and embroiled in complex relations of power. In this chapter we raise a number of questions relating to the family meal and how it has come to be understood in various school programmes and policies, as a means to secure better health and social outcomes for children and young people. We analyse how families are targeted via a number of pedagogical strategies and resources, that seek to cultivate and shape health[y] conduct. In considering the various initiatives at play, we explicitly focus our discussion on the ways in which specific pedagogies oper-ationalise notions of family mealtimes suggesting that school-based programmes and pedagogical approaches focused on 'the family meal' position schools as key mediating spaces which permit governmental imperatives to reach into the lives of families. Drawing on the work of Foucault and the field of govern-mentality studies we suggest that the valorisation of the family meal as a means to achieve specific health and social objectives does governmental work that is imbued with a variety of moral imperatives. Our discussion will interrogate the various pedagogies through which families are incited not only to be healthy, but also to form particular sets of social relations. The chapter is ostensibly divided into three sections. The first tackles the problem of defining the family meal, its forms and functions. Here, we provide a critical analysis of some of the accepted truths surrounding the notion of the 'family meal' – namely, that families are not eating together anymore; that they *should* be eating together more and that the family meal mode of dining conveys particular benefits on its participants. The second section outlines our theoretical approach which frames the analysis in the remainder of the chapter. The third examines a range of formal and informal pedagogical strategies used within schools which mobilise notions of family mealtimes to develop not only healthy eating practices amongst children, but also to model appropriate civilised modes of dining. We suggest that these pedagogical strategies and devices reinforce idealised notions of families that overlook the complexities, tensions and power dynamics of intergenerational encounters and furthermore that these strategies pedagogicalize families in new ways.

The mythology of the family meal

> It's shocking. Children never talk to their parents, they don't have a time when they sit down and discuss everything. It's one of the causes of our dysfunctional society, a reason why children behave so badly. It's not just that they're getting stuffed with junk food, they don't have a family meal that draws them together. If you never talk to granny you don't mind banging her on the head (Leith, 2007).

The above comments reflect recent and ongoing concerns that families are no longer sitting down to eat a 'proper family meal' at the table. 'Did you know that 80 per cent of households never sit down for a meal together? They don't even have a table', suggests Prue Leith the chair of the UK based charity The Children's Food Trust until 2010. The decline of the family meal is a powerful discourse that has generated a range of campaigns hoping to encourage more families to eat together more frequently (see Back to the Table campaign 2004–2009, Round the Table campaign sponsored by Quality Meat Scotland 2013, The Family Dinner Project – ongoing). However, as many have pointed out, the idea of the family meal, conceived of as a heterosexual nuclear family sitting and eating an evening meal together around a table is a relatively recent invention (Cappellini and Parsons, 2012, Cinotto, 2006) and concerns over its demise have been circulating since the 1920s (Murcott, 1997). Consequently, it is problematic to assume that we are 'no longer' sitting down to a family meal since 'we' may never have done so. Furthermore, while it is assumed that everyone knows what is meant by a proper meal, terminology is variously applied and the requisite structural components are contested (Douglas, 1972; Murcott, 1982; and Kerr, 1988; Levi-Strauss, 1997; Mitchell, 1999). A lack of consensus about what constitutes a family meal, which family members need to be in attendance (Cook and Dunnifon, 2012) and where the family meal should take place, means that the family meal is often considered in isolation outside the context of wider familial relations (Capellini and Parsons, 2012). Our suggestion is that concerns about the demise of the family meal may be emblematic of wider concerns about the family and that valorisation of the family meal may relate more to its ideological and symbolic power rather than lived experiences of everyday family mealtime encounters. As Wilk (2010) notes and as our opening vignette demonstrates, the realities of family mealtimes 'rarely live up to the ideal' (p428).

Despite increasing evidence that points to the complexities and ambiguities of family relations during family mealtimes, the idealized notion of the family meal proves remarkably resilient and indeed, has been invested with a bewildering range of beneficial attributes that position it as a panacea for contemporary social ills. Both the frequency and form of the family meal are regarded as significant in the prevention of drug and alcohol use (White and Halliwell, 2010), anti-social behaviour (Eisenberg et al, 2009), obesity (Fulkerson et al, 2009; Hammons and Fiese, 2011; Neumark-Sztainer et al, 2003), disordered eating (Hammons and Fiese, 2011, Neumark-Sztainer et al., 2008) and poor communication skills. Engaging in family meals is thought to reduce the risk of children smoking (Eisenberg et al, 2004) bringing improvements in family relationships (Neumark-Sztainer et al, 2004; Jacobs and Fiese, 2007; Fiese et al, 2006), improving nutritional intake (Neumark-Sztainer et al, 2003; Taveras et al., 2005; Videon and Manning, 2003, Larson et al, 2007; Hammons and Fiese, 2011), and academic performance (Eisenberg et al, 2004). Despite the number of studies advocating the beneficial effects of family meals, it is difficult to correlate this wide range of beneficial outcomes with the family meal itself, rather than any other aspect of family life and relationships. Furthermore, reliance on self-reported survey data in some of research in this area can also be problematic. Nevertheless, despite some of the conceptual and methodological challenges associated with defining and assessing the prevalence of family mealtimes, wildly ambitious and unsubstantiated claims are made for the family meal in which increasing its frequency and prevalence will 'nourish ethical thinking' (The Family Dinner Project), enhance social cohesion and generally address the causes of our 'dysfunctional society'. As Wilk (2010) points out, this way of thinking about the family meal is ultimately hegemonic so that any 'alternatives are unthinkable. There is no oppositional position, no shading of opinion, and no praise of solitary eating' (p429). It is this hegemonic positioning of the family meal which occludes the complexities, tensions and ambiguities that characterise the realities of family dining and which imbues the family meal with almost mythical properties for addressing social ills that is mobilized in schools to do governmental work within families.

Governing families, governing food – the role of pedagogy

Following Dean (2010) we have suggested elsewhere that families are currently bombarded by a myriad of initiatives that seek to explicitly shape, sculpt, mobilize and work through the health choices, desires and aspirations, needs, wants and lifestyles of parents, children, and the family unit as a whole (Pike and Leahy, 2012). While the family has long been a target for governmental intervention (Donzelot, 1979), Burrows (2009) suggests in contemporary times there has been an intensification of the governmental strategies directed at prescribing the health[y] conduct of 'families'. In order to understand this proliferation of governmental strategies and in turn how they work to govern parental food practices, including modes of family dining we draw on the field of Foucauldian inspired governmentality studies. Foucault defined government as 'the conduct of conduct' stating that government relates to the 'way in which the conduct of individuals or groups might be directed: the government of children, of souls, of communities, of families, of the sick … to govern in this sense, is to structure the possible field of action' (Foucault, 1982, pp220–221). His various analyses of government explored questions related to how conduct, and attempts to shape conduct, were imagined and enacted within different historical epochs, states and sites (Gordon, 1991).

According to Dean (2010, p18) government refers to:

> … any more or less calculated and rational activity, undertaken by a multiplicity of authorities and agencies, employing a variety of techniques and forms of knowledges, that seeks to shape conduct by working through our desires, aspirations, interests and beliefs, for definite but shifting ends and with a diverse set of relatively unpredictable consequences, effects and outcomes.

Within this context we understand some of the strategies within schools that aim to promote the family meal, as governmental devices that provide a 'contact point' for government (Burchell, 1996) connecting questions of government, politics and administration to the space of bodies, lives, selves and persons (Dean, 2010, p20). In essence, some of the pedagogical approaches in schools, particularly those that invoke hegemonic notion of family meals, provide an opportunity to explicitly shape, sculpt, mobilize and work through the food choices, desires and aspirations, needs, social relations and lifestyles of parents, families and children.

In the remainder of this chapter, our subsequent analysis shows that while traditionally students have been the targets of school governmental interventions, some of the strategies that promote the family meal, position families and more specifically mothers as the objects and targets of these pedagogies. Not only do schools encourage future generations to become self regulating citizens, but they also to extend their reach beyond the school gates through increasingly porous boundaries to reach out to mothers and families (Pike and Colquhoun, 2012; Leahy et al, 2016). In this respect there is increasing recognition of the pivotal pedagogical work that families do. Furthermore, the championing of the family meal as the preferred mode of dining constitutes a new line of force that traverses school dining rooms, classrooms and other school spaces, bringing family pedagogies 'closer in' than ever before.

Contemporary policy and practice then is predicated on the imperative to 'educate' parents and families with regard not only to what they feed their children, but also how they feed them and children themselves are increasingly tasked with performing this governmental work, shaping and regulating modes of dining at home. While there are many different spaces that perform this work, it is the role of schools, as appropriate sites for the 'pedagogicalization' of parents and families that is the focus of this chapter.

Modelling the family meal

In this section we consider a range of pedagogical approaches and resources constructed to teach children about what constitutes the 'proper way' to eat as a family (and conversely what is not proper). For the purposes of this chapter we focus our attention on three worksheets used by Health and Physical Education teachers within primary schools in Australia that provide us with illustrative examples of the ways in which the mythological family meal functions pedagogically. The first worksheet was developed by the Bakers IDI Heart and Diabetes Institute (2003) and is part of a larger resource package called *Primary Fight Back: Healthy Eating and Physical Activity: A Resource for Teachers, Students & Their Parents*. The second and third worksheets we discuss were developed by teachers as part of their classroom unit of work that focuses on 'eating well'. Despite the different origins of the worksheets, the same pedagogical force fuels all three. This force, as we have suggested above, consists of a constellation of discourses about food, health, risk, morality and changing family structures and in turn invokes particular approaches to learning about how families should (and should not) eat.

The worksheet entitled *Family Eating* (see Figure 7.1) forms part of a larger resource package designed to teach primary school aged children about eating well and exercising. The worksheet features a character called Popcorn

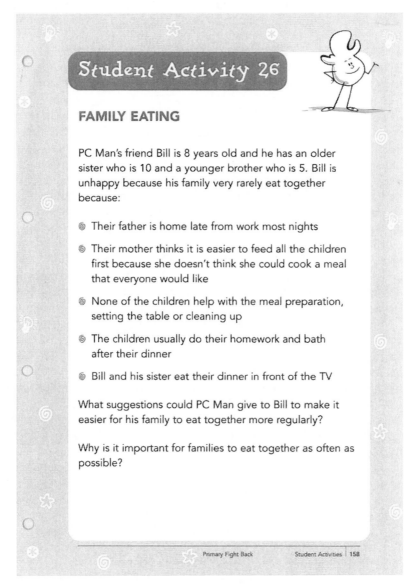

Figure 7.1 Family Eating
Source: Baker IDI Heart and Diabetes Institute, 2003

Man or PC Man (see top right-hand corner of the worksheet) who provides advice to children to help them make appropriate choices about what and *how* to eat.

In this scenario Bill (an eight-year-old boy) is unhappy because his family does not eat together. Based on the worksheet we can surmise the following: Mum makes the dinner without any help and prepares two different meals to account for different generational tastes. Dad is more often than not late home from work. Instead of eating together Bill and his siblings eat their meals in front of the TV. They then have their bath and do their homework. Upon reading through the problem, students are then invited to help PC man advise Bill on how to make it easier for his family to eat together more regularly. Students are then asked 'Why it is important for families to eat together as often as possible?'

The second worksheet, which was developed by a health education teacher, adopts a similar approach to the worksheet discussed above. This time the family of interest is *The Simpsons*. The worksheet's title is 'What is wrong with this picture?' The picture is of the Simpsons eating dinner in front of the television. Marge, Homer and Lisa are on the couch eating their dinner from dinner trays placed on stands. Bart is lying on his stomach on the floor in his underwear, fork poised near his mouth. Maggie and Snowball (their cat) are sitting on the floor and Santa's Little Helper (the family dog) is asleep. The kids all have their eyes set firmly on the TV, as does Snowball. Marge is looking sideways at Homer's can of beer with a disapproving look on her face. Homer is gazing longingly at Lisa's plate. The image operates as a prompt for analysis for students. Students are required to address the following three questions which appear directly below the image 'What is wrong with how *The Simpsons* are eating their dinner?' 'List the health effects of eating dinner in this way?'; and, finally, 'How could *The Simpsons* change how they eat the family meal so that it is better?'

The third worksheet consists of various pictures that capture different approaches and ways of eating. The worksheet was developed by a primary classroom teacher for her grade 4 class as part of a unit on food. The pictures on the worksheet were drawn by hand and included the following: someone eating in front of the TV alone, someone walking into McDonalds, a nuclear family sitting around a kitchen table eating dinner (on a plate, meat and vegetables are clearly discernible), a young girl sitting on her bed eating cake (alone and upset), someone snacking out of the fridge, a couple eating a junk food dinner in front of the TV, a man sitting alone at the table eating dinner on a plate (again meat and vegetables), and a nuclear family sitting around a dinner table eating junk food. According to the instructions students are required to make a series of judgements, placing a tick next to the images that they regard as good, and crosses next to the ones that they think are bad.

It is clear from all three worksheets that eating around a table, with all members of the nuclear, heterosexual family in attendance, is regarded as the preferred mode of dining. It is good. Students are invited to classify all other modes of eating that do not conform to this model, solitary eating, eating in front of the television, parents and children eating separately, as 'bad'. Students must consider the health implications of these ways of eating and why they are wrong. The dividing of different eating practices into discrete binary categories of 'good' and 'bad' not only prevents any 'shading of opinion' (Wilk, 2010) but it also performs an important governmental function whereby the family meal becomes a necessary and unquestioning intervention designed to produce particular health and social outcomes. Students are invited to think about what could be done to make the 'bad' eating scenarios better (i.e., more like a family meal). In the first example, eight-year-old Bill is tasked with the responsibility of making it easier for his family to eat together, presumably by intervening in those areas where he is able to exert some influence, for example helping to prepare the meal, set the table or clear the dishes. However, students may also suggest that Bill could challenge his mother who mistakenly *'thinks* it is easier to feed all the children first' or to challenge his father to return promptly from work since all family members in this scenario contribute to the failure to uphold the family meal model. Such encouragements overlook the generational and gendered power dynamics which operate in many families, particularly around mealtimes and food provision (Dobash and Dobash, 1980; Burgoyne and Clarke, 1983; Ellis, 1983; Charles and Kerr, 1988).

Furthermore, in classifying particular modes of eating as good or bad, it is clear that children are encouraged to do far more than simply judge the eating practices of others; they are also required to identify with Bill or Lisa and Bart Simpson and to judge their own family eating practices accordingly. Following Michel Foucualt, Vaz and Bruno (2003) suggest that:

> … the classification of each individual along the polarity ranging from normal to abnormal achieves its goal if it is active in the interior of individuals, if it makes them judge and conceive themselves according to this polarity (Vaz and Bruno, 2003, p277).

The pedagogical use of these scenarios then can be read as an attempt to encourage children to measure eating practices within *their own* home against the normative model of family meals, and if necessary intervene to change how their own families eat. In attempting to cultivate these particular modes of conduct, schools become an important governmental technology in shaping the conduct of children and their families. Families become responsible for regulating what and *how* family members eat and for regulating the conduct of individual members.

The use of family scenarios in the worksheets outlined above reveals how the mythological family meal is conceptualized within the everyday practices of education. However, what is less clear is how teachers deploy these resources in the classroom and how the discursive construction of family mealtimes is taken up, modified or challenged by students. It is hard to imagine, given the simplistic, binary renderings of the family meal and that students would not raise further questions. For instance, students who are familiar with *The Simpsons* might notice that Homer is not wringing Bart's neck in the TV dinner scenario whereas at the dinner table this is common practice. Or they might even challenge the dominant construct of the family and the gender roles being portrayed in Bill's family. Research suggests that students do challenge what they are taught about food (see Leahy and Gray, 2014; Leahy and Pike, 2015) and that when students problematize the intended 'message', teachers can find it difficult to allow the contradictions, complexities and tensions to emerge, flourish and flow (see, for example, Cliff and Wright, 2010; Leahy and Gray, 2014). Questioning the preferred model of the family meal detracts from the imperatives and forces driving the pedagogical strategy.

Conclusion

This chapter has attempted to review some of the ways in which the family meal is constructed by a selection of pedagogical resources used to promote healthy eating in schools in Australia. We suggest that the valorization of the family meal as a panacea for a range of social ills, and the concomitant attempts to persuade, entice or cajole families into these preferred norms of consumption, is problematic on a number of counts. First, as we have suggested in our initial vignette and subsequent discussion, the reality of family mealtimes is often very different from the imagined and idealised constructions of family meals deployed by educators. Such a construction of family mealtimes ignores the wider social context in which they occur and overlooks the power relations and dynamics which characterize everyday family mealtime encounters. Promoting the family meal as the preferred and 'proper' mode of dining not only occludes other possible ways of eating, but it is taken as a signifier of healthy consumption, effective parenting and functional family relations, a ritual where loving, nurturing, healthy family relationships are enacted and performed. Those who do not or cannot engage in such rituals are somehow regarded as ineffective parents raising problem children. Second, the perceived health and social benefits of family meals are predicated upon tenuous assumptions. The claims that family mealtimes can protect against such a wide range of detrimental health and social outcomes are conceptually ill defined and methodologically flawed. Such claims are embedded in discourses of crisis, reflecting contemporary concerns around young people's health, obesity, eating disorders, substance misuse, crime and general concerns over young people's moral character or lack thereof. As we have suggested in the first part of this chapter, evidence that the prevalence of family mealtimes is declining in modern times is far from persuasive. Third, attempts to shape family dining practices pedagogicalize families in new ways that extend beyond the school gates. Family mealtimes become a site for intervention where family members must judge and regulate their own and each other's eating practices against a highly normative model. The knowledge and expertise of parents in terms of what works best for their family, is inferior to the expertise of the school. Finally, children are positioned as both target and technology of government and encouraged to take responsibility for how family mealtimes are structured. This has important implications which appear to be overlooked within the pedagogical resources described, as the mythology of the family meal is upheld without question. Given the tensions and complexities of family dynamics depicted within the family meal scene in *August Osage County* it is difficult to see how children such as Bill might intervene to shape family eating practices. While eight-year-old Bill might help with setting the table, preparing food, cleaning the dishes, effective strategies in other families may more closely resemble wrestling a parent to the ground, towering over them and bellowing 'You don't get it, do you? ....I'M RUNNING THINGS NOW!'

References

Burchell, G. (1996) Liberal government and techniques of the self. In A. Barry, T. Osborne and N. Rose (eds.), *Foucault and political reason*. Chicago, IL: University of Chicago Press, pp19–37.

Burgoyne, J. and Clark, D. (1983) You are what you eat: Food and family reconstitution, in A. Murcott (ed.) 1983. *The Sociology of Food and Eating*. Aldershot: Gower Publishing Company Ltd, pp153–163.

Burrows, L. (2009) Pedagogizing families through obesity discourse. In J. Wright and V. Harwood, eds., *Biopolitics and the obesity epidemic: Governing bodies*. New York, NY: Routledge, pp127–140.

Cappellini, B. and Parsons, E. (2012) Sharing the meal: Food consumption and family identity, *Research in Consumer Behavior*, 14, 109–128.

Charles, N. and Kerr, M. (1988) *Women, Food and Families*. Manchester: Manchester University Press.

Cinotto, S. (2006) 'Everyone would be around the table': American family mealtimes in historical perspective, 1850–1960, *New Directions for Child and Adolescent Development*, 111, 17–33.

Cliff, K. and Wright, J. (2010) Confusing and contradictory: Considering obesity discourse and eating disorders as they shape body pedagogies in HPE, *Sport, Education and Society*, 15, 221–233.

Cook, E. and Dunnifon, R. (2012) *Do Family Meals Really Make a Difference? Parenting in context*, New York: Cornell University.

Dean, M. (2010) *Governmentality: Power and rule in modern society* (2nd ed.). London: Sage.

Dobash, R. and Dobash, R. (1980) *Violence against Wives*. Shepton Mallet: Open Books.

Donzelot, J. (1979) *The Policing of Families*. New York: Random House.

Douglas, M. (1972) Deciphering a meal, *Daedalus*, 101 (1), 61–81.

Eisenberg, M., Olson, R., Neumark-Sztainer, D., Story, M. and Bearinger, L. (2004) Correlations between family meals and psychosocial well-being among adolescents, *Archives of Pediatric and Adolescent Medicine*, 158, 792–796.

Eisenberg, M., Neumark-Sztainer, D. and Feldman, S. (2009) Does TV viewing during family meals make a difference in adolescent substance use?, *Journal of Preventive Medicine*, 48, 585–587.

Ellis, R. (1983) The way to a man's heart: Food in the violent home, in Murcott, A. (ed.) *The Sociology of Food and Eating.* Aldershot: Gower Publishing Company Ltd, pp164–167.

The Family Dinner Project.Org (nd) *The Family Dinner Project.Org.* Available from http://thefamilydinnerproject.org/ [accessed 20 September 2015].

Fiese, B., Foley, K. and Spagnola, M. (2006) Routine and ritual elements in family mealtimes: Contexts for child well-being and family identity, *New Directions for Child and Adolescent Development*, 111, 67–89.

Foucault, M. (1982) The subject and power. In H. Dreyfus and P. Rabinow, eds. *Michel Foucault, beyond structuralism and hermeneutics.* Chicago, IL: University of Chicago Press, pp208–226.

Fulkerson, J., Kubik, M., Story, M., Lytle, L. and Arcan, C. (2009) Are there nutritional and other benefits associated with family meals among at-risk youth?, *Journal of Adolescent Health*, 45, 389–395.

Gordon, C. (1991) Governmental rationality: An introduction. In G. Burchell, C. Gordon and P. Miller, eds., *The Foucault effect: Studies in governmentality.* Chicago, IL: The University of Chicago Press, pp1–52.

Hammons, A. and Fiese, B. (2011) Is Frequency of Shared Family Meals Related to the Nutritional Health of Children and Adolescents?, *Paediatrics*, 127 (6), e1565–e1574.

Jacobs, M. and Fiese, B. (2007) Family mealtime interactions and overweight children with asthma: Potential for compounded risks?, *Journal of Pediatric Psychology*, 32, 64–68.

Larson, N., Neumark-Sztainer, D., Hannan, P. and Story, M. (2007) Trends in adolescent fruit and vegetable consumption, 1999–2004: Project EAT, *American Journal of Preventative Medicine*, 32 (2), 147–150.

Leahy, D., Burrows, L., McCuaig, L., Wright, J. and Penney, D. (2016) *School health education in changing times: Curriculum, pedagogies and partnerships.* New York: Routledge.

Leahy, D. and Pike, J. (2015) Just say no to pies: Food pedagogies, health education and governmentality. In R. Flowers and E. Swan, eds., *Food pedagogies.* Surrey, England: Ashgate.

Leahy, D. and Gray, E.M. (2014) Popular pedagogical assemblages in the health education classroom. In P. Benson and A. Chik, eds., *Popular Culture, Pedagogy and Teacher Education: International perspectives.* London: Routledge, pp184–208.

Leith, P. (2007) *Prue Leith's radical recipe: Free school meals and eating with a knife and fork.* Available from http://www.telegraph.co.uk/news/uknews/1571327/Prue-Leiths-radical-recipe-free-school-meals-and-eating-with-a-knife-and-fork.html [accessed 20 September 2015].

Letts, T. (2008) *August, Osage County.* New York: Theatre Communications Group.

Levi-Strauss, C. (1997) The culinary triangle. In C. Counihan and P. Van Esterik, eds., *Food and Culture: A Reader.* London: Routledge, pp28–35.

Mitchell, J. (1999) The British main meal in the 1990s: Has it changed its identity?, *British Food Journal*, 101 (11), 871–883.

Murcott, A. (1982) On the Social Significance of a 'Cooked Dinner' in South Wales, *Social Science Information*, 21, (4–5), 677–696.

Murcott, A. (1997) Family meals – a thing of the past? In P. Caplan, ed., *Food, Health and Identity.* London: Routledge, pp32–49.

Neumark-Sztainer, D., Eisenberg, M., Fulkerson, J., Story, M. and Larson, N. (2008) Family meals and disordered eating in adolescents: longitudinal findings from project EAT, *Archives of Pediatrics and Adolescent Medicine*, 162(1), 17–22.

Neumark-Sztainer, D., Hannan, P., Story, M., Croll, J. and Perry, C. (2003) Family meal patterns: Associations with sociodemographic characteristics and improved dietary intake among adolescents, *Journal of the American Dietetic Association*, 103, 317–322.

Neumark-Sztainer, D., Wall, M., Story, M. and Fulkerson, J. (2004) Are family meal patterns associated with disordered eating behaviors among adolescents?, *Journal of Adolescent Health*, 35, 350–359.

Quality Meat Scotland (nd) *Campaign encourages family to get back 'Round the Table'*. Available from http://www.qmscotland.co.uk/news/campaign-encourages-families-get-back-%E2%80%98round-table%E2%80%99-0 [accessed on 20 September 2015].

Pike, J. (2008) Foucault, space and primary school dining rooms, *Children's Geographies*, 6 (4) 413–422.

Pike, J. and Colquhoun, D. (2012) Lunchtime lock in: Territorialisation and UK school meals policies. In P. Kraftl, J. Horton and F. Tucker, eds., *Critical geographies of childhood and youth: Contemporary policy and practice*. Bristol: Policy Press, pp133–150.

Pike, J., and Leahy, D. (2012) School food and the pedagogies of parenting, *Australian Journal of Adult Education*, 52, 434–460.

Taveras, E., Rifas-Shiman, S., Berkey, C., Rockett, H., Field, A., Frazier, A., Colditz, G. and Gillman, M. (2005) Family dinner and adolescent overweight, *Obesity Research*, 13, 900–906.

Vaz, P., and Bruno, F. (2003) Types of Self-Surveillance: From abnormality to individuals 'at risk', *Surveillance and Society*, 1, (3), 272–291.

Videon, T. and Manning, C. (2003) Influences on adolescent eating patterns: The importance of family meals, *Journal of Adolescent Health*, 32, 365–373.

White, J., and Halliwell, E. (2010) Alcohol and Tobacco Use during Adolescence; The Importance of the family meal time environment, *Journal of Health Psychology*, 15 (4), 526–532.

Wilk, R. (2010) Power at the Table: Food Fights and Happy Meals, *Cultural Studies Critical Methodologies*, 10 (6), 428–436.

8 Manufacturing (parental) consent

A critical analysis of the HPVV informed consent process in Ontario, Canada

LeAnne Petherick, Moss E. Norman and Geneviève Rail

Our girls aren't guinea pigs. A mass inoculation of Canadian girls against a sexually transmitted virus is under way. Is an upcoming mass inoculation of a generation unnecessary and potentially dangerous? (Cathy Gulli, *Maclean's*, 27 August 2007)

Despite evidence, parents' fears of HPV vaccine grow (Genevra Pittman, *The Globe and Mail*, 18 March 2013)

HPV doesn't make girls more promiscuous (*Peterborough Examiner*, 15 October 2012)

Spread the word not the disease (www.hpvinfo.ca)

Introduction

In 2007, families in the Canadian province of Ontario were asked to provide consent for their daughters to receive the Human papillomavirus (HPV) vaccine. Around that time, an issue of *Maclean's* magazine garnered considerable public attention and generated an explosion of anxiety, suggesting that the mass vaccination program that aimed to reduce the risks of cervical cancer associated with the HPV virus was treating Canadian girls, including those in the province of Ontario, as 'guinea pigs'. These conflicting messages meant that parents' decision about whether to vaccinate or not was not nearly as straightforward as public health professionals intended, as parents faced an impossible task of deciding between, on the one hand, being irresponsible for *having* their daughters exposed to a 'potentially dangerous' vaccine and, on the other, being negligent for *not having* their daughters vaccinated. These competing messages persist today and continue to give rise to much confusion, fear, anxiety and, in some cases, outright resistance, as families – mothers in particular – try to negotiate the multiple and conflicting health messages that circulate in popular media and public health campaigns in an effort to make an informed health decision about their daughter's long-term wellbeing.

Since its introduction in 2007, the HPV vaccine has become a more or less entrenched part of the public health immunization programs within Canadian schools, but it is not without controversy. In this chapter, we critically examine HPV vaccination informed consent documents that are circulated by eight public health agencies within the Canadian province of Ontario and argue that these documents are strategically designed to simultaneously invoke parental fears about HPV contagions, at the same time that they manage parental anxieties about the vaccine itself and, in so doing, manufacture parental consent.

In titling our chapter 'manufacturing (parental) consent,' we deliberately parody the title of Noam Chomsky's seminal book to draw attention to how the documents are not so much about informing parents about HPV vaccination as they are about compelling, or manufacturing, parental consent. In making this argument, we are not suggesting that parents are 'coerced' into consent, but rather we draw upon a neo-Foucaultian framework to highlight how the information is presented in such a way as to persuade otherwise 'free' and 'autonomous' individuals that consent is the best – if not the only – option. This is problematic because while the documents are seemingly a rational presentation of factual information, they are in fact structured in such a way as to elicit emotive responses from parents, where fear is manufactured around the issue of HPV and girls' sexual health, giving rise to a sense of urgency to consent to vaccinate. Importantly, we do not wager into the debate about whether the best option is to vaccinate or not vaccinate. Rather, we aim to push back against the evangelical-like dogma that is reflected in the 'spread the word, not the disease' HPV campaign slogan, which simultaneously generates fears of HPV-related cancers spreading uncontrollably across populations, while foreclosing a more engaged dialogue about the social and cultural complexities of the health and wellbeing of girls and women.

The HPV vaccination

The HPV vaccine is most commonly a three-stage doses injection program for reducing the effects of a sexually transmitted infection – the human papilloma virus – which has no detectable signs or symptoms and has been linked to cancer. Some research suggests that the vaccine is most effective if given prior to sexual activity (Schiffman et al, 2007) and that it protects against 70 per cent of the viruses that lead to cervical cancer and 90 per cent of the viruses for genital warts (Lowy et al, 2008). Two forms of the vaccine exist: Gardasil and Cervarix. Gardasil is the quadrivalent vaccine protecting against four different types of HPV – HPV 6, HPV 11, HPV 16, HPV 18 and genital warts in both males and females and it is the vaccine of choice provided in schools across Canada. Through a mass immunization approach, the Canadian government aims to reach young girls prior to sexual activity to inoculate them against the highest risk strains of HPV and those most linked to cancer. As a result, parents are being asked to consider the risks of a sexually transmitted infection, the long-term consequences of cervical cancer, and a lesser-known vaccination process when they make so-called informed decisions about the vaccination and the current and future health status of their children.

Theoretical background

Using a neo-Foucaultian theoretical framework, we suggest that informed consent should be examined as part of a broader neoliberal rationality whereby the state functions through a mode of 'governing at a distance' (Rose, 1999). Here, power does not operate through a centralized state apparatus that forcibly imposes its will onto its citizens, but rather through a diffuse network of discourses, institutions, and diversely situated actors that, when assembled together, function to incite, persuade and guide individuals (and families) in the art of self-governance. Here, power relations are organized in the administration of life itself, where individuals are simultaneously autonomized or accorded their 'freedoms' at the same moment that they are incited to fashion a prudent, healthy and responsible life. In other words, individuals are 'free' to choose how to live their life, but are at the same moment subjected to a host of lifestyle discourses designed to incite them to make particular, health-enhancing choices – for example, to eat in a healthy way, to exercise, to not smoke and, in the specific case of this chapter, to vaccinate against HPV. It is important to note, however, that while individual citizens are 'free' to make their own choices, these choices are not without consequence. For example, the 'choice' to eat too much, to not exercise, to smoke and to not vaccinate against HPV are morally coded as bad and irresponsible decisions and folks who make these 'poor' lifestyle choices are constructed as less-than-citizens who represent a disproportionate burden to the state. In other words, these poor decisions are understood to affect not just the individual, but also the broader population (e.g., missed workdays, increase in morbidities, greater health care costs, spread of disease). This moral coding of health practices, however, is shorn of the broader social, cultural and historical contexts in which these so-called 'choices' are made where, for instance, conditions of material (e.g., economic), structural (e.g., systemic racism), and representational (e.g., discursive) oppressions are left unexamined (McGibbon, 2012). In this way, healthy lifestyle 'choices' are not so much freely made as they are forcibly compelled, albeit through techniques rooted in the arts of persuasion more than they are state-centred techniques of command and control.

Technologies of governing at a distance are consistent with a neoliberal political rationality that aims to reduce government costs by shifting responsibility for citizen wellbeing from the big bureaucratic structures of the welfare state to the individual entrepreneurial self (Rose, 1996). Within this context, individuals are supposedly 'empowered' to take responsibility for themselves for their own health and wellbeing. Health education is one primary technique through which the shift from state- to self-responsibility has taken place (Peterson and Lupton, 1996), where individuals and families are instructed or educated on how to live a healthy, prudent life. We argue that these technologies of governing at a distance are at work in school-based HPV vaccination programs, where parents are provided (or educated) with specific types of information about HPV through informed consent documents that frame scientific facts in such a way so as to incite, persuade or manufacture parental consent.

Parenting and the HPV vaccination

In this section, we argue that the HPV vaccination programme represents one technology within a broader parenting project, whereby parents are being asked to engage in a whole host of practices aimed at guiding, safeguarding, and protecting their children towards good health for now, and into the future. Such a project is not merely about the well-being of individual children, but parents are increasingly responsible for rearing what is understood to be future generations of the nation state, and thus the family unit is an important target for governmental strategies.

Burns and Davies (2015, p74) draw attention to how individuals are currently accountable for the contemporary and future consequences of their own health practices:

> ... broadening health to include a wider range of variables and risk factors means that individual citizens are not only asked to consider and be responsible for a greater number of health promoting behaviours, they are also expected to be accountable for a greater number of health deficiencies – bad health choices, an unhealthy lifestyle, failure to consume healthy products or options, and so on.

Here, Burns and Davies (2015) highlight the pressure to manage one's own health. We would extend this and suggest that it also applies across familial networks as the risk of ill-health for children and youth intensifies parental responsibilities (especially mothers' responsibilities) for the health of their children. Thus, parents are an integral part of a diffuse network assembled together to influence the health conditions of future populations. The proliferation of potential health deficiencies facing children and youth positions parents as bearing even greater responsibility for promoting good health behaviours by directing their sons and daughters to avoid potentially health harming choices (Schulre et al, 2014). It is within the context of proliferating risks, and the competing messages that surround those risks, that parents may be overwhelmed with the diversity of health decisions that confront them, potentially giving rise to anxieties about how best to ensure the health of their children. In order to assuage these anxieties, as well as facilitate parental compliance with various governmental techniques, parenting is increasingly transformed into a technical matter, where parents are incited to take a managerial approach to family health (Connell, 2011).

Within the neoliberal context, public health messaging targets parents as managers who must make a series of rational and technical decisions about the health of their family, both for the good of the family unit as well as the population more generally. In translating what are in essence weighty health decisions into mere technical matters, much of the complexity of the decisions being made is erased and boiled down into relatively simple decisions between 'right' and 'wrong' choices. Within the contemporary vaccination culture, for instance, parents are not only treated as family managers, but they are managers given just enough information, framed in a highly selective manner, to make them think that there is only one 'right' decision and, in making this decision, that they are protecting the best interests of everyone involved, including their daughters, their family, and ultimately the State (Kitta, 2012). However, as these public health messages try and sanitize the complexity of the decisions being made into mere technical matters, the complexities of inoculation and the questioning of scientific intervention nevertheless elicit an emotional aspect of the decision-making process. In other words, despite the attempts of public health messaging to reduce complexity, these health decisions are much more than technical matters to be approached with a managerial rationality (Connell, 2011).

Scholars have noted that the decisions of whether and when to vaccinate are emotionally charged ones (Biss, 2015; Kitta, 2012; Mara, 2010). In the specific case of HPV vaccination, these emotions come from a variety of uncertainties, including, on the one hand, concerns about the vaccination itself, such as its safety, efficacy, and a general scepticism about corporate-pharmaceutical manipulations (Batt and Lippman, 2010), with many of these concerns reflected in the quotations we used to open this paper. On the other hand, parents have questions about the threat of disease and infection and its relationship to HPV, as well as questions about the onset of their daughter's sexual activity (Misha and Graham, 2010; Reiter et al, 2009). These concerns and uncertainties give rise to fears and anxieties, emotions which public health messages recognize and strategically manipulate in order to persuade parents to have their daughters vaccinated. Here, the dangers of HPV and its relationship to cervical cancer and genital warts are emphasized (Kitta, 2012), creating a culture of fear around girls' embodied sexualities that is designed to compel parents to protect their daughters through vaccination, while the anxieties about the vaccination itself are downplayed, if not dismissed outright. Public health messaging and its attendant emotions are highly gendered, as they target mothers in particular (Burns and Davies, 2014, 2015; Schulre et al, 2014).

Public health messaging emphasizes the maternal aspect of the so-called caring parent. Misha and Graham (2010) 'suggest that HPV immunization is a key example of the deeply gendered control and surveillance of bodies and bodily risk' (p58). Thus, as women's relationships with their children have historically been tied with a desire for protection (Biss, 2015; Hochschild, 1989; Polzer and Knabe, 2012), the efforts to control the future health of a population construct 'good' mothering practices as characterized by maternal love, and then deploy this ideal in calling upon mothers to protect and care for their daughters through vaccinating against HPV. This emotional interchange is a charged neoliberal approach and 'assigns mothers a moral responsibility for giving their children 'the best possible start in life', for undertaking a planning process in which their children are raised for success in a competitive world' (Connell, 2011, p53). Everything from food choices, to activity, to accessing healthcare and medical services has intensified within our contemporary health-crazed culture and, for mothers in particular, this leaves them with a greater burden of investing in their children's current and future safety (Biss, 2015; Hochshild, 1989; Mara, 2010; Polzer and Knabe, 2012).

Methods

In overviewing the types of information presented to parents of grade 8 girls as they wager into the vaccination decision-making process, we conducted an analysis of the informed consent documents from eight public health units in the province of Ontario, Canada. These eight public health units were selected as they represent a range of geographical areas within the province and were selected as a matter of convenience as the complete documents were readily available online. What we are referring to as the informed consent documents are comprised of both vaccination information or 'fact' sheets and the statement of consent. It should be noted that informed consent is required by law for people under the age of 18 years to receive the HPV vaccination in Canada; thus parents are ultimately responsible for the vaccination of their child within the school immunization programme.

Using a Foucaultian theoretical framework enables us to ask questions of how information related to the HPV vaccination is presented to parents in the informed consent process. For Foucault (1980), health information or 'facts' are not unmediated, objective 'truths', but are instead the expression of power relations. Once knowledge is removed from its privileged position as an unassailable and objective truth, as it is in a Foucaultian-informed discourse analysis, it is then possible to examine how the 'facts' are framed and with what effects. In this way, we were able to pose a number of questions to the informed consent documents, including: what information about HPV and the HPV vaccine is included in the documents and what information is excluded? How is the information presented and what are the effects (and affects) of framing the 'facts' in this way? And, finally, how do the informed consent documents interpellate or hail parents/guardians who read them and how do such inter-pellations work to forcibly materialize particular subjectivities (for example, responsible or irresponsible parents/mothers)? In so doing, we have looked to expose the moral coding that constructs parents and parenting as an entrepre-neurial endeavour whereby governing at a distance, as Rose (1999) suggests, places parents at the centre of an assemblage of health professionals and dis-courses shaping health decisions. Thus, the consent process is important to analyse, we argue, because it represents that critical moment in the parenting project when parents are asked to make an important decision about the health of their daughter – that is, it is the moment when parents are asked to consent (or not) to have their daughter vaccinated.

In our analysis, each author independently read and re-read the informed consent documents, coding them for how the information about HPV and the vaccine was framed. We then came together and compared notes and developed thematic codes ranging from biomedical information related to HPV and sexual health, vaccination procedures and process, and social and cultural messages about gender and health. After these initial themes were identified, further coding was performed using a critical discursive lens identifying the power relations circulating in the types of information shared within these public documents.

Findings: Manufacturing and managing fear and anxiety

In our analysis of the informed consent documents, we found that the HPV vaccination consent process functions at once to create and manage parental fears and anxieties. On the one hand, the documents work to create fears about HPV and non-vaccination, while on the other, they serve to manage those fears by suggesting that dangers associated with HPV are preventable through vaccination. We identified three general strategies that were deployed in creating fears and managing anxieties, all in the service of manufacturing parental consent: first, the documents framed the risks of HPV as serious, but preventable; second, they minimized the 'side effects' of the vaccination, while obscuring, erasing and foreclosing complicating stories; and, finally, through emphasizing choice the economic imperative of vaccinating as soon as possible is imperative.

1 HPV as a serious, but preventable risk

Through the use of statistics, HPV-associated cancers are constructed as simultaneously pervasive, potentially deadly, but also preventable. Here, parents are confronted with a statistical story that situates HPV as both a common virus and one that potentially leads to cervical cancer and even death: 'HPV is a common virus with more than 100 strains. Some strains of HPV cause cervical cancer, which is responsible for about 400 deaths per year in Canada' (York PHU). In highlighting that the virus is 'common' with 'over 100 strains', without drawing attention to the fact that only two strains may be related to cancer, parents are left with the impression that HPV is both rampant and that HPV inevitably leads to genital warts and cancer (and potentially death). In other words, the narrative framing of the statistics serves to erase the complex etiology of the relationship between HPV and disease (i.e., that the vast majority of HPVs are benign) and, in so doing, constructs the virus as deadly, commonplace and in need of immediate action. In this sense, the informed consent functions to create fear amongst parents about HPV, and this fear warrants an urgent, but prudent, response. This response is then offered in the form of the HPV vaccination itself: 'Some types of HPV can cause cancer of the cervix in women, and other types can lead to genital warts and other cancers in men and women. Fortunately, most HPV infections and cervical cancers can be prevented with the HPV vaccine' (Timiskaming, PHU). The resulting numeric picture that is conjured within the informed consent documents is reflective of the State's investment in constructing HPV-related cervical cancer as something that reaches significant numbers of people but can be stopped through medical intervention. Powell and Leiss argue that there is an inherent problem in communicating risk because it is comprised of what they refer to as 'two languages' of risk: 'the scientific and statistical language with experts on the one hand and the intuitively grounded language of the public on the other' (1997, cited in Kitta, 2012, p3). We are arguing that the framing of risks associated with the HPV strategically uses these two languages – the legitimate and authoritative language of positivist science, embedded within the intuitive language of the public – to create what Massumi (2010) refers to as an 'affective fact' or a fact whose truth lies not in some unassailable validity, but rather because it is *felt* to be true (see Evans, 2010). Therefore, descriptions that identify the volume of strands of HPV, the number of deaths and an alarming ratio of who is at-risk of infection are packaged together in such a way as to garner an affective response of fear and anxiety about the pervasiveness of the HPV virus, which conjures alarm in parents about the health of their children, and compels an urgent response.

Our concern with how HPV is explained to parents is less with the use of statistics and more with how the statistics are framed, where the commonness and threat of the virus are emphasized, giving the impression that everyone, everywhere is vulnerable to this looming threat, without also acknowledging that the vast majority of virus strains are inconsequential to health. Moreover, we are also critical of how the fear that is generated through this framing is then used to incite parents to consent to have their daughters vaccinated. Positioning HPV-related diseases as serious but preventable operates to render the informed consent process as a part of a broader technology of govern-mentality, where parents are simultaneously accorded their 'powers of freedom' (Rose, 1999), the power of consent in this case, at the same time that they are responsibilized with making the 'right' choice which, given the discursive framing in the documents we reviewed, can *only* be the choice to consent to vaccination.

2 Minimizing potential side effects

The information disseminated to parents works to minimize any anxieties parents might have about the 'side effects' associated with the vaccination itself. We opened this chapter by describing the broad public anxiety surrounding vaccinations generally, and HPV vaccinations specifically. Such anxiety is largely an outcome of the contemporary postmodern condition, where multiple and competing truths, from a diversity of sources, vie for supremacy. The proliferation of medical truths means that parents must negotiate a complex and fluid terrain of meanings as they try and determine what course of action best meets the health needs of their children. One specific and highly publicized concern related to HPV vaccination is the health risks associated with the vaccination itself. As witnessed in the quotes we used to open the chapter, there has been – and continues to be – a great deal of concern about how thoroughly the vaccine has been evaluated in clinical tests and the potential long and short-term consequences of the vaccine. Concerns about the vaccine could create doubts in the parents' mind as to whether their daughter should be vaccinated and thus pose a direct threat to the efficacy of a vaccination campaign. Concerns about the vaccine were assuaged in the informed consent process through two related strategies. On the one hand, the 'risks' associated with non-vaccination were repeatedly and forcefully emphasized, while on the other, the 'potential side effects' associated with vaccination were minimized. We argue that the framing of the debate between the decision to vaccinate or not is neither neutral, nor particularly informative, and that the information is presented in such a way as to lead parents to the conclusion that vaccination is the only responsible course of action.

Indeed, in several of the informed consent packages, a pictorial representation of the costs and benefits of the vaccination decision-making process was included (see Figure 8.1, KFL&A PHU).

This pictorial representation – replete with grave statistical figures – clearly leaves the reader with the impression that the risks associated with non-vaccination outweigh the potential side effects associated with vaccination. This pictorial scale of relative risks, we suggest, essentially pits the anxieties and fears around HPV and its associated diseases against those of the vaccine itself, asking parents to engage in an emotional calculation, whereupon they are incited to come to the conclusion that vaccination is the best, if not only, option. In documents that did not include this 'scales of relative risk' image, the potential side effects of the vaccine itself were narratively framed along a spectrum of probability (e.g., more common, less common and very rare) (Ottawa PHU), and severity (e.g., mild, serious, and severe) (Waterloo PHU). Having identified the probability and severity of potential vaccination side effects, the documents than work to obscure the causes of such side effects. For instance, several of the documents explain that swelling, redness, and headaches are common side effects associated with *any* injection, including placebo injections (Hamilton PHU; Timiskaning, PHU; Toronto, PHU; Waterloo PHU). In other words, the documents create the impression that the vaccination has *no* side effects of its own beyond those associated with any injection. The point we are arguing here is made explicitly in one of the informed consent documents, where an extremely condescending – if not ridiculous – anecdote is used to impress upon parents that there are few, if any at all, side effects associated with HPV vaccination, and those there are may not be linked with certainty to the vaccination itself. While literacy levels do have to be accounted within communication strategies the following

HPV VACCINE CONSENT FORM

INSTRUCTIONS FOR PARENT
1. Read the attached information about the HPV vaccine.
2. Remove the consent form. Complete the front of this page.
3. Return the signed form to your child's teacher.

Vaccine Program
www.hamilton.ca/immunize
Phone: 905-546-2424 x7556
Fax: 905-546-4841

Hamilton
Public Health Services

1. STUDENT INFORMATION

LAST NAME	FIRST NAME	

BIRTHDAY	SCHOOL	CLASS (E.G. 8A)
YEAR MONTH DAY FEMALE		

PARENT/GUARDIAN NAME	HOME PHONE	WORK OR CELL PHONE

2. STUDENT HEALTH HISTORY

	CHECK ONE	IF YES, PLEASE EXPLAIN
Does your child have any allergies?	◯ YES ◯ NO	
Has your child ever reacted to a vaccine?	◯ YES ◯ NO	
Does your child have a history of fainting or seizures?	◯ YES ◯ NO	
Does your child have a serious medical condition?	◯ YES ◯ NO	

3. CONSENT FOR IMMUNIZATION

I have read or had explained to me the attached information about the HPV vaccine.
My questions have been answered to my satisfaction. Check **one**:

◯ Yes, please vaccinate my child with 3 doses of the HPV vaccine.

X _____   _____
PARENT/GUARDIAN SIGNATURE   DATE

◯ No, please do not vaccinate my child with the HPV vaccine.

◯ No, my child already received the HPV vaccine on the following dates:
Check one: ◯ Gardasil®   ◯ Cervarix®

DOSE 1 DATE	DOSE 2 DATE	DOSE 3 DATE

COLLECTION AND USE OF PERSONAL HEALTH INFORMATION

We are allowed by law to collect what you write on this form.
- Health Protection and Promotion Act
- Personal Health Information Protection Act

The information will be used for
- the vaccine program
- immunization records
- outbreak management
- program evaluation
- statistics and research

If you have questions about the collection of your information, contact:
Vaccine Program Manager
Hamilton Public Health Services
110 King Street West, 2nd Floor
Hamilton ON L8P 4S6
905-540-5250
Visit www.hamilton.ca/phsprivacy to learn more.

Figure 8.1 HPV consent form

example reduces the complexity surrounding the potential side effects of the vaccine. The following is taken from the Hamilton PHU:

What is an adverse event?

An adverse event is any health problem, after the vaccine is given. The event may or may not be due to the vaccine. When things happen close together it does not mean they are related. For example, if you eat an apple and then break your arm, it does not mean the apple caused the bone to break (Hamilton PHU).

| STUDENT NAME | | | | | | | ROOM | |

NURSE'S ASSESSMENT

	DOSE 1	DOSE 2	DOSE 3
Do you have a fever or are you sick today?	○ YES ○ NO	○ YES ○ NO	○ YES ○ NO
Has anything changed with your health recently?	○ YES ○ NO	○ YES ○ NO	○ YES ○ NO
Did you react to a previous dose of HPV vaccine?	○ YES ○ NO	○ YES ○ NO	○ YES ○ NO
Is there a chance you could be pregnant?	○ YES ○ NO	○ YES ○ NO	○ YES ○ NO
Do you understand what the vaccine is for? If no, health teaching provided.	○ YES ○ NO	○ YES ○ NO	○ YES ○ NO
Do you have any questions? If yes, health teaching provided.	○ YES ○ NO	○ YES ○ NO	○ YES ○ NO

VACCINE INFORMATION

GARDASIL® 0.5 mL IM

DATE	TIME	LOT #	DELTOID SITE		SIGNATURE	DATA ENTERED
			R	L		
			R	L		
			R	L		

NURSE'S NOTES

_____

_____

_____

_____

_____

Figure 8.1 (Continued)

Moreover, in the above pictorial representation (Figure 8.1), the most severe side effect of the vaccine – death – is presented as not being a risk at all, as the diagram states the risk of death is zero. However, the media has covered several high profile deaths, emergency room visits, hospitalization and disabilities that are seemingly linked to the HPV vaccine in the United States (CDC, 2014), Australia (Mercola, 2014), Japan (Mulchany, 2013), India (Berkley, 2013) and Canada (Gonthier, 2012). Given that many parents may

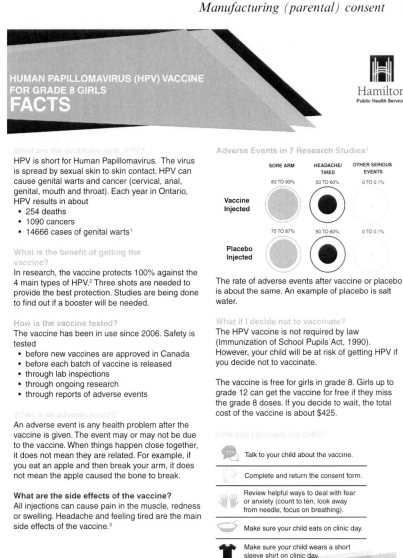

HUMAN PAPILLOMAVIRUS (HPV) VACCINE FOR GRADE 8 GIRLS
FACTS

Hamilton
Public Health Services

What are the problems with HPV?

HPV is short for Human Papillomavirus. The virus is spread by sexual skin to skin contact. HPV can cause genital warts and cancer (cervical, anal, genital, mouth and throat). Each year in Ontario, HPV results in about

- 254 deaths
- 1090 cancers
- 14666 cases of genital warts[1]

What is the benefit of getting the vaccine?

In research, the vaccine protects 100% against the 4 main types of HPV.[2] Three shots are needed to provide the best protection. Studies are being done to find out if a booster will be needed.

How is the vaccine tested?

The vaccine has been in use since 2006. Safety is tested

- before new vaccines are approved in Canada
- before each batch of vaccine is released
- through lab inspections
- through ongoing research
- through reports of adverse events

What is an adverse event?

An adverse event is any health problem after the vaccine is given. The event may or may not be due to the vaccine. When things happen close together, it does not mean they are related. For example, if you eat an apple and then break your arm, it does not mean the apple caused the bone to break.

What are the side effects of the vaccine?

All injections can cause pain in the muscle, redness or swelling. Headache and feeling tired are the main side effects of the vaccine.[3]

Adverse Events in 7 Research Studies[3]

	SORE ARM	HEADACHE/ TIRED	OTHER SERIOUS EVENTS
Vaccine Injected	83 TO 93%	50 TO 60%	0 TO 0.1%
Placebo Injected	75 TO 87%	50 TO 60%	0 TO 0.1%

The rate of adverse events after vaccine or placebo is about the same. An example of placebo is salt water.

What if I decide not to vaccinate?

The HPV vaccine is not required by law (Immunization of School Pupils Act, 1990). However, your child will be at risk of getting HPV if you decide not to vaccinate.

The vaccine is free for girls in grade 8. Girls up to grade 12 can get the vaccine for free if they miss the grade 8 doses. If you decide to wait, the total cost of the vaccine is about $425.

How can I prepare my child?

Talk to your child about the vaccine.

Complete and return the consent form.

Review helpful ways to deal with fear or anxiety (count to ten, look away from needle, focus on breathing).

Make sure your child eats on clinic day.

Make sure your child wears a short sleeve shirt on clinic day.

Figure 8.1 (Continued)

have come across media accounts of these deaths, disabilities and adverse effects, how are parents to make sense of the informed consent documents that suggest that the probability of death is zero? Once again, the point of our analysis is not to determine the truth about HPV, its relationship to disease, or the HPV vaccine and its associated side effects or risks, but rather to

It is worse to get HPV than the vaccine.

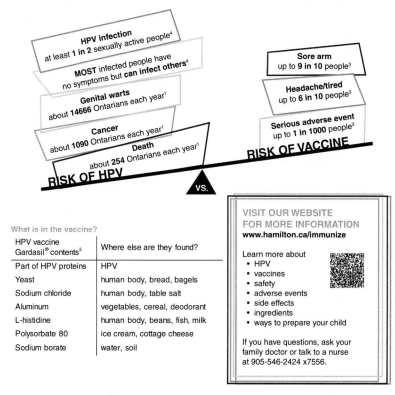

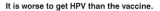

Figure 8.1 (Continued)

highlight how fear and anxiety are manufactured and managed by foregrounding some HPV stories (such as those on the risk posed by the virus itself and the risk associated with non-vaccination), while obscuring, discounting and foreclosing other stories (such as the adverse reactions to the vaccine).

In structuring the documents around the benefits and risks associated with the vaccine itself, a myriad of other concerns and considerations that parents and girls might have about HPV, the vaccination, and sexual health more broadly are also foreclosed. In so doing, the vaccination itself – a schedule of needle injections – comes to stand in for, and displace, a broader and more engaged dialogue about girls' sexual health and well-being. Here, the seeming neutrality and simplicity of the vaccination process, and the promise of protection it offers, obscures what is in fact a profoundly complex social and cultural phenomenon. For instance, most of the informed consent documents do not encourage parents to talk to their daughters about the vaccine, and none suggest that they talk about the broader issues surrounding sexually transmitted infections and their prevention. Those that do mention talking with their daughter (n=2) quite simply state 'talk to your child about the vaccine' (Hamilton PHU and Waterloo PHU). In this way, the suggested parameters of the conversation are limited to the vaccine itself, and do not extend to those other social and cultural implications related to 'nascent female sexualities' (Polzer and Knabe, 2012). Here, dialogue with the girls who are to be vaccinated is implicitly foreclosed on the grounds that they are not considered old enough to take part in what is constructed as parental decisions about the sex and sexuality of their daughters. Girls are thus positioned as passive recipients of immunization, without agency of their own, and are thus infantilized in the process, while adult parents are treated as the rightful protectors of their children. In this way, rather than providing parents with information in order to make an informed decision about consent, which is the intent behind the informed consent process, parents are confronted with an informed consent process that is designed to incite them to make the only 'right' choice and consent on behalf of their daughters.

3 The economic imperative and its relation to choice

A final technology used to incite or manufacture parental consent relates to the financial cost of the vaccination and the discourses surrounding these costs. Three of eight informed consent packages reviewed made explicit reference of the cost of the three-stage vaccination process in Ontario, listing it at over $400. These packages go on to explain that the provincial government will only cover the cost of the HPV vaccine if it is administered between grade 8 and 12 (with grade 8 vaccination being the planned ideal), after which families or individuals must pay for their own vaccination. The rationale behind this time frame, the documents explain, is that the vaccine is more efficacious if administered before girls begin to engage in sexual intercourse (Waterloo PHU). By informing parents of the economic and potential health costs of waiting to have their daughters vaccinated, the documents serve to manufacture anxiety and a sense of urgency in three inter-related ways. First, there is the obvious economic imperative underlying the rationale, where compliant families are rewarded for having their daughters vaccinated within the required time frame by not having to pay for the vaccine. Secondly, the risks associated with delaying vaccination are clearly outlined and are attributed to sexual activity that, we suggest, leads to an intensified level of anxiety in parents, which leads to our third point. By linking the risks of HPV to female sexuality and the efficacy of the vaccine, the informed consent documents implicitly construct female adolescent sexualities as dangerous and potentially pathological (Polzer and Knabe, 2012). Keeping in mind that it is 'nascent female sexualities' (Polzer and Knabe, 2012, p346) that are positioned as 'risky' and in need of protection within these documents, it is thus arguable that they reflect a continuation of historical discourses of medicalization that construct women's bodies as messy, dangerous and in need of control (Shildrick, 1997), at the same time that they implicitly suggest that women (that is, mothers) need to take responsibility for both their own sexual health and the health of their daughter (Batt and Lippman, 2010) and, in so doing, protect the broader well-being of populations.

Conclusion

In the process of informing parents about cervical cancer, genital warts and vaccination prevention strategies, we have argued that the Ontario-based consent documents that we reviewed serve to manufacture, as opposed to neutrally inform, parental consent. In making this argument, we have first shown how these documents simultaneously invoke and intensify parental fears about the risks of HPV and thus create as sense of urgency to act within parents, at the same time that they work to assuage parental anxieties about the side effects of the vaccine itself. Importantly, we deliberately side-stepped the debate about the efficacy or safety of the vaccine and instead have chosen to focus on how the presentation of 'facts' within the informed consent documents are not so much 'truthful' accounts as they are carefully constructed stories designed to compel parents to consent to have their daughter vaccinated. We suggested that in an attempt to create the appearance of only one 'right and responsible choice,' the documents worked to obscure or even erase contradicting complexities, minimize and trivialize parental anxieties, and foreclose more engaged familial dialogues. Indeed, we find that information on the vaccine, its potential harm, and its available alternative are lacking and, therefore, that informed assent is absent for girls and informed consent is absent for parents/ guardians.

From a bioethical perspective the effects of informed consent documents do little to assure parents of their daughters continued health status. Bioethicists (e.g., Weijer 1995) suggest that four criteria should be met before testing a vaccine for disease prevention in healthy individuals: (a) the vaccine should be safe; (b) the targeted sub-population should be at a clear risk for the disease; (c) the vaccine should not harm too many and help too few; (d) the vaccine should stand on its own merit and if it is tested to prevent something, other potential benefits should be considered irrelevant for the testing. At the moment, we find that the HPV vaccine fails on all four counts. In minimizing the information about disease and circumventing the risks of vaccination the complex considerations that confront parents (and erase girls' assent) about the HPV, vaccination, and sexual health to one choice – vaccination – parenting is ostensibly reduced to a technical matter, where the prudent parent-cum-manager merely has to trust public health information and consent to have their daughter vaccinated.

The third and last conclusion concerns public health. In the province of Ontario (Canada) and in places where the vaccine has been distributed in Canada, we find that the basic principles of public health have been put aside. We suggest that moving from a perspective of health promotion and disease prevention to a model of biomedicalization and pharmaceutical intervention undermines the proven public health strategy of identifying and eliminating causes of disease. In addition, introducing a short-term vaccine without proper and fully informed consent poses new threats to girls and women's subjectivities and bodies. In this sense HPV vaccination may unnecessarily manufacture anxiety and push parents into making urgent decisions, without consulting or conversing, about their daughters' long-term health.

In addition, a case could be made that these government documents target an ideal reader-parent and family structure – namely, one that takes the Euro-Canadian parent–child rearing practices for granted, thereby discounting other culturally diverse family and kinship structures. Indeed, the documents only ever refer to 'your child' or 'your daughter', thus failing to appropriately acknowledge diverse family and kinship structures that may allow for extended family or communal child-rearing practices. Recently, there has been a concerted push to expand the scope of the HPV vaccination program by including boys. The implications this will have for parents, in particular mothers, is an interesting development that warrants further study. In this sense, the informed consent process that is an essential component of the HPV vaccination program promulgates a culture of fear and moral coding of girls and their bodies while re-entrenching parental responsibility for youth health. We would suggest that the current framing of the informed consent documents in Ontario obscures the complexity of frictions that whirl around the HPV vaccine, including constructions of girls' embodied sexualities and sexual health, the commercialization of health education in schools, the risks and efficacy of the vaccine itself, and neoliberal imperatives to take up responsibility for the self that increasingly insert parents into an impossible situation.

References

Batt, S. and Lippman, A. (2010) Preventing disease: Are pills the answer? In A. Rochon Ford and D. Saibil (Eds.), *The push to prescribe: Women and Canadian drug policy* (pp47–66) Toronto: Women's Press.

Berkley, S. (8 October 2013) Why anti-vaccine campaigners need a shot of good sense, *The Guardian*, http://www.theguardian.com/global-development/2013/oct/08/anti-hpv-vaccine-campaigners-cervical-cancer.

Biss, E. (2015) *On Immunity. An inoculation*. Minneapolis, MN: Graywolf Press.

Burns, K. and Davies, C. (2014) Mediating healthy female citizenship in HPV vaccination campaigns, *Feminist Media Studies*, 74(5), 711–726. DOI: 10.1080/14680777.2013.830632.

Burns, K. and Davies, C. (2015) Construction of young women's health and wellbeing in neoliberal times: A case study of HPV vaccination program in Australia. In K. Wright and J. McLeod (Eds.), *Rethinking Youth Wellbeing: Critical Perspectives* (pp71–89). New York, NY: Springer.

Connell, R. (2011) *Confronting equality. Gender, Knowledge and Globe Change.* Malden, MA: Polity Press.

Centres for Disease Control and Prevention (20 February 2014) *Summary of HPV Adverse Events Reports.* Published in the *JAMA*, http://www.cdc.gov/vaccinesafety/Vaccines/HPV/jama.html.

Evans, B. (2010) Anticipating fatness: Childhood, affect and the pre-emptive 'war on obesity', *Transactions of the Institute of British Geographers*, 35, 21–38.

Gonthier, V. (31 January 2012) Family sues after teen dies following HPV vaccination, http://www.torontosun.com/2012/01/31/family-sues-after-teen-dies-following-hpv-vaccination.

Gottvall, M., Grandahl, M.Hoglund, A., Larsson, M., Stenhammar, C., Andrae, B. and Tyden, T. (2013) Trust versus concern-how parents reason when they accept HPV vaccination for their young daughter, *Upsala Journal of Medical Sciences*, 118, 263–270.

Hamilton Public Health Unit (PHU) (nd) Hamilton Public Health Services. HPV Vaccine Consent Form. Taken from www.hamilton.ca/immunize.

Hochschild, A. (1989) *The Second Shift: Working parents and the revolution at Home.* New York, NY: Penguin Books.

Kitta, A. (2012) *Vaccinations and public concern in history. Legend, Rumour and Risk Perception.* New York, NY: Routledge.

KFL andPHU (Public Health Unit) (nd) Kingston, Frontenac, Livingston and Addison Public Health. Human Papillomavirus Immunization Program for Grade 8 Females. Taken from www.kflapublichealth.ca.

Lowy, D. R., Solomon, D., Hildesheim, A., Schiller, T. J. and Schiffman, M. (2008) Human paopillomavirus infection and the primary and secondary prevention of cervical cancer, *Cancer Supplement*, 113(7), 1980–1983.

Mara, M. (2010) Spreading the (dis)ease: Gardasil and the gendering of HPV, *Feminist Formations*, 22(2), 124–143. DOI: 10.1353/ff.2010.0000.

Massumi, B. (2010) The Future Birth of an Affective Fact: The Political Ontology of Threat. In G. Seigworth and M. Gregg (Eds.) *The Affect Theory Reader* (pp52–70). Durham: Duke University Press.

McGibbon, E. (2012) *Oppression: A Social Determinant of Health.* Winnipeg, Manitoba: Fernwood Publishing.

Mercola (24 January 2014) HPV Vaccine Victim Sues Merck, http://articles.mercola.com/sites/articles/archive/2012/01/24/hpv-vaccine-victim-sues-merck.aspx.

Misha, A. and Graham, J. (2010) Risk, choice and the 'girl vaccine': Unpacking human papillomavirus (HPV) immunization, *Health, Risk and Society*, 14(1), 57–69.

Mulchany, N. (25 June 2013) Japan withdraws HPV Vaccination Recommendation for Girls, http://www.medscape.com/viewarticle/806645.

Ottawa Public Health Unit (PHU) (nd) *Human Papillomavirus. Get the facts on school vaccines.* Ottawa Public Health, http://ottawa.ca/en/residents/public-health/disease-and-medical-conditions/school-immunization-clinics.

Peterson, A. and Lupton, D. (1996) *The new public health: Health and self in the age of risk.* London: Sage.

Polzer, J. and Knabe, S. (2009) Good girls do … get vaccinated: HPV, mass marketing and moral dilemmas for sexually active young women, *Journal of Epidemiology and Community Health*, 63(11), 869–870.

Polzer, J. and Knabe, S. (2012) From desire to disease: Human papillomavirus (HPV) and the medicalization of nascent female sexuality, *Journal of Sex Research*, 49(4), 344–352.

Reiter, P., Brewer, N., Gottlieb, S.McRee, A. L. and Smith, J. (2009) Parents' health beliefs and HPV vaccination of their adolescent daughters, *Social Science and Medicine*, 69(3), 1–6. DOI: 10.1016/j.socscimed.2009.05.024.

Rose, N. (1996) Governing in 'Advanced' Liberal Democracies. In A. Barry, T. Osborne and N. Rose (Eds.), *Foucault and Political Reason: Liberalism, Neo-liberalism and Rationalities of Government* (pp37–64). Chicago, IL: University of Chicago Press.

Rose, N. (1999) *Powers of Freedom: Reframing political thought.* New York, NY: Cambridge University Press.

Schiffman, M., Castle, P. E., Jeronimo, J., Rodirguex, A. C. and Wacholder, S. (2007) Human papillomavirus and cervical cancer, *Lancet*, 370(9590), 890–907.

Schulre, C., DeSouza, N., and Coyne-Belsey, T. (2014) Parents' decisions about HPV vaccine for sons: The importance of protecting sons' future female partners, *Journal of Community Health*, 39, 842–848.

Shildrick, M. (1997) *Leaky bodies and boundaries: Feminism, postmodernism, and (bio)ethics.* New York, NY: Routledge.

Timiskaning Public Health Unit (PHU) (nd) *HPV Consent form for Young Females in Grade 8.* Taken from http://www.timiskaminghu.com/uploads/files/CDC/HPV%20School%20Consent-N-101a-CDC.pdf.

Toronto Public Health Unit (PHU) (nd) *Human Papillomarvirus Fact Sheet. Immunization Program for Grade 8 Girls.* Taken from http://www1.toronto.ca/city_of_toronto/toronto_public_health/communicable_disease_control/immunization/files/pdf/grade8_hpv.pdf.

Waterloo Public Health Unit (PHU) (nd) *Human Papillomavirus (HPV) Grade 8 Vaccination Program Consent Form.* Taken from http://chd.region.waterloo.on.ca/en/clinicsClassesFairs/resources/HPV_ConsentForm.pdf.

Weijer, C. (1995) Our bodies, our science, *The Sciences*, 35(3), 41–45.

York Public Health Unit (nd) *York Region. Human Papillomavirus (HPV) Immunization.* Community and Health Services Department Public Health Branch. Taken from http://www.york.ca/wps/wcm/connect/yorkpublic/5da1f363-8a4d-40ea-b739-f86cd288d110/HPV+Consent+Form+Fact+sheet.pdf?MOD=AJPERES.

9 Health and physical activity messages among ethnic minority groups

South Asian families

Whitney Babakus Curry

Introduction

It is generally accepted that the burden of disease morbidity and mortality is not shared across all ethnic groups (August and Sorkin, 2010) and that ethnic minority groups (EMGs) experience higher levels of a range of chronic diseases (Griffiths et al, 2005; Nazroo, 2003). Self-reported poor health in developed nations such as the United Kingdom (UK) is highest among EMGs (Gatineau and Mathrani, 2011). These poor health outcomes are increasingly seen in chronic disease morbidity and mortality in diseases such as diabetes, cardiovascular diseases and cancers in which EMGs develop these at higher rates and at much younger ages than their white European counterparts (Chowdhury et al, 2006). Findings from the National Survey of Ethnic Minorities indicate that health inequalities among EMGs in the UK increase with age and become more pronounced after age 30 (Nazroo, 2003).

One area in which this disparity is clearly seen to affect the health of EMGs is physical activity (PA). The positive relationship between PA and health has been well established over the past 50 years (Tremblay, 2006) and recently the role of sedentary time (ST) has been shown to adversely affect health outcomes (Owen et al., 2009). Globally, it is believed that as many as 80 per cent of the population is not physically active (WHO, 2012). In nations such as the United States, Australia and the UK, levels of inactivity among EMGs are estimated to be between 62 and 87 per cent (Antikainen et al, 2005; Dogra et al, 2010). Over the past three decades policy-makers and health practitioners have recognized the need for improved policy guidelines to encourage increased participation in PA in EMGs and to decrease ST. These guidelines, however, may not lead to an uptake of PA by those who are not physically active.

One speculation is that, particularly in developed nations, individuals are held solely responsible for their health (Benn et al, 2011) while the socio-ecological determinants of health are not being considered in the framework and implementation of health promotion and policies (Halfon and Hochstein, 2002). Socio-ecological theories (SETs) indicate that determinants include the demographic, psychological, social, cultural and environmental factors that influence health behaviour choices (Jonnalagadda and Diwan, 2005; Lord et al, 2011). Although there is evidence that suggests that an individual's agency, or ability to exert control over aspects of life, should not be dismissed, it is important to note that this agency exists within the social and cultural structures in which people live and can therefore be limited by those structures (Bandura, 1989; Depelteau, 2008; Mahler and Pessar, 2001).

Determinants exert their influence through multiple levels and pathways to influence individuals' activity patterns (King et al, 2001) and individuals negotiate through these layers in their daily lives (Benn et al, 2011). Indeed, theories of intersectionality which suggest we are all positioned within social categories such as ethnicity, race and socio-economic status, should be considered in tandem to SETs (Phoenix, 2006). Among these social categories and determinants of health, families are now becoming the focus of research aimed at improving the health of EMGs as they may be an advantageous pathway to deliver tailored health promotion messages (King et al, 2001).

Currently there is little known about how ethnic minority families transmit and absorb health messages and a major gap in knowledge of how to encourage EMGs to become more active and less sedentary, with evidence on interventions aimed at these groups showing no or limited successes in the goal (Babakus and Thompson, 2012; Bernardi, 2011; Caperchione et al, 2009). It is therefore essential for the role of families to be examined as a pathway for the dissemination of positive health messages to EMGs in order to utilize these pathways more fully and incorporate them into appropriate interventions.

Throughout this chapter data from a study on South Asian (SA) families (Bangladeshi and Pakistani families) within the UK will be used as examples for discussion. Limited research indicates that SAs living outside their native counties, do not engage in recommended levels of PA and are highly sedentary, putting them at increased risk for chronic disease morbidity and mortality (Graham, 2004; Jonnalagadda and Diwan, 2005). This chapter aims to examine how ethnic minority families, using SA families as an example, transmit and absorb health messages on PA and ST and will make recommendations for how future health promotion, policies and interventions can benefit from understanding and incorporating these lessons into their development.

Determinants of physical activity and sedentary time

A socio-ecological model of PA/ST can organise our understanding of both the internal and external influences on these behaviours. A socio-ecological model includes demographic, psychological, social, cultural, and environmental determinants of PA and ST behaviours (WHO, 2012). The complex interactions of these determinants on individuals and within communities can create barriers to increasing activity or alternatively may facilitate participation in PA (Frohlich and Potvin, 2008; Rafnsson and Bhopal, 2009). In the following section I focus specifically on the social and cultural determinants of PA and ST in EMG families.

Social determinants

Social support, defined as the help, care and companionship that others provide (Ryan et al, 2005), is an important factor in the health of EMGs. It is widely accepted that social support can provide individuals with a sense of well-being and may encourage positive health behaviours such as engagement in PA (Stephens et al, 2011). Social support offers protection against psychological stress and increases personal control (Umberson et al, 2010). Literature suggests that lack of social support influences the way EMGs perceive their health and may contribute to engaging in fewer health promoting behaviours such as PA (Caperchione et al, 2009; Jonnalagadda and Diwan, 2005). Evenson et al (2004) found that social support is one of the most consistent correlates of PA and may be equally as important as age and gender in determining PA behaviour.

Just as social support has an influence on PA and ST, the social networks in which this support takes place can have a positive or negative effect on activity. Social networks are characterized by links between an individual and others in the immediate community and those outside of the community (Umberson et al, 2010). Individuals assert their agency and make decisions within the context of the social networks to which they belong (Bernardi, 2011; Mahler and Pessar, 2001).

One significant social network is the family. It has been found that SAs immigrating to the UK were more likely to do so because they had family living there, and upon arrival they came to live in predominantly SA neighbourhoods (Smith et al, 2009). When a social network becomes ethnic-specific, the advantages that initially made the network strong such as a sense of support from familiar peers, may become limiting in that information or support from the wider society may not infiltrate the network (Ryan, 2011). A high-quality social network, such as one which extends beyond the immediate family and community, can influence health through dissemination of health knowledge, increases in healthy lifestyle activities and influence of social norms that can have a positive effect on health (Stephens et al, 2011; Yu et al, 2011).

Cultural determinants

The culture of members of a social network will often dictate what is acceptable behaviour for its members. Culture can be defined as the beliefs, abilities and customs that one acquires as a member of society (Caroppo et al, 2009). Aspects of culture can include language, diet, religious beliefs, attitudes and family traditions (Jonnalagadda and Diwan, 2002). Studies have identified that SA cultures, for example, may place a higher value on women staying in the home, dressing modestly, and promoting a sense of family and community over an individualistic ideal such as engaging in PA for one's own personal benefit (Bao and Lam, 2008; Downie et al, 2007). Faith and religion are also critical components of SA culture and central to many families. In fact Bangladeshis and Pakistanis account for 17 per cent of the Muslim community in the UK (Alexander et al, 2010). Research suggests that SAs view their religion as a large part of their identity construction (Caroppo et al, 2009; Egan et al, 2009).

While the Muslim faith encourages healthy lifestyles and family taking a central role in achieving those healthy lifestyles, familial responsibilities may take priority (Grace et al, 2008; Laird et al, 2007). In a study by Grace et al (2008) on the influence of culture on health, they found that religious leaders supported and encouraged healthy lifestyle habits such as increased PA, though a woman's duty to take care of the family was prioritized higher than taking care of personal needs. Moreover, researchers have consistently found that PA for health has little cultural meaning to SAs and activities such as sport are not usually performed by adults (Cerin and Leslie, 2008). There may also be social barriers to PA (Griffiths et al, 2005) such as social sanction or gossip about a SA woman if she participates in PA or sports since it is not commonly accepted in this culture (Curry et al, 2015; Grace et al, 2008).

South Asian families in the UK

Bangladeshi and Pakistani groups make up a significant portion of the SA population in the UK (nearly 1 million born outside of the UK but now living in the UK). UK Bangladeshis and Pakistanis have been reported to be religiously homogenous, with 92 per cent identifying themselves as Muslim in the 2011 Census (Ballard, 2011). Additionally, these groups have been reported to be the most socio-economically deprived of the SA groups and one of the most deprived populations in the UK, having high rates of unemployment and low rates of education (Alexander et al, 2010).

The following research was conducted with communities in Cardiff, Wales. In 2011 it was estimated that those of SA descent made up 4 per cent of the population and there were nearly 4838 Bangladeshis and 2637 Pakistanis living in Cardiff (Office for National Statistics, 2012). These large and comparatively young EMGs in the UK are known to have high rates of chronic disease morbidity and mortality, and engaging them in this research offers a unique opportunity to understand how PA/ST messages are transmitted and understood.

Study background

Twenty-four Bangladeshi and Pakistani mothers and adult daughters participated in semi-structured interviews with a female researcher of mixed ethnicity having in-depth knowledge of the Muslim religion. Traditionally SA women are the main caregivers and responsible for the health of the family, therefore women were targeted in this study (Curry et al, 2015). Fathers and men were not included in this study because it was thought that women would be reluctant to engage in the study and would be less likely to respond freely due to concern over confidentiality if male family members were involved. A full explanation of the methods and analyses can be found elsewhere (Curry et al, 2015). The aim of this study was to use semi-structured interviews to explore the shared experiences of SA mothers and daughters in the UK in relation to PA and ST, and investigate how active living messages are disseminated among SA families.

Main findings

Conceptualization and contextualization

Frequently the terms PA and exercise are used interchangeably in the literature to indicate bodily movement above rest that results in energy expenditure (Eyler et al, 2003). It is important to mention here that even in the literature, PA is defined in several ways. These include occupational PA, leisure time PA (LTPA) and active travel (such as cycling to work). Therefore interview questions began with asking if SA women would explain what each term meant to them. Women conceptualized PA as keeping busy or just moving around a lot. This can be seen in the many references to being active through daily housework. As one 36-year-old Bangladeshi woman described:

> Physically active to me means doing things. Being busy with life, housework, cooking, cleaning and going out and about.

Nearly all women indicated that being physically active meant being healthy. Particularly, being active was regarded as something that helped keep illnesses away. A 39 year-old Pakistani woman, when asked what she thought it meant to be physically active, commented that:

> I think it's good to be active. It's good for your health. Um, otherwise you've got all these other illnesses that come along.

The concept of being 'sedentary' was explored before asking participants how much ST they engaged in. Most women did not know what the word sedentary meant and required an explanation by the interviewer. Once defined, participants expressed the concept of being sedentary as falling into two main categories. Firstly, being sedentary was seen as resting or 'taking it easy'. Nearly all women who referred to being sedentary as resting commented on a sense of deserving a rest after a long and busy day. Many women wanted to relax after doing their housework. One 61-year-old Pakistani woman said:

I have um, something … to do all the time. Either cleaning the house or like you know … . Well in the evening I do take rest. I just um, I lay down and then I do nothing. But um, I think that I deserve [to rest] after the whole day.

Not only does this provide a picture of this woman's concept of what it means to be sedentary, but it is also a reflection of what her position is within the family unit. It is clear that it is expected that she will be busy with family-related tasks during the day and is allowed (by her family or herself) to take a rest. This cultural expectation was pervasive in interviews, with nearly all mothers and daughters indicating the importance of family responsibility before taking care of one's self. Women navigated overlap of family, cultural expectation and gender to assert their agency to determine when they were deserving of a rest.

Other women referred to being sedentary as being lazy. They conceptualized being sedentary as not keeping up with their housework and being a 'lady of leisure'. Importantly, both younger and older women remarked that after a woman becomes a grandmother (around age 40), she becomes very sedentary and stops doing things for herself. This was said to be a widespread practice in the community. The daughter-in-law was identified as being primarily responsible for taking care of the older woman and what used to be her household duties. One older (60 year-old) Pakistani woman commented:

… problem becomes when woman becomes mother-in-law and come homes and that's it. It's my time to sit now. She [daughter-in-law] will do everything. It's her responsibility. I done my job. Even mother-in-law may still be in early 40s. So that's where the thing goes wrong. Personally that's my view.

One younger (36-year-old) Bangladeshi woman agreed, but expresses difficulty in changing this cultural norm within the family social network:

They [daughters-in-law] have to encourage their mother-in-law to do a little bit of housework. Um, I know like within Asian culture it's rude to ask somebody to do that.

All mothers and daughters in this study referred to this specific cultural phenomenon. The importance of social networks are exemplified here as this message was carried from the 'home' countries of Bangladesh and Pakistan where this practice originated and is being passed to subsequent generations in the UK.

Health messages

Messages external to family

Messages on PA/ST from outside the family originated from health professionals, friends, and members of the community. Many women were advised by their GPs to be cautious about participating in PA due to ill health and injuries. One 46-year-old Bangladeshi woman described why she cannot be active:

> I try to be but my health prevents it at the moment. 'Cause I've got so many kinds of illnesses so there are certain exercises that I wanted to do which I am not able at the moment. That's because doctors told me to take things easy.

Women indicated that GPs did not spend enough time with them or give them enough guidance on what to do for PA. The only guidance they were offered was that they needed to exercise for their health. A 52-year-old Pakistani woman explained how more help from GPs would break this barrier to PA:

> I think actually give them [referring to the patient] a bit more time when they go to see you [referring to the GP]. Actually listen to your problems. No, it's true. Because half the problem is solved when the professional you speak to actually listens to you.

A need to be social during PA was found among SA women. Many women preferred to engage in PA with other women and also needed the encouragement of others to educate and motivate them to be active. When these were not in place women were less likely to engage in PA. One 58-year-old Pakistani woman described why this is the case:

> I'm more of a social person. So I find exercising or going for walks with someone enjoyable. I'm not one of those people who will just get up and go for a walk by themselves. So I always need to arrange some things.

Women did not want to be seen by others in the community as being lazy or 'sitting around doing nothing'. Women who were seen to be sitting around and seemingly not doing their housework were judged negatively. One Pakistani woman said she would call a sedentary woman a 'lady of leisure', which was emphasized as a derogatory reference. Messages on PA from friends indicated that PA outside of housework should be a social activity and enjoyed in the company of other women (though never men). SA women preferred to engage in leisure time PA if it meant that they could visit with their friends and family at the same time. In fact, many women modelled their PA behaviour after the more active women in the community.

Messages from within the family

Strong and entrenched messages on PA and ST were found to be transmitted throughout SA families. As previously discussed, becoming a mother-in-law equated to being expected to be less active as a result of traditional practices.

Among SA women in this sample there was an expectation for themselves and from the family that as they get older, they are entitled to relax. Many women explained that they had 'done their job' and that now it was time to enjoy life, which included spending a great deal of their time in ST. Others were sedentary since they had become a mother-in-law with fewer familial responsibilities.

When women were asked how to encourage older ladies to be more active, they said that mothers-in-law should not allow their daughter-in-law to do everything for them. It is a cultural tradition for this to happen, but both younger and older participants agreed that it had become an unhealthy one. Every mother and daughter interviewed expressed worry about a current disease or worry about developing a disease related to, in their words, having 'too much body fat'. Too much body fat was a concern for every woman in this study especially those who had seen a GP for a health issue, although none used the term 'obese'. Although the traditional message of the mother-in-law stepping back from housework once she has a daughter-in-law was still in effect, all recognized that due to the health consequences of inactivity, excess body fat and disease, this practice should not continue in its current state. Many women acknowledged, though, that this traditional message would be very difficult to change. One 39-year-old Pakistani woman described this:

> ... well the daughters all help the mothers anyway. But um, mothers should be active in some way and be more independent and not rely on other people. Mainly because they think they can't do it. That's the situation isn't it?

Family-caring responsibilities were expected to take precedence over all other activities in a SA woman's life. This took the form of caring for husbands, children and ageing parents. No woman in this sample was free from some type of family caring obligation. Overlapping with caring responsibilities is family pressure to prioritise housework over leisure time PA. Women frequently noted that they were expected to ensure that all family and household needs were met before engaging in any outside activities. Again, daughters-in-law caring for mothers-in-law was seen as the norm and daughters felt pressure to continue this tradition. One daughter explained that in fact it is not the daughter who can encourage mothers to be active but it is the 'younger ones and husbands. Can't forget them'.

At the social level, other family members such as a daughter or friends were the most influential in delivering messages on PA and encouraging SA women to be more active. Women said that having their daughters, sisters, and other SA women to be active with made the activity more fun, therefore they would be more likely to continue. Younger women (those not yet a mother-in-law) were the greatest source of information on activities and many made an effort to bring groups of others, both younger and older, together to engage in activity. It seemed that being active was more acceptable if the activity was conducted with other SA women, especially other female family members.

Additionally, these women were the source of knowledge on the benefits of PA as well as where activities were taking place. One 36 year-old Bangladeshi woman talks about her enjoyment of being social during PA:

> I think we go through phases where my friends and my sister, if we are doing something for an event we all get together and we perform and we dance. And that's when we're doing lots of dancing and practices.

Using cultural events to incorporate PA such as dance is one major example of a culturally responsive practice. This activity was accepted by both male and female family members as appropriate activity to engage in. It seemed that special dispensation for taking time away from family responsibilities was made for these activities because of their wider cultural importance. Although, once the cultural event was over, women were no longer expected to engage in these activities.

Many women acknowledged the importance of getting children involved in PA at a young age and having young people help to educate older women. Several mothers of younger children encouraged their children to be active. This was through after-school activities and sports. Utilizing younger people to help encourage older women to be more active was suggested by several participants, although this was seen as a difficult subject to tackle due to cultural norms.

Concluding thoughts and reflections

SA mothers and daughters in this example conceptualized PA first and foremost as being good for their health. When probed for what types of activities might constitute PA, most identified housework and 'keeping busy' as their main modes of PA. This concept of PA was transmitted throughout families and perpetuated from generation to generation as mothers and daughters reported similar conceptualizations. It is evident that if health promotion or interventions are to be successful with SA women and other comparable groups, this message of PA for health should be employed as it appears to be the most salient.

Women identified one of two conceptualizations of ST: resting or being lazy; concepts tied very closely to their family social network and cultural traditions. Since most women perceived their days to be filled with housework and family obligations that kept them busy, many believed they deserved to rest in the evenings or were expected to. In contrast, others saw it as being lazy if a woman was known to be 'sitting around'. If this was the case, she was not completing her household tasks and was therefore seen negatively by others in the community. This social pressure was pervasive within the family social networks of the mothers and daughters interviewed.

The only exception to this negative opinion was in reference to mothers-in-law. It was an accepted fact that as a mother-in-law, they were entitled to do a great deal of sitting after having raised a family and done the housework for many years. At this point in the life course, the daughters-in-law take over these responsibilities. While everyone (including the male family members, according to the women) acknowledged this was the case, all women interviewed conceded that this habit was not healthy to engage in. All women recognised that there are health risks that result from leading a sedentary lifestyle. The importance of family traditions has been found in other studies on SA women (Siddiqui et al, 2008; Sriskantharajah and Kai, 2007). These studies also found that women understood the importance of being active, but that family responsibilities and traditions often prevented them from engaging in PA.

Messages on PA and ST among SA mothers and daughters were transmitted through several key routes: family (specifically daughters and often sisters or aunts), friends, medical professionals (GPs) and members of the community. Crucially, cultural traditions and messages such as the position of mothers-in-law and the role of women in caretaking influenced family members' under-standing of PA/ST, their motivation to engage in these activities, and their own transmission of these traditions and messages. Scholars such as Bourdieu have acknowledged the strong association between the social construction of family and the social pressures exerted on individuals (Bourdieu, 1996). This is made clear in the case of the SA families in this study. Cultural customs and expectations of family were exerted on mothers and daughters and upheld by them, resulting in the aforementioned messages on PA and ST. These can be considered social and cultural determinants of PA/ST in SA families. Moreover this study exemplified the ways in which members of a group of ethnic minority women navigated within the intersectionality of determinants such as gender, socioeconomic status and ethnicity to assert their agency to be sedentary or active as they saw fit within these structures. While individual responsibility for health is highly valued and emphasised in many western countries as well as in health promotion and interventions, this emphasis may have little resonance within the confines of many EMGs. As this study example has illustrated, the cultural practices of SA and many other EMG families are largely misunderstood or ignored by health promotion and policies. Health promotion and policies would benefit from an increased understanding of how diverse families understand, transmit and act upon health messages.

References

Alexander, C., Firoz, S. and Rashid, N. (2010) *The Bengali diaspora in Britain: a review of the literature.* London: London School of Economics.

Antikainen, L., Ellis, R., Kosma, M. et al (2005) Examining Change in Theory-based Physical Activity Beliefs of Culturally Diverse Older Adults, *Journal of Applied Gerontology*, 29(4), 507–517.

August, K. J. and Sorkin, D. (2010) Racial and Ethnic Disparities in Indicators of Physical Health Status: Do They Still Exist Throughout Late Life?, *Journal of the American Geriatrics Society*, 58, 2009–2015.

Babakus, W. and Thompson, J. L. (2012) Physical activity among South Asian women: a systematic, mixed-methods review, *International Journal of Behavioral Nutrition and Physical Activity*, 9, 150–168.

Ballard, R. (2011) *The current demographic characteristics of the South Asian presence in Britain: an analysis of the results of the 2011 census.* PhD thesis. Manchester: University of Manchester.

Bandura, A. (1989) Human agency in social cognitive theory, *American Psychologist*, 44(9), 1175–1184.

Bao, X. and Lam, S. (2008) Who Makes the Choice? Rethinking the Role of Autonomy and Relatedness in Chinese Children's Motivation, *Child Development*, 44(9), 1175–1184.

Benn, T., Dagkas, S. and Jawad, H. (2011) Embodied faith: Islam, religious freedom and educational practices in physical education, *Sport, Education and Society*, 16(1), 17–34.

Bernardi, L. (2011) A mixed-methods social networks study design for research on transnational families, *Journal of Marriage and Family*, 73, 788–803.

Bourdieu, P. (1996) On the Family as a Realized Category, *Theory, Culture & Society*, 13, 19–26.

Caperchione, C. M., Kolt, G. S. and Mummery, K. W. (2009) Physical activity in culturally and linguistically diverse migrant groups to Western Society, *Sports Medicine*, 39(3):167–177.

Caroppo, E., Muscelli, C., Brogna, P.*et al.* (2009) Relating with migrants: Ethnopsychiatry and psychotherapy, *Annali dell' Ist Superiore Sanita*, 45(3), 331–340.

Cerin, E. and Leslie, E. (2008) How socio-economic status contributes to participation in leisure-time physical activity, *Social Science & Medicine*, 66, 2596–2609.

Chowdhury, T. A., Lasker, S. S. and Mahfuz, R. (2006) Ethnic differences in control of cardiovascular risk factors in patients with type 2 diabetes attending an Inner London diabetes clinic, *Postgraduate Medical Journal*, 82, 211–215.

Curry, W. B., Duda, J. L. and Thompson, J. L. (2015) Perceived and Objectively Measured Physical Activity and Sedentary Time among South Asian Women in the UK, *International Journal of Environmental Research and Public Health*, 12(3), 3152–3173.

Depelteau, F. (2008). Relational thinking: A critique of co-deterministic theories of structure and agency, *Sociological Theory*, 26(1), 51–73.

Dogra, S., Meisner, B. A. and Adern, C. I. (2010) Variation in mode of physical activity by ethnicity and time since immigration: a cross-sectional analysis, *International Journal of Behavioral Nutrition and Physical Activity*, 7, 75–85.

Downie, M., Cua, S. N., Koestner, R.*et al.* (2007) The Relations of Parental Autonomy Support to Cultural Internalization and Well-Being of Immigrants and Sojourners, *Cultural Diversity and Ethnic Minority Psychology*, 13(3), 241–249.

Eapen, D., Kalra, G. L., Merchant, N.*et al.* (2009) Metabolic syndrome and cardiovascular disease in South Asians, *Vascular Health and Risk Management*, 5, 731–743.

Egan, M., Tannahill, C., Petticrew, M.*et al.* (2009) Psychosocial risk factors in home and community settings and their associations with population health and health inequalities: A systematic meta-review, *BMC Public Health*, 8, 239–251.

Evenson, K., Olga, R., Sarmiento, L.*et al.* (2004) Acculturation and physical activity among North Carolina Latina immigrants, *Social Science & Medicine*, 59, 2509–2522.

Eyler, A. A., Matson-Kaffman, D., Young, D. R.*et al.* (2003) Quantitative study of Correlates of physical activity in women from diverse racial/ethnic groups. Women's Cardiovascular Health Network Project introduction and methodology, *American Journal of Preventive Medicine*, 25, 1–14.

Frohlich, K. L. and Potvin, L. (2008) The inequality paradox: the population approach and vulnerable populations, *Government, Politics, and Law*, 98(2), 1–6.

Gatineau, M. and Mathrani, S. (2011) Ethnicity and obesity in the UK, *Perspectives in Public Health*, 131, 159–160.

Grace, C., Begum, R., Subhani, S.*et al.* (2008) Prevention of type 2 diabetes in British Bangladeshis: Qualitative study of community, religious, and professional perspectives, *British Medical Journal*, 337, a1931–a1938.

Graham, H. (2004) *Socioeconomic inequalities in health in the UK: evidence on patterns and determinants*. Lancaster University: Institute for Health Research.

Griffiths, C., Justhna, M., Abdul, A., Ramsay, J.*et al.* (2005) Randomized controlled trial of a lay-led self-management programme for Bangladeshi patients with chronic disease, *British Journal of Medical Practice*, 55, 831–837.

Halfon, N. and Hochstein, M. (2002) Life course health development: an integrated framework for developing health, policy, and research, *The Millbank Quarterly*, 80(3), 433–479.

Jonnalagadda, S. and Diwan, S. (2002) Regional variations in dietary intake and body mass index of first-generation Asian-Indian immigrants in the United States, *Journal of the American Dietetic*, 102(9), 1286–1289.

Jonnalagadda, S. and Diwan, S. (2005) Health Behaviors, Chronic Disease Prevalence and Self-Rated Health of Older Asian Indian Immigrants in the U.S., *Journal of Immigrant Health*, 7(2), 75–83.

King, A. C., Castro, C., Wilcox, S.*et al.* (2001) Personal and Environmental Factors Associated with Physical Inactivity Among Different Racial-Ethnic Groups of U.S. Middle-Aged and Older-Aged Women, *Health Psychology*, 19(4): 354–364.

Laird, L. D., Amer, M. M., Barnett, E. D.*et al.* (2007) Muslim patients and health disparities in the UK and the US, *Archives of Disease in Childhood*, 92, 922–926.

Lord, S., Francois, S.Chastin, M.*et al.* (2011) Exploring patterns of daily physical activity and sedentary behaviour in community-dwelling older adults, *Age and Ageing*, 40, 205–210.

Mahler, S. J. and Pessar, P. R. (2001) Gendered geographies of power: Analyzing gender across transnational spaces, *Identities*, 7(4), 441–459.

Nazroo, J. Y. (2003) The Structuring of Ethnic Inequalities in Health: Economic Position, Racial Discrimination, and Racism, *American Journal of Public Health*, 93 (2), 277–284.

Office for National Statistics (2012) 2011 Census: Country of birth (detailed), local authorities in England and Wales. In *2011 Census, Key Statistics for Local Authorities in England and Wales*. Accessed April 2015 [http://www.ons.gov.uk/ons/publications/re-reference-tables.html?newquery=*&newoffset=25&pageSize=25&edition=tcm%3A77-286262].

Owen, N., Bauman, A. and Brown, W. (2009) Too much sitting: A novel and important predictor of chronic disease risk?, *British Journal of Sports Medicine*, 43(2), 81–83.

Phoenix, A. (2006). Interrogating intersectionality: Productive ways of theorising multiple positioning, *Kvinder, Køn & Forskning*, 2–3, 21–30.

Rafnsson, S. B. and Bhopal, R. S. (2009) Large-scale epidemiological data on cardiovascular diseases and diabetes in migrant and ethnic minority groups in Europe, *The European Journal of Public Health*, 19(5), 1–8.

Ryan, R. M., LaGuardia, J. G., Solky-Butzel, J.et al (2005) On the interpersonal regulation of emotional: Emotional reliance across gender, relationships, and culture, *Personal Relationships*, 12, 145–163.

Ryan, L. (2011) Migrants' social networks and weak ties: accessing resources and constructing relationships post-migration, *The Sociological Review*, 59(4), 707–724.

Siddiqui, F. R., Ur-Rahman, M., Bhatti, M. A.*et al.* (2008) Knowledge, attitudes and practices to lifestyle risk factors for coronary heart disease (CHD) and diabetes amongst South Asians in North Kirklees, England: A focus group study, *Pakistan Armed Forces Journal*, 3, 1–9.

Smith, N. R., Kelly, Y. J., and Nazroo, J. Y. (2009) Intergenerational continuities of ethnic inequalities in general health in England, *Journal of Epidemiology and Community Health*, 63, 253–258.

Sriskantharajah, J. and Kai, J. (2007) Promoting physical activity among South Asian women with coronary heart disease and diabetes: what might help?, *Family Practice*, 24(1): 71–76.

Stephens, C., Alpass, F., Towers, A.et al (2011) The effects of types of social networks, perceived social support, and loneliness on the health of older people: Accounting for the social context, *Journal of Aging and Health*, 23, 887–911.

Tremblay, M. S., Bryan, S. N., Perez, C. E.*et al.* (2006) Physical Activity and Immigrant Status Evidence from the Canadian Community Health Survey. *Canadian Journal of Public Health*, 97(4): 277–282.

Umberson, D., Crosnoe, R. and Reczek, C. (2010) Social Relationships and Health Behavior across the Life Course, *The Annual Review of Sociology*, 36, 139–157.

WHO (World Health Organization) (2012) *Social determinants of health. Report by the Secretariat*, 1–5.

Yu, G., Renton, A., Schmidt, E.*et al.* (2011) A multilevel analysis of the association between social networks and support on leisure time physical activity: evidence from 40 disadvantaged areas in London, *Health & Place*, 17, 1023–1029.

10 'Pedagogized families' health and culture

Intersectionality of race and social class

Symeon Dagkas

The 'making up' of the child in terms of 'talents' or 'abilities' is 'the product of an investment of time and cultural capital' (Bourdieu, 2004, p17). The nature of (enrichment) activities would suggest that 'unintended learning made possible by a disposition acquired through domestic [or scholarly] inculcation of legitimate culture' (Bourdieu, 1986, p28). This is 'the work of the bourgeois family' (Bourdieu, 1986, p28) and of its actors. Through activities and visits [to galleries, museums, sport centers, leisure centers and sports clubs], confrontations with conventions and institutions, the child is surely inducted into the 'caste' of 'those who understand' (Vincent and Ball, 2007, p1074).

Introduction

The quotes above are illustrative of the focus of this chapter and as a matter of fact of this whole book on the role of families in (re)shaping, (re)directing young people's dispositions towards physical culture. As researchers, we ought to investigate the range and variety of practices that underpin what is portrayed as the 'family's' activities and the way informal pedagogies shape agency. With current global economic uncertainties, recession and projected increases in poverty (Dagkas and Quarmby, 2012) especially amongst young people, understanding how diverse family formations and cultural dispositions toward physical culture and health shape young people's engagement is crucial. It is equally important to acknowledge the familial contextual differences enacted by personal histories, religious and cultural ideologies and practices towards physical culture. Families in this sense are engaged in the cultural transmission of values related to physical culture (e.g., toward physical activity participation and health) which could (re)produce dispositions, agency and perpetuate existing structural inequalities and dispositions. This chapter draws on social theory of habitus, capital and field as well as intersectionality, in an effort to explore the ways in which the intersectionality of the field of family, and other fields such as religion and socio-economic status influence young people's (particularly those of Asian and minority ethnic background) physical culture. The chapter will also examine the role of the pedagogized family in cultivating young people's dispositions towards physical culture and physical activity for health. Finally it will explore cultural practices of families in relation to health, sport and physical activity.

It is important to contextualize any notion of agency within current neoliberal doctrines that emphasise consumerism in relation to health and individual responsibility for maintenance and care of the body. According to Vincent and Ball (2007) in a neoliberal climate 'the child is understood as a project with the 'good' parent presenting a myriad of opportunities and support for the child to have a range of learning experiences' (p1065).

Furthermore, neoliberalism can be seen as a political and social doctrine that urges people to be responsible for their own personal choices for health, education and lifestyle (Macdonald, 2012). This, in turn, has significance for the way society itself and groups within society view the preservation of the body, and maintenance of good health (Macdonald, 2012). Therefore, 'the consumption behavior of parents and children needs to be understood as that of materially positioned individuals belonging to differentiated social groupings and communities' (Martens, 2005 cited in Vincent and Ball, 2007, p1066). Vincent and Ball (2007) suggest that 'this is a particular kind of individualism... embedded in the specialness and particularity of the young child, and the idea that the child should be able to realize their inherent capabilities or potential and become a self-developing subject, a person of categoric value' (p1070), especially within middle class families.

Nevertheless, personal responsibility for care of the body assumes that people, and for the purposes of this chapter, families, have the competence and resources available to make informed choices about good health, and physical activity (O'Sullivan, 2012). As many have signalled (see also Chapters 5, 9 and 12 in this volume; Hill and Azzarito, 2012), for some disadvantaged young people and those from diverse ethnical backgrounds, structural and environmental barriers restrict this capability. Rose (2006, cited in Macdonald, 2012, p38) explains that, in neoliberal societies, 'the maintenance of health and quality of life has become obligatory; negative judgments are directed towards those who refuse to adopt active and healthy behaviours'. Furthermore, Macdonald (2012) has concluded, 'the pervasiveness of neoliberalism can make the neoliberal approach to health appear somewhat natural and logical and thereby shift critique' (p42). I contend that it also has an 'othering' effect for those outside of the norm. In what follows I endeavour to contextualize the notion of the pedagogized family in the context of neoliberalism and the structural barriers that some families face in relation to health and physical culture.

The 'pedagogized' family

The parent is considered, for the purposes of this chapter, as a pedagogue and the child as a social actor (learner) in a dynamic that influences the reading of public/official discourses towards physical culture and specifically towards physical activity and health (such as the volume, intensity and patterns of activity, as well as nutrition, body ideal and presentation). I locate this discussion within macro structures of power (Evans and Davies, 2004) and control within families, which, for the purposes of this chapter, are acknowledged, as fields (Bourdieu, 1984). The discussion developed is based on Ball's (2010) suggestion that it is necessary to look beyond the school establishment if we are to explain inequalities in health, sport and physical culture. It is important therefore to examine the pedagogical practices of different types of families (especially the culturally diverse family) in relation to physical culture.

Sandlin et al (2010) describe (public/ informal) pedagogies – that is, spaces of learning that exist outside the school, as crucial to our understanding of the development of identities and social formations (in lisahunter, 2013). I draw on Tinning's (2010) explanation of informal pedagogies. He suggests that cultural transmissions, exchanges, and (re)production of cultural values constitute informal pedagogic practices. In this relational cultural practice, socially contracted sets of markers of habitus such as gender, class, race and ethnicity are used to differentiate and therefore position people (individual and group habitus) and, in the case of this chapter, families. This operates through capital endowment within fields and influences young peoples' and families' dispositions and access to capital.

The family is a pedagogic site (see also Chapters 3, 5 and 7 in this volume) which, according to Bourdieu (1984), acts as a 'field' where social (re)production takes place. These pedagogical processes contribute to the development of 'manifest embodiments', attitudes, predispositions and orientations (Evans and Davies, 2010) toward physical culture. Therefore, it can be argued that attitudes and orientations toward patterns of physical culture and participation in sport and physical activity may well be developed outside formal education. According to Ball (2010), the influence of the family environment is critical because families also invest in physical culture and sport based activities.

Family environments differ and every learner (child) learns differently based on, for example, economic resources, family income and structure, locality, place of birth, working hours (especially for the low-economic status families), and parenting practices. In addition, gender, class, race, and ethnicity, all markers of habitus, influence the family environment of young people (Dagkas and Quarmby, 2012).

The standard biological definition of the family restricts the family unit to persons related by birth, marriage, or adoption, living in the same residence. However, this definition of family fails to include various other families, those living apart and/or in multiple homes and those not blood related. Wise (2003) points to the multitude of relationships between parents and children in a household as key to defining family formations. Given the range of relationships, family formations can clearly incorporate a host of different formations. Perhaps the most common is the two-parent family where all children are the biological children of two non-divorced parents (Wise, 2003). Finally, a growing acceptance of divorce and sexual relations outside of marriage has decreased the prevalence of the heterosexual two-parent family and allowed for a more open view and existence of same sex families (Sullivan, 2004). As same sex couple families are choosing parenthood through a variety of means, the extent to which family members are biologically related can differ.

The pedagogized family and social theory

Bourdieu's notions of individual habitus suggests that individuals' personal histories and current social circumstances crucially influence young people's engagement in physical activities, particularly when considering the influence of the family as a social field. Bourdieu (1996) defined field as a site in which certain beliefs and values are established and imposed on the people within it through the various relationships and practices that occur. In this sense, fields are sites of ideological reproduction (Bourdieu, 1996). Bourdieu and Wacquant (1992, p17) argue that a field 'is simultaneously a space of conflict and competition', structured internally in terms of power relations. Individuals try to distinguish themselves from others and acquire capital that is useful or valuable within that arena and as such, fields are seen to be hierarchical (Dagkas and Quarmby, 2012). However, the boundaries of a particular *field* are demarcated by where its effects end. Consequently, such boundaries can be difficult to locate; thus, overlapping fields (family, school, physical culture, etc.) can affect the internal dynamics within them (Laberge and Kay, 2002). As such, hierarchical influences in and of the primary socialization field (family) influence practices and agency in, for example, the secondary field (school; social environment) and possibly vice versa. Markers of habitus, such as race and social class, position individuals and groups differently according to the field. Whereas one's race and ethnicity positions a young person strongly within their family field this may not be so within the schooling field. The overlapping fields of 'family', 'religion' and 'school' (see following section on intersectionality) that are carried into the daily practices of the micro field, for example of PE or physical culture, comprise a structured system of social relations that maintain physical, economic and symbolic power relations between members (Bourdieu, 1996). Therefore, family and cultural/religious fields are hierarchically structured in terms of economic capital, as I will explain later (usually lying with the agent(s)), and cultural or social capital and its symbolic value within that field.

Importantly, Bourdieu (1996) argues that it is the intersection of habitus, capital and field that produces the logic of practice. Moreover, he suggests that those who occupy the same field, or in the case here, the same family formation, with similar objective living environments, may share similar habitus and reproduce the culture of their shared fields through practice (Bourdieu, 1984). However it is evident in latest research (see also Chapters 3 and 9 in this volume) that even within similar ethnical and racial groups, the habitus of families differs and is hugely influenced by the markers of the habitus present in the given field, such as socio-economic status and economic capital, race and ethnicity. For example Dagkas and Quarmby (2012) suggested that in the low-economic capital families whom they investigated in their research study, physical culture did not occupy a place of significant value within that field and the development of a 'taste for necessity' (Bourdieu 1984) by their study participants highlighted certain beliefs and 'natural attitudes'. These natural family attitudes (their taken-for-granted assumptions) about the value of physical culture and its place within their lives could be expressed more specifically, as their family-specific doxa. This 'Doxa' was evident in Dagkas and lisahunter's (2015) study of Asian young people and their families where in the low-economic capital families physical culture held no value. Furthermore, Benn et al's (2011) study with Muslim parents and their daughters' physical activity engagement showed that physical culture held no value in the field of family and the doxa's natural practice was to abstain from formal pedagogical terrains and from the given PE field. Doxa forms part of Bourdieu's (1996) theory of practice and refers to the commonplace values and beliefs, unquestioned opinions and perceptions permeating a given field that determine natural practice and attitudes. Although, doxa is produced by a particular habitus, namely that of an individual within a field with particular symbolic power (i.e., a parent), it importantly transcends in any one particular habitus, allowing agents within a field to share similar doxic experiences and to adopt similar values and beliefs. Thus, within a given field such as a Muslim (Asian) family, doxa is fed back into multiple habitus and shared beliefs and orientations of offspring and other family members to create a legitimate family-specific doxa and shared views towards physical culture. Doxa therefore within the families in the study by Dagkas and lisahunter (2015) showed that the habitus of low economic capital families towards physical culture had no symbolic value, whereas the field of religion and culture held immense value.

However in the Quarmby and Dagkas (2015) study, it was clear that the family, as a particular social field and site of social reproduction that struggles with physical, economic and symbolic power relations (Bourdieu 1996), allowed for the development of physical activity tastes and preferences. I maintain therefore, that early family experiences intersecting with socio-economic variables 'produce the structures of the *habitus* which become in turn the basis of perception and appreciation of all subsequent experience' (Bourdieu, 1984, p78).

The 'pedagogised' family and intersections of multiple fields such as social class and religion

In short, the theoretical framework/concept of intersectionality allows for better understanding of the way multiple often-overlapping fields influence families' agency towards physical culture. I have adopted Phoenix's (2006) definition that suggests intersectionality describes 'the complex political struggles and arguments that seek to make visible the multiple positioning that constitutes everyday life and the power relations that are central to it' (p187). Skeggs (1997, cited in Gillborn, 2010) attest that 'class is a discursively, historically specific-construction, a product of middle class political consolidation, which includes elements of fantasy and projection' (p15). According to Evans and Davies (2006, pp797–798) the term social class implies 'not just a categorization or classification or people with reference to some quality, but an invidious, hierarchical ranking of people which is inherently value laden'. Social class is, for Evans and Davies (2006), a set of social and economic relations that influence, dominate, and dictate people's lives. Linking social class and family, Evans and Davies (2006) observed that middle-class families facilitated high levels of participation in sport and physical activity at an early age to retain educational superiority and, thus, class distinction. As such, middle-class families faced fewer barriers in obtaining education than working-class families (Evans and Davies, 2006). Indeed, many working-class and Asian families are constrained by the need to work unsocial hours and face associated costs that can't be met.

Another aspect of the intersectionality approach that I have adopted in this chapter that influences family's physical culture is religion/ethnicity. Religion is an under-researched domain in terms of its influence on the social self and body cultures, particularly in the fields of education and sport. Attention to the concept of embodiment of a physical identity and physical culture acknowledges the material, physical, biological as well as the social whole of the 'lived body' (Garrett, 2004, p141). For many Asian families Islamic influences can lead to preferences to embody their faith by covering arms, legs and heads (Benn et al, 2011). The contested nature of the private/public faces of religious identity within the family field, as explained in an earlier section in this chapter, is important and can justify different manifestations of religion. The 'lived religion' or the religiosity of Asian families, their degree of 'Islamization' and interpretation of their social world and environment, have to be considered, especially since Asian families have been defined as 'hard- to- reach' groups, rarely participate in research on physical culture and have also been regarded as a homogeneous group, which as explained above is clearly not the case. As with all families, Asian families demonstrate multiple and fluid positionalities.

Faith is embodied in the sense that presentation of the body, appearance, physicality, social interaction and behaviour is integral to religious identity, to the lived reality of the daily life (Benn et al, 2011). The concept of habitus can increase understanding of the significance of embodied faith (Benn et al,

2011) and hence the dilemma facing some Muslim families, and especially their girls and women when physical activity contexts deny that embodiment, creating tension between values accrued in the field of family and other often overlapping fields (such as school, social groups, PE, etc.) In a recent study by Dagkas and lisahunter (2015) young Muslims further demonstrated agency towards physical culture while simultaneously assigning to the religious beliefs conveyed by their parents. This particular trend was especially evident in those young Muslims whose family's economic capital was low as mentioned earlier. The authors supported that intergenerational embodiment of strict religious adherence amongst Muslims with low economic capital is prominent within the field of family. Benn et al (2011) supported that Asian families acquire sophisticated codes of body usage, articulated, for example, in terms of dress, behaviours in public and private, and preferred ways of displaying or concealing bodies and this I contend is highly relevant to the economic capital of the family as Dagkas and lisahunter (2015) supported in their study. It is imperative, therefore, to acknowledge that Asian families are not a homogenous group and that identities of Asian families are not static and fixed but dynamic and manipulated through the power of agency, their personal histories and their economic capital. Action in pursuit of preferences for opportunity both to participate in sporting activities and retain adherence to religious identity, demonstrates such agency.

According to Vincent and Ball (2007) involvement in 'enrichment activities' (such as children sporting activities, sport tasters, music lessons, etc.) is class specific and an indicator of 'good', 'appropriate' and 'desirable' parenting as acknowledged in the public health discourse. Parents enrol their children in numerous age-specific, organized (sporting) activities that dominate family life and they view these activities as transmitting life skills and they view their children as a project for development (Vincent and Ball, 2007). However the authors claim that working-class families are far less likely to involve their children in 'such' enrichment activities. One clear reason for this, they suggest, is financial, as many of the enrichment activities tend to be expensive and unaffordable. Therefore, the working-class parents are much less likely to see their children as a project for development unlike their middle-class counterparts. This investment, according to Vincent and Ball (2007), is clearly one way of increasing middle-class family's privilege. It is evident, then, that for high economic capital families, the 'making up' of the child in terms of particular 'talents' or 'abilities' is then 'the product of an investment of time and cultural capital' (Bourdieu, 2004, p17). Furthermore these 'enrichment' activities or in many cases the 'buying-in' of expertise through activities is one obvious way in which cultural capital is linked to economic capital. There are multiple determinations of the body involved in the production of what Vincent and Ball (2007) have called a 'renaissance child ... a child with intellectual, creative and sporting skills and experience' (p1071). In their study of middle-class families habitus and agency they suggested that 'enrolling under fives in [sporting] activities ensured that children developed physical, social and intellectual skills which would leave them in a state of learning readiness for future success at school' (p1072).

There is evidence that higher socio-economic status (SES) is linked to higher levels of involvement in physical activity. In Dagkas and Stathi's (2007) research, young people and families from low socio-economic status experience greater barriers to participation in sport than those from middle or high SES. Such barriers can be classified as financial, logistical and geographical. While participants from high SES areas report a plethora of opportunities, young people and their families living in low SES areas often comment on the restrictions they faced due to their geographic location and lack of facilities to enact physical culture. In the field of PE and generally sport, high SES parents expect teachers and schools to build on parental 'investment' in their children through their embodied practices. Such practices appear to illustrate Bourdieu's (1984) concept of intergenerational habitus as parents implicitly impart values, attitudes, predispositions and their embodied practices of physical culture involvement onto their children.

According to Burrows and Wright (2004, p90), 'it is often those parents who are already "othered" in the normalizing discourses of parenting who are further marginalized by ... moral imperatives to regulate children'. Even though it might seem that I extend this 'marginalization' and 'othering' of Asian and low SES families in this chapter by highlighting barriers and obstacles to enacting physical culture; the intention is to portray the multifaceted interlocking inequalities that exist that impact on young people's dispositions toward physical culture. In recent research findings (see, for example, Dagkas and Quarmby, 2012), it is evident that pedagogic practices within the field of the family moved from health and fitness to pedagogic practices of 'safety.' 'Good parenting' in this context reflected imperatives of 'getting home safely' and 'staying out of trouble' which derived from environmental elements and areas of residence, notions absent from the dominant health discourse that is dominated by the obsessiveness of a healthy body, the body that is free of disease. Therefore desires to enact physical culture are constrained by social influences that are accepted as 'normal' (doxa) by many of these families. Thus, Dagkas and Quarmby (2012) maintained that the understanding of what could be considered 'normal' living circumstances differed in different families and influenced the parents' pedagogic practices of physical activity participation.

Families employ specific rules related to the development of the child in relation to physical culture, albeit within given economic resources and psychosocial parameters. In a comparative study of various family formations by Quarmby and Dagkas (2015) it was evident that in two parent families, the 'pedagogized' family was influenced by the existing health discourse and the guidelines of a healthy lifestyle. Whereas in alternative family formations (i.e., lone parent families; step-families) changes in the family field influenced physical culture. In many cases, changes in the family environment (one field) directly influenced changes in the dispositions toward physical activity that directly influenced on habitus (Bourdieu, 1984); the development of the body either in terms of physical development or in terms of physical activity behaviour. However, I want to avoid further marginalizing and 'othering' of alternative 'non-normative' families and to avoid homogenization, I want to acknowledge that a change in the field of family doesn't always necessarily have a negative impact upon dispositions toward physical culture, or at least existing research evidence doesn't support this.

Concluding thoughts

Ball (2010) argued that inequalities 'are being formed and reproduced within… civil societies through institutional ordering … as forms of classism' (p158). The 'pedagogized' family as argued in this chapter reproduces class and racial distinctions and reinforces existing structural inequalities, especially when markers of habitus in multiple fields are intersecting, with regards to physical culture. Cultural transmissions (Bourdieu, 2004) within the family as presented in this chapter can influence pedagogical orientations and establish embodied practices, as evident in many middle class families and the 'renaissance child'. These cultural transmissions are closely related to economic capital, cultural and physical capital where agency within the family environment is structured through certain socioeconomic, racial and religious backgrounds that are crucial to the development of embodied dispositions, which can facilitate or constrain experiences based on place, locality, and environment. Bourdieu (1996) contended that the family (as a field) remains the key site of social reproduction and plays a vital role in maintaining social order and reproducing the structure of social space and social relations. It is also one of the key sites, as explained in this chapter, for the accumulation and transmission of various forms of capital. I want to maintain that the family, therefore, plays a pivotal role in the reproduction of social order across generations.

To address social inequalities we need to look further into the fields where habitus is formed by intersecting economic capital with changes in the field of family. 'Interlocking inequalities' (Ball, 2003, cited in Evans and Davies, 2006, p805) embedded within everyday practices of class and family occur in a complex and dynamic interplay of structures, which involve decision-making, values, and priorities (Dagkas and Quarmby, 2012). It is, therefore, important to understand what constitutes 'the family' as a field and the way in which pedagogic practices shape embodied dispositions toward physical culture and health in this field. It is important to engage with families – especially those identified as 'hard-to-reach' families due to their cultural, racial and ethnic background that have remained silent in the public health discourse and voice the 'other' to uncover multiple intersecting markers of habitus within various fields that constitute agency and practice, and provide a clear understanding of what 'health', 'healthy body', and 'healthy lifestyles' actually mean within these families. A perception of working class or Asian

Muslim families as a homogeneous group is not helpful in understanding existing inequalities or health disparities. Families within similar social groupings taste and experience inequalities in various forms and levels. As such families adopt diverse (informal) pedagogic practices and dispositions toward physical culture despite being categorized under the same social groupings in society. Adopting a rhetoric style here I want to maintain that if we are to address existing inequalities in society, policy makers, practitioners and even researchers need to move away from monocultural doctrines to avoid further marginalising the 'others' outside of the monoculture. As I mentioned earlier in this chapter it is important to acknowledge and accept that Asian families are not a homogenous group and that identities of Asian families are not static and fixed but dynamic and manipulated through the power of agency, their personal histories and their economic capital. We need to be fully informed about the different pedagogic environments in which young people come to learn about and experience physical culture. Importantly, informal pedagogic encounters within the family may differ and clash with formal pedagogic encounters in different institutions (Dagkas and Quarmby, 2012) and, as such, Tinning (2010) argues that 'in order to better understand the impact of institutional work, there is a need to grasp the pedagogical work done by 'other cultural players that often undermines the intentional pedagogical work' carried out by specialists' (p419).

References

Ball, S. (2010) New class inequalities in education: Why education policy may be looking in the wrong place! Education policy, civil society and social class, *The International Journal of Sociology and Social Policy*, 30(3/4), 155–166.

Benn, T., Dagkas, S. and Jawad, H. (2011) Embodied faith: Islam, religious freedom and educational practices in physical education, *Sport, Education and Society*, 16(1), 17–34.

Bourdieu, P. (1977) *Outline of a theory of practice.* Cambridge: Cambridge University Press.

Bourdieu, P. (1984) *Distinction: A social critique of the judgment of taste.* New York: Routledge and Kegan Paul.

Bourdieu, P. (1986) The forms of capital, In J. G. Richardson (ed.) *Handbook of theory and research for the sociology of education* (pp241–258). New York: Greenwood Press.

Bourdieu, P. (1996) On the family as a realized category, *Theory, Culture and Society*, 13(3), 19–26.

Bourdieu, P. (2004) *In other words.* Cambridge, MA: Cambridge University Press.

Bourdieu, P. and Wacquant, L. (1992) *An invitation to reflexive sociology.* Cambridge: Polity Press.

Burrows, L. and Wright, J. (2004) The discursive production of childhood, identity and health. In J. Evans, B. Davies and J. Wright (eds.), *Body knowledge and control: Studies in the sociology of physical education and health* (pp83–95). London: Routledge.

Dagkas, S. and Stathi, A. (2007) Exploring Social and Environmental Factors Affecting Adolescent's participation in Physical Activity, *European Physical Educational Review*, 13(3): 369–383.

Dagkas, S. and Quarmby, T. (2012) Children's embodiment of health and physical capital: The role of the 'pedagogised' family, *Sociology of Sport Journal*, 29, 210–226.

Dagkas, S. and lisahunter (2015) Pedagogic practices influencing young Muslim's physical culture: exploring intersections of family, religion and social class, *Physical Education and Sport Pedagogy*, 20(5), 547–558.

Evans, J. and Davies, B. (2004) The embodiment of consciousness: Bernstein, health and schooling. In J. Evans, B. Davies, and J. Wright (Eds.) *Body, knowledge and control: Studies in the sociology of physical education and health* (pp207–217). London: Routledge.

Evans, J. and Davies, B. (2006). Social class and physical education. In D. Kirk, D. Macdonald and M. O'Sullivan (eds.), *Handbook of physical education* (pp796–808). London: Sage.

Evans, J. and Davies, B. (2010) Family, class and embodiment: Why school physical education makes so little difference to post school participation patterns in physical activity, *International Journal of Qualitative Studies in Education*, 23(7), 765–784.

Garrett, R. (2004) Gendered bodies and physical identities. In J. Evans, B. Davies and J. Wright, (eds.) *Body, knowledge and control: Studies in the sociology of physical education and health* (pp140–156). London, Routledge.

Gillborn, D. (2010) The white working class, racism and respectability: Victims, degenerates and interest-convergence, *British Journal of Educational Studies*, 58(1), 3–25.

Hill, J. and Azzarito, L. (2012) Representing valued bodies in PE: A visual inquiry with British Asian girls, *Physical Education and Sport Pedagogy*, 17(3), 263–276.

Laberge, S. and Kay, J. (2002) Pierre Bourdieu's sociocultural theory and sport practice. In Maguire, J. and K. Young (eds.) *Theory, sport and society* (pp239–267). London: JAI Press.

lisahunter (2013) What did I do-see-learn at the beach? Surfing festival as a cultural pedagogical sight/site. In L. Azzarito and D. Kirk, (eds) *Physical culture, pedagogies and visual methods* (pp144–161). New York: Routledge.

Macdonald, D. (2012) Like a fish in water: Physical education policy and practice in the era of neoliberal globalization, *QUEST*, 63(1), 36–45.

O'Sullivan, D. (2012). Justice, culture and the political: Determinants of indigenous Australia health, *Ethnicities*, 12(6): 687–705.

Pheonix, A. (2006) Editorial: Intersectionality, *European Journal of Women's Studies*, 13, 187–192.

Quarmby, S. and Dagkas, S. (2015) Informal mealtime pedagogies: exploring the influence of family structure on young people's healthy eating dispositions, *Sport Education and Society*, 20(3), 323–339.

Sandlin, J. A., Schultz, B. D. and J. Burdick. (2010) Understanding, mapping, and exploring the terrain of public pedagogy. In J. A. Sandlin, B. D. Schultz and J. Burdick (eds) *Handbook of public pedagogy: education and learning beyond schooling* (pp1–5). New York: Routledge.

Sullivan, M. (2004) *Family of women: Lesbian mothers, their children, and their undoing of gender*. New Jersey: University of California Press.

Tinning, R. (2010) *Pedagogy and human movement*. London: Routledge.

Vincent, C. and Ball, S. (2007) 'Making Up' the Middle-Class Child: Families, Activities and Class Dispositions, *Sociology*, 41(6), 1061–1077.

Wise, S. (2003). *Family structure, child outcomes and environmental mediators: An overview of the development in diverse families study.* Melbourne: Australian Institute of Family Studies.

11 Early years learning (EYL), class and ability

Julie Stirrup and John Evans

Introduction

In countries across the globe, concerns over the impact of poor quality early years learning (EYL) or early years education (EYE)[1] (see Siraj-Blatchford, 2004; Swadener et al, 2000) on future educational attainment (Sammons, et al, 2004) along with increasing health concerns focused on obesity and sedentary lifestyles (Marsden and Weston, 2007) have together precipitated renewed interest amongst politicians and academics alike in the early years education of children. Such concerns have brought to the fore the pedagogical roles that families and parents have to play in the education of their offspring and in enhancing social mobility (see Saul, 2005; Mol, 2007; Nairn et al, 2012; Vincent and Ball, 2006; Evans, 2014). Against this backdrop, this chapter focuses attention on the transactions of practitioners and children in three EYL centres in England in order to examine the claim that the 'playful' (or, rather, 'play filled') environments of EYL (both of the paid for by parents kind and free, i.e. state provided up to 15 hours a week[2]) can make a difference to the life chances of children, enhancing their education and negating inequalities. In particular, we explore how the dynamic between family and EYL settings influences children's development, affecting their subjectivities and educational opportunities. We document how 'ability hierarchies' and class relations are produced and maintained within such settings in and through the medium of play. These processes, we suggest, are critically shaped by the evaluative assumptions practitioners make both about children's family backgrounds and the knowledge they are deemed to bring to the EYL setting. We demonstrate that in order to be considered 'successful' in such contexts, children need to be 'able' to broach the gap between the play principles regulating access to the formal knowledge of EYL settings and those of the lay culture they have already embodied from home. Ultimately, our analyses attest that as currently configured the play environments of EYL far from eroding class relations and extant social hierarchies, subtly reproduces them in ways that do little to either alter or address educational opportunities and social mobility.

Parental investment and EYL

Research in the UK (echoing that of Europe and wider afield – Bertram and Pascal, 2002, 2014; Cochran, 2011; Lareau, 1987, 2000, 2003) focusing on the parent–school relationship (e.g., Crozier, 1997, 1998, 1999) has found that parents' intervention in their children's schooling is largely determined by their social class, habitus and capital. Middle-class parents with heightened knowledge of the education system, wealth at their disposal and positive experiences of school themselves are more able and (it seems) inclined to get involved in the education of their children both in and outside schools. Ball and colleagues (Ball, 2003, 2010; et al, 2004; Ball and Vincent 2005, 2007) have extensively researched parenting strategies and practices in relation to the UK education market and they, like Crozier, have observed that having large amounts of capital (not least financial and cultural) provides parents with more opportunities to acquire educational opportunities for their children. For example, economic capital enables parents to buy their children entry to (purportedly) 'better' (fee-paying independent) schools and/or supplement their children's formal education with private tuition, while social capital significantly influences the school selection process (i.e., parents deploying a variety of strategies such as moving to a 'select' catchment to ensure their offspring gain entry to the 'best' schools). Other researchers have suggested that socialization in the family influences not only children's academic development, but also their sports participation over the life span (Wheeler and Green, 2012; Wheeler, 2012; Birchwood et al, 2008; Evans and Davies, 2011) as parents invest in and transmit cultural capital in the form of sporting tastes, skills and abilities to their children (Green, 2010).

But are these parental investments reflected in the transactions between children and practitioners in the play environments of EYL, and if so, with what effect? We might surmise that the amount of time and money parents invest in their offspring's physical activity (physical capital) and educational development both in the family and outside EYL settings may influence how a child approaches the various forms of play (see Figure 11.1) they experience within EYL settings (see Table 11.1) and in turn how their corporeality is recognized and assessed by practitioners. In the analyses below we therefore begin to shed light on processes such as these as we explore how young children's 'learner identities' are constructed through play in relation to contemporary corporeal discourses (e.g., around education and social mobility) as practitioners emplace and enact EYL policies within three socially and culturally different EYL settings.

Learning in the early years

Ball et al (2004) attest that childcare settings have two main impacts: they shape children's socialization experiences; and set children on educational trajectories. In relation to socialization experiences, Melhuish et al (1990)

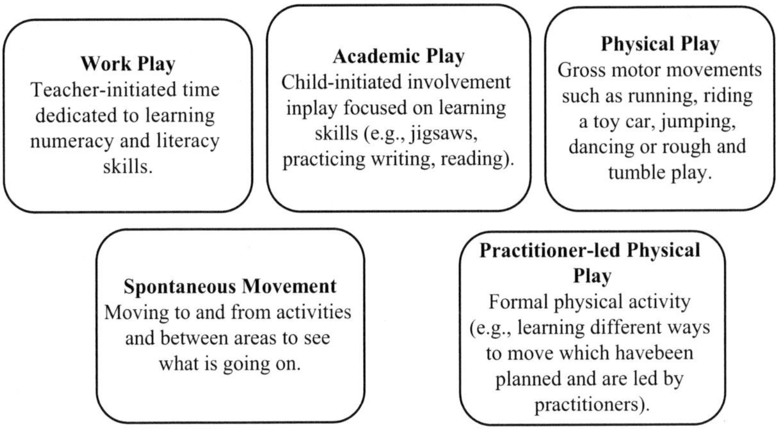

Work Play
Teacher-initiated time dedicated to learning numeracy and literacy skills.

Academic Play
Child-initiated involvement inplay focused on learning skills (e.g., jigsaws, practicing writing, reading).

Physical Play
Gross motor movements such as running, riding a toy car, jumping, dancing or rough and tumble play.

Spontaneous Movement
Moving to and from activities and between areas to see what is going on.

Practitioner-led Physical Play
Formal physical activity (e.g., learning different ways to move which havebeen planned and are led by practitioners).

Figure 11.1 Play in EYL

Table 11.1 Play differences within EYL

Time spent on each form of play	Work play	Academic play	Physical play	Practitioner-led physical activity	Spontaneous movement
*Busy Buzzy Bees***	20 min (1:1 ratio)	45 min	20 min morning	5 min (not daily)	15 min
Little People	20 min (1:5 ratio)	10 min	50 min	5 min (not daily)	30 min
Little Stars	15 min (1:5 ratio)	10 min	40 min	45 min(weekly)	40 min

have documented that child–child and child–adult interactions vary significantly between nursery settings (e.g., in terms of the time children have with practitioners) and that state and private nursery settings afford different 'social mixes' for children in the UK (Ball et al, 2004). There is also evidence of different pedagogical regimes in nurseries, with some placing more emphasis on formal learning than others (Ball and Vincent, 2007). However, despite a plethora of research on EYL we still know very little of how, or indeed whether, these processes are subject to the influences of class and culture, or if the transactions of EYL actually realize policy intentions to enhance social equity and mobility, and erode social class and ability differences and hierarchies.

Within England, teaching and learning in all EYL settings is governed and regulated by government policy as defined in the EYFS framework (DfE, 2014). Reflecting conventional wisdom in academic research and thinking on EYL (from Plowden, 1967, to present day – Broadhead and Burt, 2012) the

Table 11.2 An overview of the demographic of each setting

	Busy Buzzy Bees	*Little People*	*Little Stars*
Age of children	3–4 years	3–4 years	3–4 years
Social class* status of those who use the settings	Working (employed) middle-class parents	Mostly unemployed working-class parents	Working-class and multicultural parents
SES score**	18112	8521	1180
SES score educational attainment	28,597	3628	7556
Government-funded places (3–4 years)	Yes	Yes	Yes

* SES was based on parental occupation using the Office for National Statistics, NS-SEC occupationally based classification. Data on parental occupations was gathered from conversations with practitioners, children and in some cases the parents themselves.
** The SES score was calculated using the Office for National Statistics indices of deprivation measure. A score of 1 indicates the most deprived neighbourhood in England and a score of 32,482 indicates the least deprived neighbourhood in England

EYFS defines play as the primary medium (or rather the pedagogical mode) through which learning takes place in EYE. How that learning is to occur and the pedagogy adopted, however, is not specified and hence is likely to vary between settings. The EYFS thus contains an implicit social 'imaginary', one that advocates viewing a child as an independent learner; an individual whose needs must (and can) be met essentially through play, which may be both child and adult initiated. The EYFS (DfE, 2014) 'imaginary child' is therefore, a neoliberal child (already) made 'able and willing to be active and independent' through aspects of effective learning via independent play' (our parenthesis). How practitioners allocate value to and inscribe various identities (e.g., as 'able', 'difficult' or 'other') through their pedagogic practices in respect of this policy imperative has profound consequences for the children in their care, as we see below. In this vision, play is intended to cultivate social, emotional, intellectual and physical learning.

Play in situ

While acknowledging the idealized form of play as represented in the EYFS, academic research on EYL and literature addressing theories of play (Takhvar, 1988; Mellou, 1994; Wood and Bennett, 1999), our analysis, by contrast, documents how play actually materializes in EYL settings. Using concepts drawn from the work of Basil Bernstein (1975–2000), essentially those of 'classification and framing', 'realisation and recognition rules' (albeit implicit in this analysis but elaborated elsewhere, Stirrup 2015), we delve beneath surface appearances to describe *five* forms of play which variously featured in the settings of this research. These play forms were embedded within data collected over 180 hours of observations within each of the three settings.

The data were analysed at several levels; firstly, through analysis of the settings in relation to pedagogies used; secondly, by looking at the broader patterns and interactions which had emerged from the data to provide a landscape of interactions within each setting. The third level explored transactions at a micro level through case studies, detailing interactions between staff/children and children/children, all contextualized within time, space and place to provide insight into the social hierarchies of each setting and the opportunities children had to participate in teach form of play. The categories of play (academic, physical, practitioner led physical, spontaneous and work play; see Figure 11.1) were the inductive constructions of the researcher. The categories of ability, however, ('able', 'difficult' or 'other') were the currency of each setting used by practitioners in their description of certain children during informal conversations with the researcher.

Figure 11.1 is suggestive of five distinct, clearly bounded categories of play; however, this belies both the permeability of the categories and fluidity of children's movements between them. Notwithstanding, beneath surface appearances, over time we clearly determined that 'play' was not homogenous, but rather took many forms, each being more or less strongly bounded from the other and all present within each of the EYL settings. In each setting these 'play' forms were differently distributed in relation to the time (and value) allocated to them, as indicated in Table 11.1 illustrates.

Further elaboration on these play forms is provided below.

Research context: The three settings

The research was set within three socially and culturally different EYL settings in central England: *Busy Buzzy Bees, Little People* and *Little Stars* (see Table 11.1).

Busy Buzzy Bees is a publicly (Government) funded EYL provider located in a large midlands town. It provides 60 childcare places for children aged three months to five years old and in addition to providing care for pre-school children, the nursery is also linked with after-school clubs for primary school children, offering a range of activities including games, craft, pool, imaginary play, toys and ball games. As many of its children are from professional middle-class families it provided stark contrast to the clienteles of '*Little People*' and '*Little Stars*'.

Little People is located within a large housing estate on the outskirts of a large town within the midlands area. It serves the local community, providing childcare for children aged three to five years old, with provision of nursery education funded places for children aged three to four years old. Located within a working class area this setting facilitated exploration of the opportunities available to working class children to access EYL and their experiences of that provision.

Little Stars is a pre-school located within a market town in middle England catering for a number of ethnic groups (mainly Asian first and second generation Indian and Pakistani children) within the community. This setting was selected because of its cultural diversity. Approximately 80 per cent of the children on roll were from ethnic minorities and of that 45e per cent spoke English as an additional language.

In each of these settings practitioners enacted 'official' EYL policy, that is to say the EYFS (DfE, 2012, 2014) curriculum, rather differently, and in the process critically influenced children's sense of themselves, their learner identity and social status within (and out with) the EYL setting.

The social construction of 'ability' and identity in EYL

In each setting, 'ability' was constructed within and in relation to each of the five forms of play (see Table 11.1); it was situationally specific (i.e., valued, recognized and defined differently across settings, albeit against a normative ideal of the imaginary ideal 'able' child; see Bernstein, 2000) implicit in EYFS documentation. Three forms of play – work, academic and physical – seemed critical in the construction of ability in that they received more time and attention within each setting. Work play describes time when children choose to play indoors, often sitting around a table or carpet area playing with construction toys (e.g. Lego/jigsaws) or engaging in role play (e.g., doctors or families) during which time practitioners participate in discussions with them to assess or cultivate their knowledge. Physical play refers to time when children choose to play outdoors with bikes, on climbing frames or engage in games such as 'chases'– practitioners observe and watch the activities for health and safety reasons but do not participate in conversations with children about their knowledge around physical movement or health. In contrast, work play is *practitioner initiated* and occurs either at tables or in a specific room. It is time for children to develop their knowledge in relation to reading/writing, etc. and gives practitioners the opportunity to assess children's knowledge in a more 'formal' context. Activities observed throughout work play included – counting out food to feed the farm animals (plastic versions) and exploring if certain objects would float or sink. What, then, was required to be considered able in such contexts?

The good

The 'good' child across all three settings was characterized as having good listening skills, demonstrating an interest primarily in 'academic' play and displaying appropriate behaviour in all other play forms. To achieve the status of 'good', children not only had to recognize these characteristics but also manifest them appropriately through their bodies, in how they moved, communicated and, in some instances, dressed (e.g., actively choosing and wearing appropriate clothing for playing outdoors or at the art table). Children able to recognize and effectively enact 'appropriate play' gained more practitioner time and attention both within *Busy Buzzy Bees* and (to lesser extent)

Little People. At *Busy Buzzy Bees* the majority of children were defined as 'able' children, however, even within this setting, one or two children, such as James, stood out. James was described as particularly 'bright' because he listened, followed instructions and worked well with the other children. Despite being smaller in stature than most of the boys, he was outwardly confident and inquisitive and always first to put up his hand either to answer or ask questions of practitioners. He even questioned the 'silliness' of storybooks (e.g. 'Why does the duck have wellies on inside? They are for outdoors!'). James had attended nursery full time since he was a baby (at not inconsiderable cost to his parents). In the perspective of practitioners his parents had invested heavily in his education and enrichment inside and outside EYL. Unsurprisingly he now conformed to the setting's concept of being 'school ready' and as such was often asked first if he would like to take part in a task, and at times was given more 'difficult' tasks to perform. In effect, James was the embodiment of the ideal EYFS 'imaginary' child.

Rhianna was regarded by all *Little People* practitioners as a 'lovely chatty child' very 'able' and 'mature' compared to most of the other children (John – practitioner). Indeed, she was one of the very few so defined in this setting, largely because she was the eldest in the class (already four) – her parents deciding she should attend nursery for an extra year to ensure she is 'school ready'. Rhianna, however, was not afforded the same parental investment that James at *Busy Buzzy Bees* enjoys. James regularly discussed with staff and children alike how many activities he does at the weekend and after nursery. For example, when asked by Helen (practitioner) if he had a good weekend, James responded: 'I went to play world with mummy and saw some trains and went walking in the forest. Today I go Little Ninjas and then swimming with daddy.'

In contrast, Rhianna, when asked if she took part in any activities outside nursery, commented: 'I'm not allowed to go to dance; mummy doesn't let me.' Rhianna often assisted practitioners with tasks such as tidying up, telling the other children when it is 'tidy up time' and is often rewarded for her 'good behaviour' more than other children, by being allowed to select songs to sing or numbers to count up to during 'gathering'.[3] While most of the children participate in these 'helping' tasks, Rhianna did them more frequently and consequently received greater amounts of practitioner time and attention. Claire (practitioner) described her 'like another little member of staff isn't she', while John (practitioner) saw her as 'in control, other children listen to her'.

The difficult

Difficult children were much more commonly found in *Little People* and *Little Stars*, rarely in *Busy Buzzy Bees* and those such as Jordan (at *Little Stars*) and Patryk (at *Little People*) were defined as such because they either could not or would not display desired behaviours (e.g., sitting still, talking quietly). This was perhaps in part due to cultural and class differences between the home and EYL learning environments. Their inability/unwillingness to recognize the appropriate regulative rules for behaviour and interaction *in situ* often led to negative interactions with practitioners and peers. Patryk, a Polish child, struggled to speak English and consequently found it difficult to communicate with both staff and children, often speaking in Polish to them but without getting a response. Small in height but athletic in build, Patryk engaged in more rough and tumble play than the other boys, demonstrating his strength by lifting 'heavy' blocks (sometimes two at a time) while others carried one between two during 'physical play'. He was thus seen by staff as a 'problem child', not (they stressed) because he is Polish but rather because his listening skills are considered poor and they believe he *wilfully* pretends not to understand when being reprimanded, often finding it funny to have staff chase after him. Claire (practitioner) described Patryk as 'naughty, he knows what he is doing, and finds it funny and he's aggressive with the other children'. This opinion was shared by other practitioners. John described him as 'one to watch out for' when playing with others on the soft play area. Patryk, then, was not only considered difficult but 'deviant' in the EYL setting by both practitioners and his peers alike.

Jordan was taller and 'bigger' than the rest of her peers at *Little Stars*. Often the first child to be noticed within the setting, she was very loud with a distinctive scream, overpowering and overwhelming some of the smaller, less vocal girls. She was viewed by staff as a 'difficult' child whose behaviour was 'very poor', often aggressive and rude to other children. She was one of three girls viewed in this light but considered 'the worst of them' by practitioners. She was frequently observed playing 'inappropriately', ignoring practitioners, scaring other children and disrupting singing time (work play), behaviour practitioners believe to be accepted as 'normal' at her home, as Mrs Jones (practitioner) commented:

> She just doesn't listen, not even to mum when it's home time. Mum doesn't seem bothered by it; she just waits until Jordan is ready to leave. Not very helpful when we're trying to tell her off for this behaviour at nursery!

In both these contexts, then, practitioners believed that children of this 'type' (i.e., Jordan and Patryk were not afforded the kind of parental investment that, for example, James at *Busy Buzzy Bees* received from his parents). Jordan and Patryk, like others, spent relatively little time in these settings (up to the maximum free 15 hours) compared to children at *Busy Buzzy Bees*. Furthermore, in the view of practitioners such pupils have little opportunity to participate in enrichment activities outside of nursery and they believed that the rules of the home are not those of the EYL setting. For example, conversations with practitioners revealed that the only time he gets to play outside regularly is at nursery:

> Patryk can be very good when he's playing outside and exploring things, building things. But he is often too rough with other children. He doesn't

have the same opportunities to socialise and explore outside of nursery as some of our children do.

(Jane, practitioner)

Similarly, practitioners at *Little Stars* suggested that:

Physical activity and playing outside aren't things she (Jordan) does at home. Many of our children don't have the financial resources at home to go to sessions and many don't have gardens to play in either.

(Mrs Jones, practitioner)

Parental investment (time, money and other resources) in children's learning opportunities (within and outside the home) manifestly influences how practitioners 'read' children's play behaviour and the identity they subsequently impute them. Bluntly, James and Rhianna are perceived to arrive at their EYL settings with far more 'appropriate' capital/ parental investment (albeit James the most) and hence an 'ability' to engage in appropriate play, than Patryk and Jordan. They have already acquired and embodied those skills (rules of listening, playing with others, demonstrating learning) which practitioners (guided by EYFS imaginaries) associate with a 'good' learner identity.

The odd

These children were found across all three settings, but not in equal numbers. At *Busy Buzzy Bees* Adam was considered 'a complex' child who occasionally engaged with staff and other children, but for the most part remained on the outskirts of his peer group, often playing by himself (academic play) or with one or two other children of similar social status as himself within the group. Physically, he was small in comparison to the other children, immature in relation to sharing toys and sitting still, and unlike most of the others, enjoys playing with bags, especially carrying bags around with him and playing 'mummies and baby', which in the practitioners' view, highlights what they consider to be his 'alternative' personality. He was one of the very few (three) children viewed as 'odd' by practitioners in this setting. To some extent, Adam blended into the background, occupying a low social position both amongst his peers and in the perspective of the practitioners largely because he tended to wander aimlessly from play activity to play activity and often his only contact with practitioners was when he was, in their terms, 'poorly behaved'.

Similarly, at *Little People* Liam was considered a well-behaved child who listened to practitioners but who found it difficult to form relationships with other children, especially the boys in any of the forms of play. On several occasions, he was observed on the periphery of the boys' games, always looking on but never being accepted into the game. He was physically slight and looked 'delicate', often crying if someone bumped into him as they moved around the setting. Consequently, while neither dominant nor difficult, staff deemed him 'odd', finding it hard to talk to him especially when he was upset because often there was no apparent reason for it. Liam became increasingly anonymous within the setting. His lack of confidence meant that unlike other children he was unable to assert himself within activities and, due to the number of children and the 'demanding' nature of some, he never really registered on the practitioner's radar. Liam's physical body has presence but little authority; it is out of kilter with the contextual rules and meaning systems of the setting which require him to communicate with other bodies and demonstrate a preparedness to 'play appropriately' and fit in. Failing to meet both 'formal' (EYFS and practitioner) and 'informal' (peer) expectations of propriety Liam suffers the associated alienation. For example, while playing 'honey bears', Rhianna tells Liam he is not 'on' because he is not sitting still. Liam begins to cry:

> Sarah (practitioner): Liam, it's Rhianna's game, you must listen to her.
> [Liam continues to cry.]
> Jane (practitioner): He just cries when he doesn't get what he wants; he is not able to share and doesn't like playing with others. Rhianna, just play on and ignore him … Liam, will you come and sit next to me?'
> [Liam ignores Jane and continues to cry.]

The 'ability' to play and playing to succeed

On the surface, all three settings looked very similar organizationally (i.e., in terms of pacing, resource allocation, the range of play activities on offer, and structure of the day). However, such surface appearances belied significant but subtle differences in approaches to knowledge construction and pedagogical transaction and, consequently, the kind of learner a child was expected to become. At *Busy Buzzy Bees*, a largely middle-class setting, 'academic play' was very highly valued, reflected in the amount of time dedicated to it each day (see Table 11.2). Although on the surface it was a context of fluid 'free play' and independent learning, practitioners predetermined activities (and play forms) for the children to 'choose' from – encouraging certain activities rather than others. In this context there was a clear hierarchy of knowledge to be derived from the different forms of play, at the top of which lay 'academic play'. What's more, it was clear that children in this setting possessed the pre-dispositional resources (symbolic and physical) to readily engage in this form of play to further develop and reproduce their social and physical capital; such resources reflecting parental investments in enrichment activities both inside and outside the home. Consequently, few children in this setting were viewed as either 'difficult' or deviant as they either met or approximated the EYFS play ideal.

In contrast, at *Little People* and *Little Stars*, high value was placed on physical play, with children spending most of their time in this form of activity with little input (guidance and/or encouragement) from practitioners. Whereas children *at Little People* and *Little Stars* tended to have 'free' choice over their activities and could choose only those they enjoyed, at *Busy Buzzy Bees* children were encouraged (and expected through subtle guidance) to play with different 'academic' toys since practitioners chose what equipment children could choose from each day. Consequently, quite different and distinct identities dominated these settings albeit featuring some fluidity. Some children routinely moved from 'good' to 'difficult' identity, depending on the requirements of a task and their engagement with it. For example, Adam (at *Busy Buzzy Bees*) invariably floated between being 'odd' (when in academic play) and 'good' because music/dancing was of interest to him and he was good at it. However, the majority of children in this setting were seen as both 'good' and 'able' for most of the time because they were able to consistently display through play valued knowledge and behaviour appropriate to the expectations of both the EYFS and practitioners. They were the ideal 'imaginary child'. In the perspectives of practitioners, family socialization had already equipped them to recognise and value the skills of listening, engaging in quiet play, playing with others and displaying their knowledge overtly and correctly. Across all three settings these learner identities (good, difficult and odd) brought from the home to the EYL setting, informed the pedagogic practices of the practitioners and influenced the type of curriculum valued within each setting.

Conclusion

So, what of policy ideals, social mobility and erosion of social and educational inequalities through the practices of EYL? Children at *Busy Buzzy Bees* were predominately identified as 'good' by practitioners, i.e., they approximated the official EYFS 'imaginary child' because parents were deemed to have invested in their children's academic and work play through enrichment activities. They had already acquired what Bernstein (1975) would describe as the recognition and realisation rules[4] of the setting and were by in large able to enact them. Hence there was no dislocation between home and school (EYL) setting. *Little People* and *Little Stars* catered for families of very similar working-class background and very few of their children, in their behaviour, approximated the EYFS ideal. At *Little Stars,* which catered for employed and unemployed working-class families, the majority of children were deemed to arrive unable (or unwilling) to recognize and display appropriate play behaviours (e.g., sitting still, listening, and 'kind hands') for learning. Class and cultural difference and dissonance between home (predominately Eastern European or Bengali) and white British middle-class rules and codes of EYFS setting may well partially account for this disjuncture. At *Little People* (which also catered for employed and unemployed working-class families) 'good' children (albeit very few in number) were those able to recognize and realize *in situ* discipline rules and demonstrate some interest in 'academic' play.

Identities in all three contexts were thus situationally specific and if adjudged by *Busy Buzzy Bees* standards (also the ideal imaginary child of EYL policy) the 'able' child at *Little People* was more 'able' than that at *Little Stars*, but never quite as 'able' as those at *Busy Buzzy Bees*.

At the intersection of family and EYL cultures and pedagogies, parents and practitioners together play their part not only in the construction and consolidation of learner identities (Dufur et al, 2012) but also the reproduction of social inequalities. The physical and cultural capital derived from the combination of home/family and EYL provisions, clearly help sections of the UK population (i.e., middle-class families at *Busy Buzzy Bees*) (enabled and endorsed by the implicit imaginaries of Government EYL policy) to maintain their position in the education market and wider social and cultural hierarchies. Against this background, further investment in EYL (especially of a kind that better serves the interests of working-class and diverse cultures) may be a very necessary and worthy ideal, but insufficient to alter (let alone erode) social class inequities or enhance social mobility.

Note

1 In this chapter, the term EYL will be used to refer to learning which occurs in formal nursery/preschool settings, while ECE will refer to a more comprehensive learning in the early years incorporating that which occurs within and outside EYL settings.
2 Within England and Wales, the government offers 15 hours per week free childcare to children aged up to three years old; since 2013, all two-year-olds from 'disadvantaged backgrounds' were to receive 15 hours free education and this was to be extended to other families by September 2014 (DfE, 2014).
3 Gathering at *Little People* is similar to registration at *Busy Buzzy Bees*, but happened in the morning and just before the children left for the end of the day.
4 Recognition rules create the means to distinguish between contexts and therefore recognize what constitutes knowledge, while realization rules regulate the creation and production of specialized relations within texts (in this case, appropriate behaviours within different forms of play).

References

Ball, S. and Vincent, C. (2007) Education, class fractions and the local rules of spatial relations, *Urban Studies*, 44(7), 1175–1189.

Ball, S., Vincent, C., Kemp, S. and Pietikainen, S. (2004) Middle class fractions, childcare and the 'relational' and 'normative' aspects of class practices, *The Sociological Review*, 52(4), 478–502.

Bernstein, B. (1975) *Class, codes and control vol. iii: Towards a theory of educational transmissions*. London: Routledge and Kegan Paul.

Bernstein, B. (2000) *Pedagogy, symbolic control and identity: Theory, research and critique* (Revised Ed.). London: Rowman and Littlefield.

Bertram, T. and Pascal, C. (2002) *Early years education: An international perspective*. Birmingham, UK: Centre for Research in Early Childhood.

Bertram, T. and Pascal, C. (2014) *Early years literature review.* Birmingham, UK: Centre for Research in Early Childhood.

Birchwood, D., Roberts, K. and Pollock, G. (2008) Explaining differences in sport participation rates among young adults: Evidence from South Caucasus, *European Physical Education Review*, 14(3), 283–298.

Broadhead, P. and Burt, A. (2012) *Understanding young children's learning through play: Building playful pedagogies.* Oxon: Routledge.

Cochran, M. (2011) International Perspectives on Early Childhood Education, *Educational Policy*, 25(1): 65–91.

Crozier, G. (1997) Empowering the Powerful: A discussion of the interrelation of Government policies and consumerism with social class factors and the impact of this upon parent interventions in their children's schooling, *British Journal of Sociology of Education*, 18(2): 187–200.

Crozier, G. (1998) Parents and Schools: Partnership or Surveillance?, *Journal of Education Policy*, 13(1): 125–136.

Crozier, G. (1999) Is it a case of 'We know when we're not wanted?' The parents' perspective on Parent-Teacher roles and relationships. *Educational Research*, 41(3): 315–328.

DfE (2012) *Early Years Foundation Stage/Curriculum*, http://webarchive.nationala rchives.gov.uk/20130401151715/https://www.education.gov.uk/publications/standa rd/publicationDetail/Page1/DCSF-00261-2008, accessed August 2014.

DfE (2014) *Early Years Foundation Stage/Curriculum*, https://www.gov.uk/governm ent/uploads/system/uploads/attachment_data/file/335504/EYFS_framework_from_ 1_September_2014__with_clarification_note.pdf, accessed October 2014.

Dufur, M., Parcel, T. and Troutman, K. (2012) Does capital at home matter more than capital at school? Social capital effects on academic achievement, *Research in Social Stratification and Mobility*, 31, 1–21.

Evans, J. (2014) Equity and inclusion in physical education PLC, *European Physical Education Review*, 20(3), 319–334.

Evans, J. and Davies, B. (2011) New directions, new questions? Social theory, education and embodiment, *Sport, Education and Society*, 16(3): 263–278.

Green, K. (2010) *Key themes in youth sport.* London: Routledge.

Lareau, A. (1987) Social class differences in family-school relationships: the importance of cultural capital, *Sociology of Education*, 60(2), 73–85.

Lareau, A. (2000) Social class and the daily lives of children: a study from the United States. *Childhood*, 7(2), 155–171.

Lareau, A. (2003) *Unequal childhoods: class, race and family life.* Berkeley: University of California Press.

Marsden, E. and Weston, C. (2007) Locating quality physical education in early years pedagogy, *Sport, Education and Society*, 12(4), 383–398.

Melhuish, E., Lloyd, E., Martin, S. and Mooney, A. (1990) Type of childcare at 18 months: Relations with cognitive and language development, *Journal of Child Psychology and Psychiatry*, 31(6), 861–870.

Mellou, E. (1994) Play Theories: A contemporary review, *Early Child Development and Care*, 102(1), 91–100.

Mol, M. J. (2007) *Outsourcing: design, process and performance.* Cambridge: Cambridge University Press.

Nairn, K., Higgins, J. and Sligo, J. (2012) *Children of Rogernomics. A neoliberal generation leaves school.* Otago: Otago University Press.

Sammons, P., Elliot, K.Sylva, K., Melhuish, E., Siraj-Blatchford, I. and Taggart, B. (2004) The impact of pre-school on young children's cognitive attainments at entry to reception, *British Educational Research Journal*, 30(5), 691–712.

Saul, J. (2005) *The collapse of globalism and the reinvention of the world*. Camberwell: Viking.

Siraj-Blatchford, I. (2004) Educational disadvantage in the early years: how do we overcome it? Some lessons from research, *European Early Childhood Education Research Journal*, 12(2), 5–20.

Stirrup, J. (2015) *Early Years Learning (EYL) and embodiments: a Bernsteinian analysis*. PhD thesis. Loughborough University.

Swadener, B. B., Kabiru, M. and Njenga, A. (2000) *Does the village still raise the child? A collaborative study in changing child-rearing and early education in Kenya*. New York: State University of New York Press.

Takhvar, M. (1988) Play and theories of play: A review of the literature, *Early Child Development and Care*, 39(1), 221–244.

Vincent, C. and Ball, S. (2006) *Childcare, choice and class practices*. London: Routledge.

Vincent, C. and Ball, S. (2007) 'Making up' the middle-class child: Families, activities and class dispositions, *Sociology*, 41(6), 1061–1077.

Vincent, C. (2006) *Childcare choice and class practices: middle class parents and their children*. London: Routledge.

Wheeler, S. (2012) The significance of family culture for sports participation, *International Review for the Sociology of Sport*, 47(2), 235–252.

Wheeler, S. and Green, K. (2012) Parenting in relation to children's sports participation: generational changes and potential implications, *Leisure Studies*, 33(3), 267–284.

Wood, E. and Bennett, N. (1999) Changing theories, changing practice: exploring early childhood teachers' professional learning, *Teaching and Teacher Education*, 16 (5–6), 635–647.

12 Who cares? Physical activity, families and children in care

Thomas Quarmby

Introduction

The purpose of this chapter is to explore an often under-represented group, children in care, when discussing critical issues in youth health and physical activity. As such, this chapter first offers a brief conceptualization of who children in care are, before problematizing the notion of 'family' for this particular group of individuals. It will then explore the benefits of physical activity, specifically for children in care, with regard to their broader health and well-being. The chapter concludes with a discussion of how children in care might 'make sense' of physical activity within their daily social and cultural environment, and the related constraints and enablers that impact on engagement with physical activity.

Children in care (or looked after children as they are also known) constitute those individuals who have been removed from their 'families' and become the responsibility of the state, often being placed in alternative, out of home care (NSPCC, 2015). While this can happen voluntarily by parents struggling to cope, it is often through an intervention by children's services because a child is thought to be at risk of significant harm. Reports from England, the US and Australia all suggest that children primarily move into care due to neglect or abuse, with a large proportion suffering physical, sexual or emotional abuse prior to their entry to care (Australian Institute of Health and Welfare [AIHW], 2014; Welfare Information Gateway [CWIG], 2013; Department for Education [DfE], 2014). However, parental illness, marital violence and breakdown, and parental imprisonment are also common reasons for children being taken into care (DfE, 2014).

Unfortunately, the figures for this group of young people continue to increase. In March 2014 there were approximately 68,840 children in care in England, an increase of 7 per cent from March 2010 (DfE, 2014); while in the US, there were an estimated 399,546 children in care as of September 2012 (CWIG, 2013). The most recent statistics from the Australian Institute of Health and Welfare (AIHW, 2014) also indicate that, as of June 2013, there were 40,549 Australian children living in out-of-home care. Though these figures are relatively small compared with overall population statistics, the number of children in care continues to increase and, clearly, attention needs to be paid to this largely 'hidden' group of young people, particularly with regard issues of health and physical activity.

Family and children in care

As is evident throughout this book, the role of the family in shaping young people's health and physical activity dispositions is crucial; enabling children to develop knowledge, beliefs and attitudes about physical activity and other health behaviours. However, while the traditional two parent family may be capable, ready and willing to invest in the physical activity of their offspring, many alternative family formations, including those young people living in care, may not be supported in the same way. Moreover, their conceptions of family may be radically different from those of their peers.

Undoubtedly, family remains a powerful symbol in our cultural imaginations and a central feature in today's neoliberal society. Yet, the family environment for children in care is often considerably different from that of their peers. Family, for many children in care, challenges what could be considered, traditional family norms. For instance, children in care tend to live in a variety of placement settings including, but not limited to, foster and residential care. In fact, foster care has been, and remains, the most common form of state provision for children in care globally. In England last year, 75 per cent of those in care lived in a foster placement, in comparison to around 9 per cent who were cared for in residential children's homes (DfE, 2014). Foster care involves a child or children being cared for by a person or people who are not members of their own birth family and it is thought that this type of placement offers a family environment that is better able and more suited to meet the needs of children. In contrast residential care involves children living in a stable and safe environment, with 24-hour support from skilled staff. Due to an increasing emphasis on foster care, residential care is increasingly being used for older children with more serious difficulties or who may have difficulty settling in foster care (Berridge et al, 2012).

However, the rate of disruption for both of these placements is high, with many moving among or between settings while in care (Lipscombe et al, 2003). Placement instability is therefore a common feature of the lives of children in care and may contribute to their over-representation in a number of vulnerable groups, including those who are not in education, employment or training, teenage parents, young offenders and drug users (Broad and Monaghan, 2003). This instability may also have ongoing repercussion for how they view family, what constitutes family for children in care and how physical activity dispositions are developed in different and changing family environments.

While traditionally, family has constituted a set of concrete ties and feelings, Gubrium and Holstein (1990) have argued that family may also be understood as a way of thinking and talking. Viewing family in relation to the conditions and understandings of everyday life and then listening to the way children in care think, feel and talk about people may provide insights into who they deem as family and how family subsequently shapes their actions. There is a growing recognition in the sociological field of family studies that families can be defined more by 'doing' family things than by 'being' family. The 'doing' of family refers to understanding the meaning of family practices. That is, families may be defined by sets of activities that have a particular meaning for those associated with them (Finch, 2007). In this sense, individuals are active in making and negotiating family (Williams, 2004). This perspective of 'doing' family places an emphasis on 'practices, identities and relationships' (Finch, 2007, p69) and, thus, understanding family for children in care may centre on how individuals talk and act with each other and the assumptions that are made about those relationships (Finch, 2007).

The notion of conceptualising family with regard to the relationships that exist may be particularly pertinent for children in care since a recent study found that it is not simply family per se that helps children, but rather the quality of relationships with carers (Holland and Crowley, 2013). Hence, it may be the quality of these relationships that matter most to children in care, not the family form in determining their outcomes across a range of different domains (with health and physical activity among them). In fact, children can overcome stigma and thrive in a range of circumstances if they have the opportunity to form quality relationships (Holland and Crowley, 2013). Ironically, being placed in care and then subsequently transferred from care setting to care setting may lead to further instability of the relationships they experience (Scott, 2011). If developing quality, key relationships is essential for children in care to help foster positive behaviours, aspirations and a sense of belonging, then staying in a stable placement for a prolonged period of time is paramount. Yet, for some this simply isn't the case.

It is also noteworthy that most young people enter care during their early to pre-teenage years when they are beginning to form an understanding of themselves and their relationship with physical activity. This is also a period when younger children are dependent on family members for shaping their views and perspectives, and in supporting their involvement in wider physical culture. At this point, foster carers and staff in residential homes will have to deal with a range of unresolved issues from the child's past (Lipscombe et al, 2003), while also trying to manage the young person's relationship with their own family and the inevitable tensions and competing beliefs and values this may entail.

Benefits of physical activity for children in care

The decision to take a child into care may have far reaching consequences for the child and their family. Across different care and welfare systems in different nation states, collective studies from England, the US and Canada reveal that there are many shared experiences for this population (Holland and Crowley, 2013). Regardless of their care placement (foster care or residential home) and the fact that their experiences are incredibly complex, most outcomes for children in care highlight their disadvantage across a range of different domains (e.g., health and well-being, education, etc.), though this is not necessarily a product of the care system itself. That said, a few studies would suggest that engagement in physical activity may play a role here in helping to alleviate some of the earlier disadvantage experienced by children in care.

For instance, children in care are four times more likely to have a mental health problem compared to their peers (Meltzer et al, 2003) and therefore, the link between activity and mental health is especially relevant for these young people. In fact, there is 'a higher prevalence of both psychosocial adversity and psychiatric disorder' for children in care 'than the most socio-economically disadvantaged children living in private households' (Ford et al, 2007, p323). As well as physical activity having a potential to enhance physical and psychological well-being (Ford et al, 2007), Gilligan (1999, 2000) also adds that regular engagement enables children in care to develop resilience; a 'capacity to do well despite adverse experience' (Gilligan, 2000, p37). Positive engagement with physical activity for a group of particularly underserved youth is therefore thought to foster 'normal' development, strengthen assertiveness, build self-esteem and confidence in one's abilities, and help develop skills required in later life (Gilligan, 1999).

As alluded to above, instability in care placement has been identified as having a considerable impact upon young people's emotional development, attainment of positive social relationships and personal identity establishment (Scott, 2011). There is a risk that those facing adversity may have a restricted range of socially valued roles, and may instead develop a stigmatised and, ultimately, all-embracing 'master' identity such as 'child in care' (Gilligan, 2008). The social roles played by a person underpin their identity and sense of self and so, diversifying this repertoire of social roles may help to alter one's identity (Gilligan, 2008). Hence, Gilligan (2000, 2008) argues that regular participation in physical activity may allow children in care to generate a sense of identity because structured physical activities such as sport and other recreational settings offer opportunities to acquire socially valued roles that may also confer many health and social benefits.

Finally, it is thought that engagement in physical activity, particularly structured extracurricular activities that have regularly scheduled practices, may provide a sense of structure to children's lives that is otherwise missing due to substantial, continual changes in care placements (Farineau and McWey, 2011). Prolonged participation in physical activities or extracurricular clubs was previously found to be an important source of stability and consistency for those living in or leaving care (Hollingworth, 2012). Moreover, Fong et al (2006) proposed that if placement stability is not possible for certain children in care, then continuity of activities would allow that young person to maintain regular, familiar and/or normalizing activities, which might minimize the disruptive effect of placement in care. As well as serving as protection against the effects of disruption, the opportunity for children in care to continue in their favoured activities may help to establish more permanent physical activity dispositions.

Making sense of physical activity

Considering the proclaimed benefits of physical activity for children in care it is surprising that little empirical work has explored how children in care view physical activity or whether or not they can readily access it. What the narrow range of literature does however suggest is that physical activity may not form a central role in the lives of children in care. For instance, a recent case study by Quarmby (2014) explored the role of sport and physical activity in the lives of four male, looked after children. After spending nine months visiting a residential children's home in the North of England, and employing a range of participatory research methods to engage participants, the findings revealed that physical activity did not feature prominently in their lives. Instead, when they did engage in activity they used it as a means to an end; to spend time with friends and develop stocks of social capital, not for fun, enjoyment or health and fitness reasons (Quarmby, 2014).

This is, perhaps, not surprising since studies from England and Norway have suggested that engagement in physical activities can open new social relationships beyond the care system (Gilligan, 1999; Säfvenbom and Samdahl, 2000). Participation in social physical activities offers children in care an opportunity to widen their social network and mix with those who are not in care (Hollingworth, 2012). This is what Putnam (2000) refers to as 'bridging'. Unlike 'bonding', a process of relationship building through activities with individuals from similar backgrounds, 'bridging' concerns a process by which social capital is gained by engaging in activities with people from different social backgrounds (Putnam, 2000). Bridging is therefore key to societal integration and central to children in care who may "experience a sense of being set apart from their community" (Murray, 2013, p1349).

In the case study outlined above, despite limited engagement in physical activity, the four children in care saw the value of engaging in activity in an effort to integrate with other young people (Quarmby, 2014). While this offers an initial insight and first few tentative steps in the field, little is still known about how children in care come to make sense of physical activity, nor how they negotiate activity within their immediate environment. Negotiating activity for some children in care may be particularly problematic since they are constrained by a variety of institutional constraints that may shape access. For instance, studies in England and America both indicate that residential home policies may include rules that affect access to physical activity opportunities (e.g., the provision of transportation to activities and scheduled activity time) (Gay et al, 2011; Quarmby, 2014). Moreover, a lack of time has been reported as a key factor restricting leisure activities (Hollingworth, 2012) that may also result from structural and organisational policies. For instance, having to eat evening meals at set times and needing to negotiate time for activities with carers (Gay et al, 2011; Quarmby, 2014).

It is perhaps here where children in care's views and values concerning physical activity are impacted most by the type of family formation they live in. While children in most families have to negotiate access to activity in some form (e.g., through discussions with parents), rarely do children in two parent, lone parent or step-families have to try and arrange activities around policies that shape day to day living as they do in children's homes. This could have a significant impact upon how they view physical activity. Likewise, for children living in foster care, while policies may not impact in the same way, their pre-established beliefs, values and dispositions about physical activity may differ considerably to those of their foster carer, who may also be trying to manage the competing demands of their own biological child(ren) and their foster child(ren).

Constraints and enablers for children in care

Undoubtedly, for children in care their family environment may present numerous challenges that may make accessing physical activity problematic. Evidence from an American study that employed a seven-day physical activity recall with 13,246 young people in grades 6 to 12 would appear to confirm this. It found that both boys and girls in care (from foster care and residential homes combined) were considerably less active and less likely to achieve recommended levels of activity that those young people in other family formations including two parent, step parent and lone parent families (Ornelas et al, 2007). However, since many children in care come from disadvantaged backgrounds, it is likely that they are already comparatively excluded from some physical activities and broader physical culture prior to their entry to care.

Once in care however there are a range of additional barriers that may prevent access to physical activity. In a UK study, Hollingworth (2012) highlighted a number of restrictions that prevented participation in physical activities for those aged between 18 and 24, living in or leaving care. For most, a lack of financial support was cited as a major barrier to their involvement in leisure and social activities (Hollingworth, 2012), with cost appearing to be a primary reason for many children and young people not participating in 'positive' activities (Department for Education and Skills, 2007). As mentioned before, a number of young people in the study reported that entering care and subsequent placement moves were barriers to social and leisure activities (including physical activities) since placements were often a considerable distance from schools. This meant participation in after-school clubs and activities was restricted by the availability of public transport or taxis (Hollingworth, 2012).

This raises another concern with regard the fact that for many disadvantaged young people, school activities may be a primary source of their engagement and experience of physical culture. Yet, for the majority of children in care, school attendance is problematic because many experience changes in placements and consequently schools, and are also more likely to be permanently excluded (Harker, 2011; Murray, 2013). Thus, children in care often miss out on school-based physical activities and may be more dependent on out-of-school activities than other children.

Outside of school, exploring physical activity for children living in residential care in America, Gay and colleagues (2011) suggested that opportunities to be active included access to on and off-site physical activity programmes, equipment and facilities. It was thought that the promotion of such opportunities through formal (e.g. promotional material) and informal (e.g., adult encouragement and involvement) messages within the immediate social environment of the care home may influence activity choices (Gay et al, 2011). They also suggest that the opportunities associated with each residential care home were subsequently influenced by the geographic location in which it resides (e.g., in rural or urban locations) (Gay et al, 2011). For instance, children living in care homes in rural locations were typically more active than their counterparts in urban homes (Gay et al, 2011), possibly due to a greater availability of outdoor space.

In America, it has been argued that residential children's homes with a recreation director offered significant opportunities to engage in physical activity (Gay et al, 2011). This is particularly important since a recreation director may act as a role model and provide the encouragement that may otherwise be missing on a daily basis for those living in residential homes. Within these studies however, little is known about the individual characteristics of the young people living in care (i.e., special education needs), or the characteristics of the homes themselves (i.e., number of children in care) and whether this impacted on access, opportunity and choice of physical activity. While this raises questions of who might act as roles models for those children in residential care, it also raises questions about whether foster cares value physical activity in the same way.

In addition to those barriers experienced by the most vulnerable families in society (including finance and transport opportunities), children in care also face a myriad of problems unique to their social circumstance when trying to accessing physical activity (Armour et al, 2011). As mentioned above, the negative impact of placement instability (Hollingworth, 2012) is thought to reduce children in care's ability to regularly engage in such activities while, potentially, a lack of interest in physical activity or support by some carers and residential staff may also prove to be a barrier. In England, for instance, Gilligan (1999) found that local authority social workers and other professionals working with children in care tended to discount mainstream activities and the value of the 'ordinary' that already exist within children's social networks. This is may also be apparent in America where it was reported that only around a quarter of children in residential care recalled playing sport with their primary carer (Gay et al, 2011). This suggests that the influence of care givers in promoting physical activity to children in care may be an important consideration when trying to understand the value they place on such activities.

Equally, a poor understanding of the value of physical activity by carers and young people themselves coupled with non- or poor school attendance (Armour et al, 2011) is also likely to restrict engagement in physical activity. However, it should be noted that children in care, living in the UK or abroad, do so in unique settings that vary according to location, social (family) environment, access and policy with regard to physical activity.

Conclusions

Often identified as being disadvantaged and 'othered', children in care clearly face multiple threats to their physical and psychological wellbeing even before entering into the care system. Once there, they frequently experience disruption and are subjects of vulnerability and social marginalisation. As discussed above, there is some evidence to suggest that access to regular physical activity might provide an opportunity to enhance their physical and psychological well-being and develop a variety of life skills to help them navigate the challenges of their daily lives. However, research exploring how children in care make sense of and access physical activity is still in its infancy.

Despite the numerous challenges children in care may face to accessing physical activity, and the fact that there are no quick fixes given the challenges with policy at local and national levels, there may still be a few 'solutions' that those key adult allies in residential care, and foster carers themselves, can do to help facilitate engagement. For foster carers and those key adults who support young people in residential care there is first a need to be aware of young people's physical activity beliefs and values, what they enjoy and what activities they do or used to engage in. In addition, staff in residential homes and foster carers, in particular, could try to engage in activities together with the young people in their care. Engaging in joint physical activity may help generate positive relationship, foster physical activity dispositions and, as discussed earlier, help to re-conceptualize their understanding of family through 'doing' and 'displaying' family activities. In foster care, specifically, young people need to establish a secure base in the foster family at the same time as they are striving to establish their autonomy (Lipscombe et al, 2003). During this time they may be also trying to form their own identify whilst separated from their birth families (Lipscombe et al, 2003) and therefore engagement in joint physical activity may serve several purposes for young people in care.

In order to better understand physical activity in the lives of children in care there is a need to understand who the key social actors are who play a significant role for them. It would then be possible to explore who may influence their engagement and enjoyment of physical activity. This approach may also help to understand whether children in care receive competing messages about physical activity from their biological family, who they may still see, and those who care for them on a daily basis.

Finally, there is a need for our attention to be directed to issues of social justice and democratic ideals when conducting research with children in care. In conditions of social justice, young people, regardless of background and upbringing, are not marginalized or 'othered' and can choose to access physical activity as readily as their peers. Hence, there is clearly a need for a focus on social justice issues so that we can ensure that all children in care have the right to access physical activity in ways that are meaningful to them.

References

AIHW (Australian Institute of Health and Welfare) (2014) *Child Protection Australia 2012–2013* (Child Welfare Series No. 58). Canberra: AIHW.

Armour, K., Sandford, R. and Duncombe, R. (2011) Right to be active: looked-after children in physical education and sport. In Armour, K. (ed.) *Sport Pedagogy: An introduction for teaching and coaching*. London: Prentice-Hall, pp214–225.

Berridge, D., Biehal, N. and Henry, L. (2012) *Living in children's residential homes*. London: Department for Education.

Broad, B. and Monaghan, B. (2003) *Talking sense: messages from young people facing social exclusion about their health and well-being*. London: The Children's Society.

CWIG (Child Welfare Information Gateway) (2013) *Foster care statistics 2012*. Washington, DC: U.S. Department of Health and Human Services, Children's Bureau.

DfE (Department for Education) (2014) *Children looked after in England (including adoption and care leavers) year ending 31 March 2014*. London: Department for Education.

DfES (Department for Education and Skills) (2007) *Care Matters: Time for Change*. London: Department for Education and Skills.

Dowda, M., Saunders, R., Hastings, L. et al (2009) Physical activity and sedentary pursuits of children living in residential children's homes, *Journal of Physical Activity and Health*, 6(2), 195–202.

Farineau, H. and McWey, L. (2011) The relationship between extracurricular activities and delinquency of adolescents in foster care, *Children and Youth Services Review*, 33, 963–968.

Finch, J. (2007) Displaying families, *Sociology*, 41(1), 65–81.

Fong, R., Schwab, J. and Armour, M. (2006) Continuity of activities and child well-being for foster care youth, *Children and Youth Services Review*, 28, 1359–1374.

Ford, T., Vostanis, P., Howard, M. et al (2007) Psychiatric disorder among British children looked after by local authorities: Comparison with children living in private households, *British Journal of Psychiatry*, 190, 129–225.

Gay, J., Dowda, M., Saunders, R. et al (2011) Environmental determinants of children's physical activity in residential children's homes, *Journal of Physical Activity and Health*, 8, 636–644.

Gilligan, R. (2008) Promoting resilience in young people in long-term care – the relevance of roles and relationships in the domains of recreation and work, *Journal of Social Work Practice*, 22(1), 37–50.

Gilligan, R. (2000) Adversity, resilience and young people: the protective value of positive school and spare time experiences, *Children and Society*, 14(1), 37–47.

Gilligan, R. (1999) Enhancing the resilience of children and young people in public care by mentoring their talents and interests, *Child and Family Social Work*, 4, 187–196.

Gubrium, J. and Holstein, J. (1990) *What Is Family?* Mountain View, CA: Mayfield Publishing.

Harker, R. (2011) *Children in Care in England: Statistics, Standard Note SN/SG/4470.* London: House of Commons Library.

Holland, S. and Crowley, A. (2013) Looked-after children and their birth families: Using sociology to explore changing relationships, hidden histories and nomadic childhoods, *Child and Family Social Work*, 18(1), 57–66.

Hollingworth, K. (2012) Participation in social, leisure and informal learning activities among care leavers in England: positive outcomes for educational participation, *Child and Family Social Work*, 17, 438–447.

Lipscombe, J.Farmer, E. and Moyers, S. (2003) Parenting and fostered adolescents: skills and strategies, *Child and Family Social Work*, 8, 243–255.

Meltzer, H., Gatward, R., Corbin, T., Goodman, R. and Ford, T. (2003) *The mental health of young people looked after by local authorities in England.* London: The Stationary Office.

Murray, C. (2013) Sport in care: Using freedom of information requests to elicit data about looked after children's involvement in physical activity, *British Journal of Social Work*, 43, 1347–1363.

NSPCC (2015) *Children in care* [Online], NSPCC. Available from http://www.nspcc.org.uk/preventing-abuse/child-protection-system/children-in-care/ [Accessed 20 May 2015].

Ornelas, I., Perreira, K. and Ayala, G. (2007) Parental influence on adolescent physical activity: a longitudinal study, *International Journal of Behavioral Nutrition and Physical Activity*, 4(3), 1–10.

Putnam, R. (2000) *Bowling alone: The collapse and revival of American community.* New York: Simon and Schuster.

Quarmby, T. (2014) Sport and physical activity in the lives of looked-after children: a 'hidden group' in research, policy and practice, *Sport, Education and Society*, 19(7), 944–958.

Säfvenbom, R. and Samdahl, D. (2000) Leisure for youth in residential care: an important context for intervention, *International Journal of Social Welfare*, 9, 120–127.

Scott, J. (2011) The impact of disrupted attachment on the emotional and interpersonal development of looked after children, *Educational and Child Psychology*, 28(3), 31–43.

Williams, F. (2004) *Rethinking Families.* London: Calouste Gulbenkian Foundation.

Part 3

Family Physical Education and youth sport

13 Teachers' perspectives on the school–family–health nexus

Eimear Enright, Rebecca Johnson, Doune Macdonald, Louise McCuaig and Anthony Rossi

Introduction

In her seminal work on teachers' caring, Grumet (1988, p33) claims schooling carries the critical objective of 'providing a passage from domestic and maternal nurturance to public institutions and patriarchal identifications', serving to mediate the 'passage between the specificity of intimate relations and the generalities of the public world' (p14). Schools and their teachers thus straddle the public–private domains of Western societies and have long been exhorted to complement, enhance or act as substitutes for the perceived suspect practices of parental care and training of children and young people. As such, Western schooling was thought to compensate for the problematic capacity of the modern family to achieve its dominant strategic function, the training of apprentice citizens in the arts of modern citizenship (Hunter, 1994; Kay-Shuttleworth, 1974). From this perspective, schools and their teachers have been deployed as 'governmental technologies' (Rose, 1999) to ensure each citizen acquires the necessary principles and practices to become healthy and productive members of a nation's population.

In this chapter we draw on data collected within the context of the Teachers as Health Workers (Macdonald et al, 2013–2015) project conducted in Queensland, a state of Australia. As schools are increasingly positioned as critical in the promotion of children and young people's health and well-being, this research seeks to understand the contemporary nature of health-related work being undertaken by teachers in Australian schools and what facilitates and constrains this work. Two underpinning theoretical frameworks of the study are Bourdieu's concepts of field and practice to locate and understand teacher's work, and Foucault's notion of biopolitics to understand how it is that individuals and populations come to comply with or resist responsible citizenship as it is enacted within schooling. These Australian data suggest that while teachers place a high priority on communicating with parents, this is often done from the perspective that teachers are compensating for what they consider are deficit parenting practices, particularly in relation to the co-production of healthy citizens.

Pushing back the welfare state

Shrinking the welfare state is an ideological objective of the neoliberal project and the contemporary context within which schools conduct health work. Wallace (2007) has described how Australia became a libertarian nation by stealth under governments across the political divide. A consequence of this is that the 'neoliberal imaginary' as described by Ball (2012) has become part of the everyday lived experience of Australians in which the discourses of entitlement and personal responsibility are being debated (see Hockey, 2012, in the case of Australia). In the United Kingdom similar debates have occurred and Liam Fox (2013), a former Tory cabinet minister, argued that the 'Great socialist coup of the last decade' had to be reversed. As Nadesan (2010) drawing on data from the US argues, the market is promoted as being the primary (some might argue only) technology capable of distributing the resources of a society both fairly and efficiently. The consequence of this is, as Nadesan (2010, p14) states, 'Social welfare apparatuses remain viable within neoliberal logics only to the extent that they can deliver cost savings', in this case, cost savings in health. Schools and the education sector, we suggest, are seen as a frontline technology to absorb some of the cost of health promotion and care, with little or no increase in funding, staffing or professional development for teachers.

Governing the family

According to Rose (1999), childhood is the most intensively governed sector of personal existence and his argument has received considerable support from authors across the social disciplines (see for example Meredyth and Tyler, 1993; Bessant, 1991; Hultqvist and Dahlberg, 2001; McLeod and Malone, 2000; Kelly, 2001). According to Hultqvist and Dahlberg (2001, p.4), childhood has been about the 'formation of the self-guiding child and citizen and thus the narrative of childhood thought has been about the child's natural route to self-governance and reason'. The child in Western liberal democratic societies is 'positioned as a special category of person who lacks for a time the complete range of capacities necessary to function fully as a citizen' (Tyler, 1993, p35). As an innocent and natural state, childhood must be preserved, a state of affairs that has led to more rather than less adult surveillance, supervision and control (Bessant, 1991).

From eugenicists to teachers, doctors to judges, psychologists to social workers, all have been mobilized to ensure a safe and preferred transition of the subject from childhood to adult citizen. Nonetheless, critical scholarship suggests that young people's transition from child to adult is a multifaceted experience requiring a multiplicity of strategies and sensitivity to the complexities of youth (Wyn and White, 1997; MacLeod and Malone, 2000). What is evident across the work of these researchers are the critical intersections between health and education discourses within the lives of young people

(Mayall, 1996; Wright and Macdonald, 2010). As Nadesan (2010, p62) summarizes, 20th-century concerns with the vitality and productivity of the population have resulted in:

> ... the institutionalization of social welfare programs aimed at 'helping' poor children 'at risk' particularly through the technologies of health ... and the pedagogical disciplines aimed at mothers at home and children in the schools.

Institutions such as the family and schools have been shaped by authorities to provide social sites through which the state can mobilize strategies of surveillance and normalisation to achieve a continuous regulatory and corrective action on the individuals who comprise the population (Rose, 1999). In his exploration of eighteenth century strategies of familial organisation, Foucault (1984, p281) reveals the state's interest in the family–children complex as comprising the 'first and most important instance for the medicalization of individuals'. Indeed he argues, that 'a private ethic of good health' (p281) was to become the reciprocal duty of parents and children, a strategy mobilized through the assignation of the family as comprising 'a linking role between general objectives regarding the good health of the social body and individuals' (p281). In early modernity, the family institution was transformed into a pre-eminent bio-pedagogical site. However, modern authorities were to consistently problematize the members of this institution as being 'either incapable or unwilling to adopt the required moral, ethical, economic and social responsibilities and obligations' (Kelly, 2001, p30) underpinning this role.

Changes and constraints occurring within the planning and production of contemporary selfhood have produced new demands on education, care and therapy (Beck, 1992). According to Rose (1999) and Beck (1992), expertise functions as a critical relay between the desired objectives of national strength and the shaping of citizens' life biographies. As individual teachers and the school community enact their caring roles, they judge and shape students' health related practices and attitudes according to criteria of normal health and wellbeing (McCuaig and Tinning, 2010). Other professions such as community child health nurses providing governance from community health services have adopted similar practices (e.g., Larsen, 1999). Where students and their families fail to meet anticipated standards, teachers are motivated to conduct intervention strategies or programs that can assist their students in their projects of healthy living (Vander Schee, 2009). While these intervention strategies are still usually targeted at the level of the individual student, it is increasingly acknowledged that ensuring the health and wellbeing of the child requires the support and strengthening of families (Lawson, 1998, 2005; Stuart and Jose, 2014).

This opens an important debate for schools as to the nature of their relationships with parents. Reflecting neoliberal tendencies to introduce privatisation and competition into schooling sectors (e.g. 'charter school' movements in the US, UK and Australia), parental voice and choice in education is welcomed. In Norway, research suggests that parents want their rights to engage with schooling extended (Tveit, 2009) while in Greece, recent research indicates that Principals would welcome a more extensive engagement with parents in schooling (Lazaridou and Kassida, 2015). The intersection of health education and more broadly health work undertaken by teachers with the rights and responsibilities of parents is a delicate touchstone in the school-family nexus given the governance of children's bodies and health practices is so contested (Foucault, 1979; Knowles, 1996).

Methodology

This was a mixed methods study that included a teacher survey, semi-structured interviews and field notes. All teachers were volunteers from within 12 schools recruited across the state of Queensland. This chapter draws upon survey and interview data gathered from participating teachers. Pseudonyms are used throughout this chapter to refer to these teachers and their schools. The sample of primary and secondary schools was drawn from all schooling sectors across urban, regional and remote environments.

Demographically, the average age of the teacher survey participants was 42.34 years (SD, 11.98), 32 per cent were male and 68 per cent female. The data showed that 24.1 per cent had one to six years' teaching experience, the largest proportion of respondents, 33.4 per cent, had been in the teaching profession for between 7–18 years, followed by 29.3 per cent that had 19–30 years' experience, while 13.2 per cent reported being in teaching 31 years or more.

Teacher survey

The 35-question survey covered three broad potential areas of health-related work – namely, the curriculum, the pastoral system and extra-curricular programmes. Sub-questions within each of these strands included: teaching health education; food and nutrition; health screening and referrals; school health policy and compliance; pastoral care work; communicating with parents and leading physical activity. Teachers were asked to consider how much time they spend on various aspects of this work in a typical week, and rate their perceived levels of confidence, expertise, and satisfaction. Surveys were administered through attendance at staff meetings or electronically via a web server-based software package with assured anonymity for all respondents.

Semi-structured interviews

The interview sought a deeper exploration of trends arising from the survey data related to the core 'health-work' themes, and included questions about the breadth and purpose of teachers' work, raising discussion about relationships with families. The interviews occurred across the school, for varying time durations, depending upon accessibility to the teachers.

Interviews were transcribed and coded using N-Vivo according to various themes identified deductively during the qualitative analysis process. Some prominent themes included families, crisis, cost/benefit economics, welfare, boundary spanners and health work classification. Often themes were deconstructed further into sub-themes – for example, researchers noted within the concept of 'families' teachers had described various aspects including the benefits of parental involvement, and also some of the disadvantages and costs.

Findings and discussion

Quantitative data from the teacher survey provide insight into teachers' patterns of engagement with parents while qualitative data were generated from the school case studies around the themes 'parents as deficit' and 'parents as strength'. Together it demonstrates the complexity of contemporary teachers' engagement with parents and the sensitivities of schools and families co-producing healthy citizens.

Patterns of engagement with parents

Across school systems, the investment by teachers in communicating with parents averaged over one hour weekly (65.9 minutes/week) in both government and non-government schools. The survey provided data on the teachers' sense of confidence, satisfaction, expertise and importance in undertaking this liaison role with families when compared to other health-related work. Table 13.1 indicates that alongside 'pastoral care', 'communicating with parents' is highly ranked in terms of teacher confidence, satisfaction, expertise and importance.

The patterns of responses suggested that, overwhelmingly, teachers had a very high or high (85.7 per cent) sense of the importance of communicating with parents while the teachers' satisfaction derived from this communication was more measured, as was their sense of expertise in doing so. Data indicate the significance of the relationship between confidence and expertise suggesting that this type of work could be supported with more extensive professional development. However, as the following qualitative data suggests, the nature of this communication may frequently be an interaction in which the teachers were compensating for what they considered as poor or neglectful parenting.

Parents as deficit

While there are undoubtedly many profound and persistent regularities associated with teachers' work, there are also many 'new' challenges, choices and demands facing teachers (Hargreaves, 1994; Sugrue, 2013). The teachers in this study frequently spoke about the way their work is changing. There was

Table 13.1 Teacher rankings of health-related work (ranked on a 5–1 Likert scale where 5 = 'very high')

Perceived expertise	Satisfaction
Communicating with parents (3.77)	Pastoral care (4.02)
Pastoral care (3.60)	Communicating with parents (3.89)
Health policy adherence (3.42)	Extra-curricular physical activity
Extra-curricular physical activity (3.37)	(3.66)
Leading physical activity (3.05)	Health policy adherence (3.46)
Teaching health education (2.87)	Leading physical activity (3.32)
Extra-curricular food and nutrition	Teaching health education (3.29)
(2.78)	Extra-curricular food and nutrition
Health screening and referrals (2.74)	(3.26)
	Health screening and referrals (3.12)

Confidence	**Importance to student health**
Communicating with parents (4.05)	Pastoral care (4.41)
Pastoral care (3.87)	Communicating with parents (4.37)
Health policy adherence (3.62)	Health policy adherence (4.25)
Extra-curricular physical activity (3.57)	Extra-curricular physical activity
Teaching health education (3.26)	(4.24)
Leading physical activity (3.25)	Leading physical activity (4.17)
Extra-curricular food and nutrition	Teaching health education (4.17)
(3.16)	Health screening and referrals (4.17)
Health screening and referrals (2.91)	Extra-curricular food and nutrition
	(4.10)

general agreement that the roles and responsibilities of teachers have expanded over time:

> I think the role of a teacher has changed dramatically over my teaching career. Where it used to be basically you're a teacher, now you're a doctor, you're a nurse, you're a welfare worker, you're a social worker, you're a guidance counsellor, you're a mum, you're a dad, you're everything really (Grant).

Like Grant, numerous teachers noted different combinations of what they saw as their multiple roles and identities: 'Parent' was, however, a consistent inclusion in all of these lists. Indeed much of the qualitative data suggests that many teachers spend a great deal of time assisting parents with what these teachers consider to be parenting and child rearing skills. The degree and nature of this assistance varied from taking on 'a little bit of a parent role at times' (Angela) to teachers who are 'commonly called dad' by students from 'broken families who don't see their dad or their dad is in jail or whatever' (Steven).

An array of reasons were provided as to why it is becoming increasingly necessary for teachers to adopt parental roles and responsibilities, and there was a notable difference in teachers' perceptions of parents from different socio-economic backgrounds. There are always significant theoretical and practical tensions involved in defining social class (see Reay, 1998; Vincent et al, 2008) and speaking about families in terms of class or economic binaries. Given this chapter is primarily based on teacher perceptions, however, we have relied on the language our teachers used to categorize certain types of parents, while acknowledging the binaries these categories create are far from ideal. The most common categorisations made by our teachers were 'parents from poorer backgrounds' and 'parents from more affluent backgrounds'.

Teachers offered the following explanations for why parents from poorer backgrounds were not doing the parental work they 'should' be doing: poverty, drug abuse, incarceration, parents' own health issues, lack of interest and parents' poor personal experience of schooling and family life:

> Some [parents] are just so busted, broke … the kids are coming and going. Some kids haven't come to school because they haven't got food (Pippa).
>
> … young people, they don't get health anywhere else. They don't get to go to a doctor regularly because either their parents can't afford it or they don't have the transportation to do so (Focus Group, Devon Secondary College).
>
> I might have to actually make an appointment for a parent to take their child to the doctors or to get a hearing assessment. Sometimes … [because parents] don't have a car or they're just – it's a lack of – for want of a better word – a lack of interest – or they don't think it's necessary (Kristie).

Many teachers found establishing and maintaining communication with these parents quite difficult:

> I've got no chance, because the parent won't even return any communication. Refuses (Peter).
>
> I have to go to feed little Johnny for the 16th time in a row, but they (teachers) just do it. They have the conversation with parents: why aren't you feeding them, blah, blah, blah, but then if you start hammering that, then they stop coming to school. So it's *Catch 22*. We ring them and we say why aren't they [students] at school? Oh, we don't have any food. Send them to school, we'll feed them. So it's – you get on their back too much, then they pull the kids away; whereas they just come, we just feed them and we just do it … . Most of the teachers – they just do it (Kristie).

Inability to communicate effectively with parents together with a desire to work in the best interests of the student meant that for some teachers, feeding, brushing hair and teeth, toileting, and medical referrals simply became part of the work they did with and for students on a daily basis.

In contrast, the story told most frequently about why and how parents from 'more affluent' social groups were shirking their parental responsibilities was quite different. Busyness was the most frequently cited rationale provided for why more affluent parents are not fulfilling what teachers perceived as parental responsibilities:

> Then there are other more affluent parents that both parents are working and I can see their children have been put in day care before school, after school-care... . Mum and dad are so busy. So, I'm looking at huge behavioural issues that are not necessarily associated with food or lack of money but it's about attention (Sue).
>
> I think parents these days are very busy themselves, spend a lot of their time on IT and technology. There's a lot of – it's not the quantity of time, it's the quality of time and they'll thrust an iPad or an iPhone at a two year old and say this will entertain you. Sit you in front of the TV, that will entertain you, I'm too busy (Simon).

Again, for various reasons, communicating with these 'time-poor' parents was perceived as difficult and a number of teachers remarked that the only time these parents did communicate with them was when they perceived something was wrong:

> I mean the feedback we get from parents is generally if something's wrong we'll know about it and if something's right you kind of don't know about it... . I think broadly parents are a bit more like, "We're happy" and they're not going to talk to you if everything's happy at home, but the minute something might be going wrong, or there's a concern, then we sort of get to hear about it a bit (Ebony).

One teacher referred to these kinds of parents as 'helicopter parents':

> Helicopter parents. They're the ones who will send you an email ... at 10 o'clock at night and you read your email and it could be quite negative – not particularly (an) attack on you – but on the system of school, and it's co-related back to you. ... So those helicopter parents will drop email bombs. They'll drop comments and they'll expect you to deal with it and fly off and you're left to pick up all the pieces (Simon).

Teachers, therefore, constructed different types of parents as inadequate, failing and blameworthy (Broadhurst, 2009; Wood and Warin, 2014) and cited an array of parental deficiencies. Unlike the findings of other work (Goldson and Jamieson, 2002; Jones, 2011), however, the pathological construction of parents was not specific to the less affluent, minority-ethnic, working-class parents. Many teachers in this study believed that, increasingly, busy working parents from more affluent backgrounds were abdicating their parental responsibilities and expecting teachers and schools to pick up the slack. Vincent and colleagues (2008, p6) have suggested that when parental deficits are created, parenting is 'redefined as a public rather than a private issue'. Many of the teachers in this study certainly felt the need to compensate for, and/or counter, what they saw as problematic parental practices by helping students to engage with the necessary principles and practices to become healthy and productive members of the population (Grumet, 1988).

Parents as strength

While the parents as deficit construction was certainly the most prevalent in our data, a minority of teachers did speak about parents, and communicating with parents, in positive terms. Parents' appreciation and support of teachers' work features in all of these more positive comments:

> ... generally the parents are very, very supportive. I do have quite a few parents who talk to me regularly and they just tell me how their children are going and how much they're enjoying it, which is lovely, which means I must be doing something right (Jeremy).
> The parents will come up at the end and they will thank you. Most of them appreciate that you've tried. If you don't try, then, you don't deserve anything. But most of the parents appreciate that we've put in a pretty hard day – you know (Peter).

Also worthy of note is that while much of the data about the changing nature of teachers' work was underpinned by a certain romanticization of the past, a small number of teachers spoke about how societal changes had resulted in a positive recasting of the parent-teacher relationship:

> My mother only came up the other day to talk about the olden days and schooling and how times have changed and that. Back in the day, the parents never went anywhere near the school or the teacher. Now I have parents that actually touch me and – oh thank you, Mrs Smith and can I give you a hug, which is lovely (Sue).

Parental practices that were positively appraised by teachers included the provision of healthy lunches, support for co-curricular health-related offerings, and openness to engage with teacher and school communication:

> We seem – we're fairly fortunate in that the children that come here are well – they seem well fed. Their lunchboxes have healthy foods. We're able to communicate to parents through newsletters about things that we like to see and we get a good response. They're all very willing to want the best for their children. They're well dressed and it's not cheap to clothe them here.... We're very lucky in that respect that we have their support. We have a lot of co-curricular offerings after school and children and their parents take advantage of those opportunities (Clare).

In several schools we observed parents as co-workers with teachers, assisting with, for example, reading, art, physical activity and cooking, as well as differing levels of involvement in what is frequently referred to as 'Parents and Friends' association activities, such as serving on the school canteen/tuckshop, supporting excursions and fundraising. Boarding schools were particularly strong examples of where teachers have a sense of a partnership with parents to collaboratively care for the students' well-being.

A close reading of both the 'parents as deficit' and 'parents as strengths' constructions reveals that, common across the teachers' responses, was a seemingly quick attribution of blame or praise to parents. While at the beginning of conversations teachers often used socio-economic background or perceived work pressures to contextualise their responses, all teachers cited parental engagement as a significant, if not the most significant, influence on student health knowledge and practices. Unsurprisingly these teachers also frequently emphasised family-centred not just student-centred practices as vital in meeting the needs of their students (Lawson, 1998):

> ... it's got to have the student, the parent and the teacher or the school, they've got to be working together in that triad, I talk about the triad, and if one of those are missing, you're stuffed. You are powerless (Peter).

Issues of 'cost' on teachers

It is simplistic to suggest the cost of engaging with parents is 'stress'. Teachers have long engaged with parents in a variety of ways including parent-teacher interviews, on the side line at sporting events or at the myriad of school concerts and celebrations. We suggest, however, that the changing nature of teachers' work to which we refer here, where 'health work' is seemingly the new 'doxa' (Bourdieu, 1977), brings with it different demands and different types of relationships. The demands to address students' 'health' concerns have, for the teachers in this research, increased greatly. Taken together, the teachers conveyed a sense of confidence in what health practices were appropriate for their students (e.g., nutrition, hygiene, medical attention, being valued, promoting independence), regardless of the students' backgrounds. Although some of the teachers described the relationship with parents as stressful, especially where it was associated with students' health, it was frequently the time in the day that was available for such relationships that was the biggest challenge. One teacher described how she had always liked to get to work early to prepare for the day ahead. However, this turned into an opportunity for parents to seek a one-on-one conversation with her. She found that she was unable to set her classroom up for the day so started to stay later after school knowing full well that her early mornings would be taken up with parent meetings. What this teacher then shared with us was that invariably these conversations were not only about their children's health and well-being, but focused on the health difficulties the parent was experiencing. Realizing that she was beginning to assume a responsibility way beyond her training or experience (even though it was over 20 years), she started to lock the classroom door when she arrived at school and ensured she could not be seen from the outside.

Another teacher described how the nature of the work associated with health and well-being of the school children extended into her home and family time. In order to ensure that parents were aware of progress their children had made or whether she needed to flag concerns about children, her work continued as soon as she got home:

> Oh yeah, probably. There's probably a cost to my family, to my kids because sometimes I go home and I'm not thinking about them at all; I'm thinking about Donald or Katy [her students] ... I don't have to worry about my own kids (Rhiannon).
>
> Yeah but your head space is probably not always where it should be.... So I will sit here till seven o'clock at night making sure that they're [the parents] getting the text messages otherwise the whole thing falls to pieces because the kids think oh well they don't even tell mum anyway; so trying to keep on top of all of that.' (Rhiannon). (Square parentheses added)

We can see that in the case of Rhiannon, she took the chance that her own children could 'make do' without her attention and to some extent was able to rely on a supportive partner. This provides another example of what Bourdieu (1990) calls the 'juridical boundaries' becoming blurred. This teacher regarded this work as crucial, yet how might this work be described: education or health? The logic of the practice as described by these two teachers means that there is a cost to teachers in terms of time and stress (which we discuss below) at a personal level as well as incurring an institutional cost. If the work described by the teachers here borders on allied health, then that 'time' is lost to the educational sector. It is an argument we take up elsewhere (see Rossi et al, in press).

Inevitably the stresses of this kind of work, especially as we found in areas described as low socio-economic status (though, we should add, not exclusively), were often profound. For one teacher, there were days of intensity at school that often involved connections to parents, telephone calls, visits, requests for visits, and emergencies which parents had to be informed about. As she said:

> Oh days that I have to deal with that emotionally it's very draining and the millions of conversations you have to have about it. I don't deal well with drama. I can't stand [it] – if I have to ring the police and I have to do things like that or the ambulance or whatever, I'm a mess and I don't particularly like it (Rhiannon).

Another teacher (Sara, a year coordinator) described a programme that she ran for year 8 girls (who were about 12 years old). The programme was about being a valuable person and being 'valued'. It is important to note that this part of the interview became particularly emotional. She described how one girl in the group had not before experienced the feelings of being valued. Sara described it this way:

> We've got one little girl who came in very meek and wouldn't interact at all. Even made a comment that she said that she's never felt that way before, so never felt like she's been valued, and she's actually starting to participate and have her say in the class. So that's a real positive because you can see that she's starting to value herself.

We might readily recognize this as a common approach in pastoral care; however, Sara found it difficult to accept that these young children were not valued in their own home. The 'cost' to Sara is significant. The interview continued:

> But then socially and emotionally for me it's huge ... like it's very detrimental. There are often times that I'll go home and just cry because it's so overwhelming. [At this point Sara started to cry.]

These teachers' emotional responses are, perhaps, unsurprising given some of the cautions shared in the literature about the relationship between those involved in 'helping professions' and the people they serve. Lawson (1998, p12), for example, suggests 'the well-being of vulnerable people and the professionals who serve them often decline in parallel fashion'.

Working across fields

Regardless of the socio-economic profile of the school, parents had a strong sense of the permeability of the fields of practice of the school and the family (Bourdieu, 1990). Data suggested that for some schools and students, one field compensates for another, most frequently schools for families. Drawing on Rose's (1999) work, Nadesan (2010) explains new instantiations of compensatory education and its remit of remediating poverty. New forms of governance that permeate in, and across, the family and school require a combined effort to produce a healthy, active, and productive citizen/child. The ever-increasing emphasis on teachers' and their students' performances in national and global high-stakes testing sharpens the teachers focus to have all students ready and able to learn. The provision of food, health tests and clean clothing by teachers is, in some schools, a piece of the performative puzzle. Also part of the performative puzzle are the high expectations of middle class parents to produce children who can compete successfully in a global marketplace. These children need seamless efforts across multiple fields – schooling, family, the arts, sport – to develop a habitus that is globally highly valued.

Another way of seeing the high investment of teachers' effort in communicating with, and compensating for, parenting reflects what Ecclestone and Hayes (2009, pxi) consider is the 'dangerous rise of therapeutic education' in which the therapeutic turn of schooling reflects the 'diminished self'. Their argument is that schools, as in other fields of practice, have come to position the self and families as defective and requiring of increased attention to their more pronounced deficits. They argue that dominant therapeutic discourses saturate schools' and teachers' priorities. Yet, many of the experienced teachers in this study would 'speak back' to this hypothesis saying that students are in need of more attention upon arrival at school and if teachers do not attend to the students' needs, who will? As discussed elsewhere (Noddings, 1992), the drive to care is a significant referent for many who enter the teaching profession and the health work undertaken by teachers on behalf of families is but one dimension of this disposition.

Conclusion

Regardless of the school or the schooling system, teachers were acutely aware of their relationship with parents and rated it as a significant dimension in their health-related work. While many were critical of parents, and specifically parental support of their children's health practices, most teachers emphasised that children's health was a shared responsibility, best supported through parent-teacher partnerships. There was, however, less agreement and insight into how best to establish and negotiate this 'shared stewardship' (Lawson, 1998). Indeed, the stories told about the active engagement of 'helicopter parents' highlight how parental engagement can be more of an interference than a support to both the teacher's day and the child's independence. That being said, in general, the importance of good communication with parents ranked very highly amongst the teachers. They considered that this communication was important to students' health, was often satisfying and, for the most part, teachers communicated with confidence and expertise. As the qualitative data elucidated, much of this relationship with parents addressed compensatory practices that differed in their nature depending on the socio-economic profile of the families and schools. This sense of teachers' expertise is particularly interesting at a time when expertise can be so exacting, so field specific. Yet, even without reported professional development, teachers were comfortable with this role.

Teachers do not want to be parents to their students. Despite many teachers feeling that they are expending significant time and effort compensating for parental deficits of one kind or another, all reported, that regardless of whether they thought it should be their work, they will always put children's unmet health needs first. This is an important point as, on the one hand, it represents a form of governmental technology and, on the other, it reflects a form of civic professionalism that extends beyond the private world of the classroom to the public sphere (Wilkinson, 2007).

This chapter constitutes a partial response to a question about the school–family–health nexus. A more complete data set for this aspect of our study would include parents' and students' voices and their perceptions of, and aspirations for, the health work of teachers. Given the high investment of time by teachers in health work (Rossi et al., in press), there is much to be learned about this significant dimension of teachers' work and how it is judged and valued by families and students.

References

Ball, S. (2012) *Global education inc.: New policy networks and the neo-liberal imaginary.* Abingdon, Oxon: Routledge.

Beck, U. (1992) *Risk Society: Towards a New Modernity.* London: Sage.

Bessant, J. (1991) Described, measured and labelled: Eugenics, youth policy and moral panic in Victoria in the 1950s, *Journal of Australian Studies*, 31, 8–28.

Bourdieu, P. (1977) *Outline of a theory of practice.* Cambridge: Cambridge University Press.

Bourdieu, P. (1990) *The logic of practice (trans Richard Nice).* Cambridge: Polity Press.

Broadhurst, K. (2009) Safeguarding children through parenting: How does every parent matter? In Broadhurst, K., Grover, C. and Jamieson, J. (eds.) *Critical perspectives of safeguarding children.* West Sussex: Wiley-Blackwell, pp111–131.

Eccleston, K. and Hayes, D. (2009) *The dangerous rise of therapeutic education.* London: Routledge.

Foucault, M. (1979) *Discipline and punish.* New York: Vintage Books.

Foucault, M. (1984) The politics of health in the eighteenth century. In Rabinow, A. (ed.) *The Foucault reader: An introduction to Foucault's thought.* London: Penguin Books, pp273–289.

Fox, L. (2013) Britain must not live beyond its means, *Telegraph* [online]. Available from: <http://www.telegraph.co.uk/news/politics/9922579/Liam-Foxs-speech-to-the-Institute-of-Economic-Affairs-in-full.html> [Accessed 15 October 2013].

Goldson, B. and Jamieson, J. (2002) Youth crime, the 'parenting deficit' and state intervention: A contextual critique, *Youth Justice*, 2(2), 82–99.

Grumet, M. R. (1988) *Bitter milk: women and teaching.* Amherst: University of Massachusetts Press.

Hargreaves, A. (1994) *Changing teachers, changing times: Teachers' work and culture in the postmodern age.* New York: Continuum International Publishing Group.

Hockey, J. (2012) The end of the age of entitlement, *The Age* [online]. Available from: <http://www.theage.com.au/national/the-end-of-the-age-of-entitlement-20120419–20120411x8vj.html> [Accessed 13 October 2013].

Hultqvist, K. and Dahlberg, G. (2001) Introduction. In: Hultqvist, K. and Dahlberg, G. (eds.) *Governing the child in the new millennium.* New York: Routledge Falmer, pp1–13.

Hunter, I. (1994). *Rethinking the school: Subjectivity, bureaucracy, criticism.* St Leonards, New South Wales: Allen & Unwin.

Jones, O. (2011) *Chavs: The demonisation of the working class.* London: Verso.

Kay-Shuttleworth, J. (1974) *Sir James Kay-Shuttleworth on popular education.* New York: Teachers College Press.

Kelly, P. (2001) The post-welfare state and the government of youth at-risk, *Social Justice*, 28(4), 96–113.

Klein, N. (2007) *The shock doctrine: The rise of disaster capitalism.* New York: Metropolitan Books.

Knowles, C. (1996) *Family boundaries.* Toronto: Broadview Press.

Larsen, A. C. (1999) Governing families with young children through discipline, *Journal of Sociology*, 35(3), 279–296.

Lawson, H. A. (1998) Rejuvenating, reconstituting, and transforming physical education to meet the needs of vulnerable children, youth, and families, *Journal of Teaching in Physical Education*, 18(1), 2–25.

Lawson, H. A. (2005) Empowering people, facilitating community development, and contributing to sustainable development: The social work of sport, exercise, and physical education programs, *Sport, Education and Society*, 10(1), 135–160.

Lazaridou, A. and Kassida, A. G. (2015) Involving parents in secondary schools: Principals' perspectives in Greece, *The International Journal of Educational Management*, 29(1), 98–114.

Macdonald, D., Tinning, R., Rossi, A., Mangan, J. and McCuaig, L. (2013–2015) *Educating healthy citizens: The health work of teachers in Australian schools.* ARC Discovery Project.

MacLeod, J. and Malone, K. (eds.) (2000) *Researching youth.* Hobart: Australian Clearing House for Youth Studies.

Mayall, B. (1996) *Children, health and the social order.* Buckingham, UK: Open University Press.

McCuaig, L. and Tinning, R. (2010) HPE and the moral governance of pleasurable bodies, *Sport, Education and Society*, 15(1), 39–61.

Meredyth, D. and Tyler, D. (eds.) (1993) *Child and citizen: Genealogies of schooling and subjectivity.* Brisbane: Griffith University.

Nadesan, M. (2010) *Governing childhood into the 21st century.* London: Routledge.

Noddings, N. (1992) *The challenge to care in schools: An alternative approach to education.* New York: Teachers College Press.

Reay, D. (1998) *Class work: Mothers' involvement in their children's primary schooling.* London: University College Press.

Rose, N. (1999) *Governing the soul: The shaping of the private self, 2nd edition.* London: Free Association Books.

Rossi, T., Pavey, A., Macdonald, D. and McCuaig, L. (in press) Teachers as health workers: Patterns and imperatives of Australian teachers' work, *British Educational Research Journal.*

Stuart, J. and Jose, P. E. (2014) The protective influence of family connectedness, ethnic identity, and ethnic engagement for New Zealand Māori adolescents, *Developmental Psychology*, 50(6), 1817.

Sugrue, C. (2013) Teachers' lives and work: Back to the future?. In Flores, M. A., Carvalho, A. A.Ferreira, F. I. and Vilaça, M. T. (eds.) *Back to the future: Legacies, continuities and changes in educational policy, practice and research.* Boston: Sense Publishers, pp39–56.

Tveit, A. D. (2009) A parental voice: Parents as equal and dependent – rhetoric about parents, teachers, and their conversations, *Educational Review*, 61(3), 289–300.

Tyler, D. (1993) Making better children. In Meredyth, D. and Tyler, D. (eds.) *Child and citizen: Genealogies of schooling and subjectivity.* Brisbane: Griffith University.

Vander Schee, C. (2009) Fruit, vegetables, fatness, and Foucault: Governing students and their families through school health policy, *Journal of Education Policy*, 24(5), 557–574.

Vincent, C., Braun, A. and Ball, S. J. (2008) Childcare and social class: Caring for young children in the UK, *Critical Social Policy*, 28(1), 5–6.

Wallace, C. (2007) Libertarian nation by stealth, *Griffith Review*, 16(1), 115–128.

Wilkinson, G. (2007) Civic professionalism: Teacher education and professional ideals and values in a commercialised education world 1, *Journal of Education for Teaching*, 33(3), 379–395.

Wood, P. and Warin, J. (2014) Social and emotional aspects of learning: Complementing, compensating and countering parental practices, *British Educational Research Journal*, 40(6), 937–995.

Wright, J. and Macdonald, D. (2010) *Young people, physical activity and the everyday*. London: Routledge.

Wyn, J. and White, R. (1997) *Rethinking youth*. St Leonards, N.S.W: Allen & Unwin.

14 Families, youth and extra-curricular activity

Implications for physical education and school sport

Andy Smith and David Haycock

Introduction: Families, parents and parenting

Family life, relationships between parents and their offspring, and the social process of parenting have long been of concern to government, policy-makers and academics. Parents are also increasingly regarded as being responsible for their children's learning and well-being, and parenting is frequently identified in social policy as an important mechanism for reducing the gap in educational achievement and improving other social outcomes (Hartas, 2014). According to Hartas (2014, p3), embedded within existing policy is a paradox in which parenting is presented, on the one hand, as 'an all-encompassing act in the political sphere where parents are to tackle underachievement and raise children to become model citizens', while, on the other hand, 'what parents do has been undermined through overregulation and deficit perceptions about some parents as being vulnerable and fragile at best, or ignorant and potentially dangerous at worst'. More particularly, the prevailing policy context presents parents and families as being responsible, among other things, for the health and well-being of children; securing future employment opportunities for children in ways that enhance their ability to make a social and economic contribution to society; and providing their offspring with opportunities to develop talents and skills as a worthy and responsible approach to childrearing (Hartas, 2014).

The tendency to focus on families as sites of formal and informal pedagogic practices that improve the life chances of children and young people, however, diverts attention from the socially structured inequalities that beset their lives, and instead focuses attention on individuals (such as parents) who are held to be responsible for their own and others' (i.e., their children's) well-being. Inequality in family life, as in other spheres (Wilkinson and Pickett, 2010), has thus 'been recast as lack of ambition, a decline in family and parenting styles and a culture of poverty rather than a culture of reduced opportunities and stagnant social mobility' (Hartas, 2014, p11). As we shall make clear in this chapter, parents do indeed matter to their children's socialization and wellbeing but so, too, do social inequalities (especially those related to social class) which continue to make a significant contribution to the lives of children and young people.

These introductory remarks provide the context for this chapter, the central object of which is to consider briefly some of the links which exist between families, the growth of extra-curricular activity as a formal and informal pedagogic practice, and young people's sport participation. More specifically, we examine:

1   the growth of extra-curricular activity under conditions of increased privatisation in education and as a part of the ideology of 'good parenting';
2   the importance of social inequality in family life for childhood sport socialization; and
3   how the formation of sporting habits during childhood and youth may be associated with extra-curricular activity in schools.

Before we consider these issues, however, it is important to note that such has been the considerable growth in the provision of activities which are now variously referred to as 'extra-curricular', 'enrichment', 'organized' or 'out-of-school' activities, and which are provided by an expanding variety of providers (state, private, voluntary) alongside the work of families, it is increasingly difficult to delineate between 'extra-curricular' and other activities undertaken formally and informally during 'leisure time'. In the context of physical education (PE) and school sport, extra-curricular time has traditionally been defined as 'the provision of activities outside of the formal PE curriculum, most often after school and at lunch times, but also in some schools at weekends and/or before school' (Penney and Harris, 1997, p42), though as we make clear below, teachers now represent just one group who deliver extra-curricular activity in schools.

The growth of extra-curricular activity

As Vincent and Maxwell (2016, p269) have noted, there has been an 'exponential rise, especially since the 1990s, in out-of-school learning and enrichment activities', including engagement in formal and less formal extra-curricular activities such as art, music, sport, drama and dance. These activities are not simply provided by the state or institutions such as schools, but increasingly by a diverse range of private providers whose activities are targeted at young people and their families through the accelerating privatisation of schools and schooling.

In the context of PE and school sport (PESS), the growth of extra-curricular options and activity has been facilitated by the increased outsourcing of activity in schools, in the UK (e.g., Evans and Davies, 2010, 2014; Smith, 2015) and elsewhere including Australia and New Zealand (Williams and Macdonald, 2015; Williams et al, 2008). The growth of outsourcing sports, services and goods, as part of what has traditionally been conceived of as extra-curricular

PESS, is often justified on a number of grounds. These include the educational benefits to young people of engaging in extra-curricular activities; the use of human resource or capital (e.g., qualified sports coaches) available only from external providers; accessing specialized facilities and equipment needed to facilitate participation; and, particularly among those attending schools serving more middle-class pupils and their families, the ability to obtain important symbolic value from working with prestigious private providers (Ball, 2012, 2013; Ball, 2015; Williams and Macdonald, 2015). In this regard, young people, through extra-curricular activities such as PESS, and other elements of schooling relations, are constrained to adopt two so-called 'neoliberal imaginaries' associated with the privatisation of education (Ball, 2012, 2013; Evans and Davies, 2014). As Evans and Davies (2014, p871) have noted, these are, first, the view 'that individuals are self-responsibilising, ameliorating and actualising across their life courses ... [and] are assumed to be equipped with knowledge, desires and fiscal resources that enable them to accumulate social and economic capital in deregulated markets'; and, second, that 'private enterprise is intrinsically better than state enterprise and, either alone or in partnership with governments, can provide better-allocated, more cost efficient services than the state unaided'.

Important though the growth of privatized provision in extra-curricular PESS is for young people's participation and experiences, as we noted earlier there has been a parallel growth in the social expectations on parents to play an active role in schooling and to regard the family home and extra-curricular activities (such as sport) as important sites for formal and informal pedagogic practice. For reasons explained below, it is clear that many families, regardless of social position, are involved in formal and informal pedagogical work, but the degree to which parents are able to transmit advantages to children and young people is to a large extent associated with their social class background and is more commonly seen among the middle-classes (Evans and Davies, 2010, 2014; Hartas, 2014). Indeed, despite the rapid growth of extra-curricular participation among school-aged young people, such participation remains socially skewed. For example, data reported by the Sutton Trust (2014) indicate that, between 2009 and 2014, the proportion of 11- to 16-year-olds in England and Wales who received private or home tuition has increased from 20 to 23 per cent. However, children from the most affluent families were more likely to have received private tuition (27 per cent) compared to those from the least affluent families (15 per cent), while almost twice as many young people living in London (37 per cent) did so compared with an average of 20 per cent elsewhere (Sutton Trust, 2014). An Ipsos MORI survey of 309 parents of 5- to 16-year-olds also revealed that three-quarters (76 per cent) of respondents reported that their child had regularly participated in extra-curricular activity in the last 12 months, though this was more commonly reported by more middle-class and degree-educated respondents. Sport and exercise (52 per cent) was the most widely reported extra-curricular activity in which young people engaged, followed by Scouts/Guiding (16 per cent), dance/ drama (15 per cent) and music (14 per cent) (Sutton Trust, 2014).

Data from studies in the United States have also indicated that participation in extra-curricular activities rise markedly in line with parents' social class, and that engagement in these activities helps produce and reproduce class-related outcomes (including education and labour market performance) which are associated with distinctive cultural practices (e.g., Bennett et al, 2012; Covay and Carbonaro, 2010; Lareau, 2011; Weininger et al, 2015). Some authors have argued that the economic and material resources, time and work flexibility available to parents help explain much of the association between social class and engagement in extra-curricular activity compared to parental values and cultural practices (e.g., Bennett et al, 2012). For example, Bennett et al (2012) have argued that working-class parents were just as likely to be enthusiastic about, and promote, their child's engagement in organized extra-curricular activities as their middle-class peers, and to incorporate these into their broader parenting strategies. Sport and cultural activities, in particular, were undertaken by significant numbers of young people from all class backgrounds in the study, but the parents of working-class young people relied far more heavily on cheaper activities provided by schools, rather than private providers, and were more likely to emphasize how activities helped to provide children with access to safe spaces in which to participate. Middle-class young people, in contrast, were 20 times more likely to engage in costly elite extra-curricular activities (e.g., foreign language lessons, music tuition, and dance classes) (Bennett et al, 2012).

For Bennett et al (2012), working-class parents do value extra-curricular activities but middle-class young people participate in more and often different activities. They also argued that the class-related differences in overall participation would be much wider if schools did not play what they regard as a 'critical avenue through which the lives of children of working-class families become involved in organized activities' (Bennett et al, 2012, p145), even though inequalities in the types and range of activities available to young people were produced and reproduced in schools. The evidence presented in Bennett et al's (2012) study was thus said to indicate how differences in extra-curricular participation between the social classes were not so much a question of class cultures or parents' cultural logics (e.g., what parents valued and regarded as important), but were instead associated with the class-related conditions in which families find themselves (e.g., the financial and other resources needed to support participation) that were to a large extent structurally unequal and disproportionately advantaged middle-class young people.

Other authors have emphasised that extra-curricular participation represents a form of 'concerted cultivation' in which cultural, rather than structural, constraints are more likely to explain patterns of engagement and experiences of extra-curricular activity (Lareau, 2011; Weininger et al, 2015). In her ethnographic study of African American and white families, Lareau (2011) argued that working- and middle-class families adopted different cultural logics and strategies towards childrearing, including their engagement in structured extra-curricular activities or letting children play unsupervised outside of school. Middle-class families, it was claimed, engaged in concerted cultivation to treat children as developmental projects on which to work, while working-class families were more concerned with allowing their offspring to achieve an 'accomplishment of natural growth' by being less directly engaged in their daily lives (Lareau, 2011). It is through concerted cultivation, in particular, that parents are said to most commonly develop children's engagement in organized leisure activities, and such has been the growth of families' (especially parents') engagement in concerted cultivation, Vincent and Maxwell (2016, p278) have claimed that it is now possible to point towards its 'normalisation ... as a parenting strategy for all'. Accordingly, they argue that 'there is a risk that parents not able to or willing to engage in such activities will be positioned as offering inadequate parenting' (Vincent and Maxwell, 2016, p278; see also Chapter 10 in this book). We shall explore some of the links between good parenting and extra-curricular activity next.

Good parenting and extra-curricular activity

As we noted earlier, engagement in extra-curricular activities is not an exclusively middle-class phenomenon, although middle-class families often make more and different kinds of use of them (Vincent and Ball, 2007; Vincent and Maxwell, 2016). For Vincent and Maxwell (2016, p271) this is often because 'engaging in extra-curricular activities is becoming a fundamental part of what is understood as constituting a "good" childhood amongst affluent populations, and, thus, an indicator of being a "good" parent is that s/he provide such opportunities to their children'. It is also part of the increasingly neo-liberal emphasis on self-responsibilization and the growing responsibilization of parents, particularly of mothers (Hartas, 2014; Vincent and Maxwell, 2016). Who are regarded as being 'responsible for generating their children's biographies through the development of the children's intellectual, social, cultural, physical and emotional skills' (Vincent and Maxwell, 2016, p273).

For young people on middle-class life courses, encouragement into extra-curricular activities represents an important symbolic investment in their futures by parents concerned with securing education and labour market advantages for their children, and accruing positive behaviours (e.g., good health, socially important networks, and valued cultural knowledge and tastes) (Vincent and Ball, 2007; Vincent and Maxwell, 2016). The young people of better-off, more middle-class, families are thus better able to draw upon the additional class-related advantages enjoyed by their parents outside schools, including their greater ability to fund, access and sustain engagement in extra-curricular activities such as sport (Vincent and Maxwell, 2016). For Vincent and Ball (2007, p1062), the provision of and support offered for extra-curricular activities is 'one response to the anxiety and sense of responsibility experienced by middle-class parents as they attempt to resist "fears of falling" ... and "make up" a middle class child in a social context where reproduction appears uncertain'. Conceptualized in this way, the engagement of more middle-class young people in different kinds of extra-curricular activities is supported by parental attempts to secure privilege for children and young people through the purposive investment of economic, social and cultural resources which are not available to the same degree, or at all, to less well-off families.

It should be noted, however, that anxiety around social reproduction and the inter-generational transmission of advantage is not the sole reason for why middle-class parents encourage engagement in extra-curricular activities (Irwin and Elley, 2011; Vincent and Maxwell, 2016; Vincent et al, 2012). As in sport and other forms of cultural participation, it is the internal differentiation of middle- and working-class groups – as well as the differences between them – that shapes the degree to which young people engage in and experience extra-curricular activities. Irwin and Elley (2011), for example, have noted that the involvement in extra-curricular activities of many of the middle-class parents in their study was underpinned less by class anxiety, and more by their recognition of the class advantages they inherited from their own parents and how these could enhance their children's futures. For these parents, the relative structural material security of their middle-class lifestyles was perceived as assisting them to 'pass on' their class-related advantages to children in relatively straightforward, taken-for-granted ways. Other middle-class parents adopted 'a more strategic orientation to their children's education, notably where circumstances and background meant they were less likely to assume their children's educational success' (Irwin and Elley, 2011, p492). In this regard, Irwin and Elley (2011, p492; emphases in original) argue that 'anxiety about facilitating a good future for their children is a *particular*, rather than *general*, account of middle-class parenting experiences'. Much diversity also existed in the perceptions of working-class parents many of whom, like their middle-class peers, valued education (including extra-curricular activities) and saw it as an important part of preparing children for the future, but others (especially the most disadvantaged) felt less confident that their strategic investment in educational opportunities would guarantee their children a better future (Irwin and Elley, 2011).

But to what extent can the foregoing discussion help us to understand young people's engagement in extra-curricular PESS? If young people's family background is central to their participation in, and engagement with, extra-curricular activity generally, what are the implications of this for their participation in PESS? And what does this suggest about the social inequalities which beset young people's lives and which structure other aspects of their educational experiences?

Families, social class and childhood sport socialisation

As Kay and Spaaij (2012, p79) have noted, the family is now 'rightly regarded as a crucial influence on young people's involvement with sport', which is in turn shaped by often significant variations in the ideologies and practices that exist between and within different family types (Kay and Spaaij, 2012). More particularly, the family, it is claimed, 'is a major conduit for social class differentiation in sport' (Kay, 2004, p42), including in relation to practical resources (e.g. income, transport availability, access to facilities), the transmission of values and dispositions (often emphasizing the social and health benefits of participation), the time spent participating and in which social contexts, and the degree to which sport is seen as a family priority and parental responsibility (Kay, 2004; Wheeler and Green, 2014). It is important to note, however, that the role played by the family in informal pedagogical practices is especially significant during primary socialization, which is 'the initial process through which children come to define their own identity and learn the rules and norms of the society of which they are part' (Kay, 2004, p40), as well as the various skills, dispositions and knowledge needed to play sport. During phases of secondary socialisation, the influence of immediate family members on sport participation is often thought to become less directly significant and, instead, usually complements other increasingly influential significant others such as friends and peers, as well as those in educational settings (Green, 2010).

As Lareau (2011, p386) has observed, however, conceptualizing the process of socialization in this way may run the risk of conveying the misleading picture that 'children are passive rather than active agents and that the relationship between parents and their children is unidirectional rather than reciprocal and dynamic'. Thus, it is important that socialization is conceptualized as a dynamic, reciprocal and inequitable process that occurs in multiple social contexts, whether formally and informally, directly and indirectly, explicitly and implicitly, intentionally and unintentionally, and always within the context of social relationships characterized by varying degrees of negotiation and constraint between social groups such as young people and their parents (Green, 2010; Lareau, 2011). No less importantly, given the increasing diversity of family types and parenting styles (Kay and Spaaij, 2012; Quarmby and Dagkas, 2010, 2013), the socialisation of young people into sport must be regarded as a process which is neither homogenous or heterogeneous as such; it should, instead, be seen as a differentiating and context-specific process constituted by dynamic degrees of power between the groups involved.

In studies of young people's participation in leisure-sport and physical activity, having two sports-active parents is one feature of childhood socialization which helps predict higher rates of participation among children (e.g., Haycock and Smith, 2014; Pot et al, 2016; Scheerder et al, 2005; Vandermeerschen et al, 2014), but which is less commonly reported among children in lone-parent families (Dagkas and Stathi, 2007; Quarmby and Dagkas, 2010). Echoing the findings of other international studies (e.g., Birchwood et al, 2008; Parry, 2013; Pot et al, 2016; Wheeler and Green, 2014), Scheerder et al. (2005, p12) have noted that, in Flanders, parental sports participation is a 'very important predictor of boys' and girls' participation in club-organized sports activities', with those young people participating most frequently in both domains having two parents who themselves are sports-active and regard lei-sure as an important site for personal development and the accumulation of socially significant cultural capital. Another study of youth participation in club-based sport in Flanders between 1989 and 2009 (Vandermeerschen et al, 2014) revealed that although males were more likely to participate in traditional club sports during this 20-year period, middle-class youth were much more likely to do so. The parents of these young people possessed greater stocks of sporting capital, and were more likely to 'pass on their love for sports and/or bring in their knowledge about club-organised sports to orientate and socialize their children' (Vandermeerschen et al, 2014, p10) into sport.

In their study of Australian girls attending a school in a deprived rural town, Smyth et al (2014, p16) have similarly noted that the 'family and class operate as key sites in the accumulation of cultural and social capital necessary' to promote and sustain participation via the transmission of parental values and preferences. The parents of active middle-class girls were more likely to reschedule their lives to accommodate sport and physical activity as a priority in the leisure lives of their offspring. For these girls, the significant symbolic and material investments provided by their parents facilitated their engagement in 'the hectic shuttling and prioritising necessary for them to participate in a range of physical and sporting activities outside of school' (Smyth et al, 2014, p11). In contrast, working-class girls, who were also the least active, had 'no such "sporty" role models' (Smyth et al, 2014, p11) and were more likely to be 'cared for by other siblings who were themselves overburdened with working to make ends meet often at multiple jobs' (Smyth et al, 2014, p11), which helped limit the number and range of activities in which they could participate.

Childhood, youth and the significance of habitus

Central to understanding the involvement of children and young people in sport and physical activity, including in extra-curricular contexts, is the notion of habitus. Although the theoretical development of habitus as a sociological concept is most closely associated with the work of French sociologist Pierre Bourdieu (Bennett et al, 2010), it is also central to the work of other sociolo-gists including the figurational sociology of Norbert Elias (Dunning and Hughes, 2013; Elias, 2000; Stuij, 2015). There are many similarities between Bourdieu's conceptualization of habitus and that of Elias, and 'there is much in Bourdieu's work that is compatible with the work of Elias' more generally (Dunning and Hughes, 2013: 200). In relation to habitus, however, Elias sought to move away from what he saw as the overemphasis Bourdieu placed upon bodily habitus in favour of a more generalized conception of habitus (Dunning and Hughes, 2013). For Elias, habitus refers to a person's 'second nature' or 'embodied social learning' which, he argued, acts as an 'automatic, blindly functioning apparatus of self-control' (Elias, 2000, p368) that develops within their historically produced and reproduced relational networks which stretch across generations.

To overcome the difficulties associated with Bourdieu's more static conception of habitus (Bennett et al, 2010; Stuij, 2015), Elias sought to demonstrate how the organization of psychological make-up into a habitus is a dynamic process that begins at birth and continues throughout a person's life as the changing networks in which people find themselves become more or less complex, and are perceived as more or less compelling (Dunning and Hughes, 2013). It is childhood and youth, in particular, which typically constitute the most impressionable phase of habitus formation and development (Elias, 2000) where sporting habits and predispositions become deeply embedded and internalised in sport participants' emerging habituses during early socialisation (Green, 2010; Haycock and Smith, 2014; Stuij, 2015). The findings of our own study (Haycock and Smith, 2014) of young adults' sport participation revealed that the clearest differences in present-day participation lay in their different experiences of childhood sport socialisation, and especially in their unfolding habituses during childhood and youth. The habituses of the more frequent (four times or more per week) participants tended to have been shaped by the involvement of two sports-active, supportive and encouraging parents who experienced fewer financial and transport constraints than other parents. These parents also appeared better able to shape the developing habituses of their offspring by purposively investing them with various emotional, financial and cultural resources that formed the basis of their childhood predispositions towards sport and subsequent sporting biographies (Birchwood et al, 2008; Evans and Davies, 2010; Haycock and Smith, 2014; Roberts and Brodie, 1992).

The construction of sporting habituses and socialization practices which are associated with higher rates of sport participation and longer-running sport careers have, however, also been shown to operate relatively independently of social class (Birchwood et al, 2008; Pot et al, 2016). As with middle-class families, less well-off working-class parents in the Netherlands, for example, have been shown to socialize their offspring into sport through a variety of support mechanisms (e.g., transport, finance, attending events), providing advice about performance, and passing on 'what the family considered important values and behaviours' (Pot et al, 2016, p327). In particular, as the main socialising agents in introducing their offspring to sport and in the early construction of their sporting habituses, parents were said to be 'extremely important for the predisposition to play sports and for transferring the socio-cultural aspects of sporting capital. Parents not only introduced children to the social context of the sporting club but also guided the formation of sports-related values and behaviour' (Pot et al, 2016, p332).

Some implications for extra-curricular physical education and school sport

The evidence reviewed in this chapter and elsewhere has identified that unequal propensities for sport participation are to a large extent related to social inequalities acquired and reproduced outside of sport and education

(Coalter, 2013), the roots of which typically lie in childhood and family life (Evans and Davies, 2010; Haycock and Smith, 2014; Quarmby and Dagkas, 2010). But what are the implications of this for young people's engagement in extra-curricular PESS?

It would be churlish to suggest that engaging in curricular and extra-curricular PESS has no impact on young people's sport participation, or on their sporting predispositions and biographies which are structured by, and structuring of, their broader social relations and habituses. Several decades of research has amply demonstrated that in many complex and varied ways the relationships developed between young people and their teachers, peers and significant others does indeed help to shape participation in, and experiences of, (extra-) curricular PESS. The diet of sports and physical activities provided in extra-curricular time by teachers (and increasingly coaches, especially in primary schools) are further mediated by the local contexts of schools (e.g., sporting traditions, availability of facilities and resources, and the 'kinds' of pupils who attend them), and by other activities associated with wider social processes (e.g. the privatization, marketization and commercialization of schooling) that characterize educational systems in many national and international contexts.

But whether the content, organization and delivery of extra-curricular PESS encourages present-day and future sport participation by young people will depend on the predispositions, habits and experiences they obtain through formal and informal pedagogical activities that occur outside of schools, including in the family home and in publicly and privately organized settings. Data from the 1970 British Cohort Study (BCS70), for example, indicate that 'the influence of parents and the home environment on children's early experiences of physical activity are the primary driver of positive experiences of physical activity both outside and inside school' (Parry, 2013, p49). Findings from the BCS70 also revealed that children socialised into sport outside of school by their parents during childhood were already more active and had more favourable experiences of sport than those who were not, and that any school-based sports made little impact on pre-existing differences in sport participation outside of schools (Parry, 2013).

The differences in sport participation generated during childhood appear to have long lasting effects for, as Evans and Davies (2010, pp768–769) have observed, upon leaving compulsory schooling in England there are often few alterations in 'social patterns and inequalities and the predispositions for sport amongst individuals and populations' in their leisure time. This, they argued, is frequently related to the class-based practices and other processes of social reproduction evident in the ways (usually middle-class) families spend their leisure time, including through investments made in their offspring that enable them to develop the 'right kinds' of sporting 'ability' and predispositions that enable them to 'get ahead' (Evans and Davies, 2010, 2014). It is also true that extra-curricular PESS has for several decades remained largely independent of developments in curricular PE and heavily dominated by competitive team sports that are often regarded as being for the most 'able' and 'talented' young people (Green, 2010; Penney and Harris, 1997; Wilkinson and Penney, 2014). Penney (2006, p575), for example, has argued that despite claims of 'much apparent change', including that brought about by the introduction of private providers and services, there has been 'very little *real* change' (Penney, 2006, p575; original emphasis) in the extra-curricular PESS programmes activities available to pupils. More recently, Wilkinson and Penney (2014, p2) have noted that 'coaches' organization and pedagogical enactment of extra-curricular PE can be seen to reaffirm discourses and practices that legitimate and contribute to the ongoing perpetuation of inequities in PE, physical activity and sport that arise from narrow conceptualisations of ability, masculinity and femininity'. It might be argued, then, that the increased involvement of external agencies such as coaches and other private enterprises in extra-curricular time appears to have done more to reinforce, than challenge and breakdown, traditional and deep-seated social inequalities that are expressed in the content, organization and delivery of extra-curricular PESS. In other words, might it be that, as in other areas of schooling and education more broadly, the increasingly privatized delivery of aspects of PESS is helping to widen, rather than narrow, prevailing inequalities that disproportionately advantage young people from more middle-class backgrounds? This is clearly one area to which more attention is needed.

Conclusion

Our concern in this chapter has been to examine some of the links that exist between families, the growth of extra-curricular activity as a formal and informal pedagogic practice, and young people's sport participation. In doing so, we have argued that while school-based experiences of extra-curricular PESS might make a contribution, it is the inequalities that characterize young people's lives that are formed largely outside of schools, and often expressed in the pedagogical practices of parents and families, which play a greater role in the development of young people's unequal sporting predispositions and habituses. Greater consideration in policy and research thus needs to be given to how the influences of social inequalities are frequently stronger and more pervasive than the actions of parents and their pedagogical practices. Rather than perpetuating the moralizing blame culture which underpins suggestions that parents are responsible for hampering or remedying their children's development, it is essential that we recognise that the 'home lives of children are unequal and [that] this inequality is translated into educational inequality, a part of larger systemic patterns of inequality that persist across generations' (Hartas, 2014, p48). While costly and very probably politically uncomfortable, tackling these patterns of inequality and growing social polarisation is likely to be more successful than the cheaper, more convenient, and simplistic attempts to encourage all parents to internalise 'practices of parenting that are typically seen as middle class to maximise their children's educational opportunities and social advancement' (Hartas, 2014, p59).

References

Ball, S. (2012) *Global education inc. New policy networks and the neoliberal imaginary.* London: Routledge.

Ball, S. (2013) *The education debate* (2nd ed). Bristol: Policy Press.

Bennett, T., Savage, M., Silva, E., Warde, A., Gayo-Cal, M. and Wright, D. (2010) *Culture, class, distinction.* London: Routledge.

Bennett, P., Lutz, A. and Jayaram, L. (2012) Beyond the schoolyard: the role of parenting logics, financial resources, and social institutions in the social class gap in structured activity participation, *Sociology of Education*, 85(2), 131–157.

Birchwood, D., Roberts, K. and Pollock, G. (2008) Explaining differences in sport participation rates among young adults: evidence from the South Caucasus, *European Physical Education Review*, 14(3), 283–298.

Coalter, F. (2013) Game plan and the Spirit Level: The class ceiling and the limits of sports policy?, *International Journal of Sport Policy and Politics*, 5(1), 3–19.

Covay, E. and Carbonaro, W. (2010) After the bell: Participation in extracurricular activities, classroom behaviour and academic achievement, *Sociology of Education*, 83(1), 20–45.

Dagkas, S. and Stathi, A. (2007) Exploring social and environmental factors affecting adolescents' participation in physical activity, *European Physical Education Review*, 13(3), 369–384.

Dunning, E. and Hughes, J. (2013) *Norbert Elias and modern sociology. Knowledge, interdependence and process.* London: Bloomsbury Academic.

Elias, N. (2000) *The civilizing process.* Oxford: Basil Blackwell.

Evans, J. and Davies, B. (2010) Family, class and embodiment: why school physical education makes so little difference to post-school participation patterns in physical activity, *International Journal of Qualitative Studies in Education*, 23(7), 765–784.

Evans, J. and Davies, B. (2014) Physical Education PLC: Neoliberalism, curriculum and governance. New directions for PESP research, *Sport, Education and Society*, 19(7), 869–884.

Green, K. (2010) *Key themes in youth sport.* London: Routledge.

Hartas, D. (2014) *Parenting, family policy and children's well-being in an unequal society.* Basingstoke: PalgraveMacmillan.

Haycock, D. and Smith, A. (2014) A family affair? Exploring the influence of childhood sports socialisation on young adults' leisure-sport careers in north-west England, *Leisure Studies*, 33(3), 285–304.

Irwin, S. and Elley, S. (2011) Concerted cultivation? Parenting values, education and class diversity, *Sociology*, 45(3), 480–495.

Kay, T. (2004) The family factor in sport: a review of family factors affecting sports participation.In Sport England (Ed), *Driving up participation: the challenge for sport* (pp39–60). London: Sport England.

Kay, T. and Spaaij, R. (2012) The mediating effects of family on sport in international development contexts, *International Review for the Sociology of Sport*, 47(1), 77–94.

Lareau, A. (2011) *Unequal childhoods. Class, race, and family life* (2nd ed). Berkeley, CA: University of California Press.

Parry, W. (2013) *Experiences of physical activity at age 10 in the British Cohort Study.* London: Centre for Longitudinal Studies, Institute of Education.

Penney, D. (2006) Curriculum construction and change. In D. Kirk, D. Macdonald and M. O'Sullivan (Eds) *The handbook of physical education* (pp565–579). London: Sage.

Penney, D. and Harris, J. (1997) Extra-curricular physical education: more of the same for the more able?, *Sport, Education and Society*, 2 (1), 41–54.

Pot, N., Verbeek, J., van der Zwan, J. and van Hilvoorde, I. (2016) Socialisation into organised sports of young adolescents with a lower socio-economic status, *Sport, Education and Society*, 21(3), 319–338.

Quarmby, T. and Dagkas, S. (2010) Children's engagement in leisure time physical activity: exploring family structure as a determinant, *Leisure Studies*, 29(1), 53–66.

Quarmby, T. and Dagkas, S. (2013) Locating the place and meaning of physical activity in the lives of young people from low-income, lone-parent families, *Physical Education and Sport Pedagogy*, 18(5), 459–474.

Roberts, K. and Brodie, D. (1992) *Inner-city sport: Who plays, and what are the benefits?* Culemborg: Giordano Bruno.

Scheerder, J., Vanreusel, B., Taks, M. and Renson, R. (2005) Social stratification patterns in adolescents' active sports participation behaviour: a time trend analysis 1969–1999, *European Physical Education Review*, 11(1), 5–27.

Smith, A. (2015) Primary school physical education and sports coaches: evidence from a study of School Sport Partnerships in north-west England, *Sport, Education and Society*, 20(7), 872–888.

Smyth, J.Mooney, A. and Casey, M. (2014) Where has class gone? The pervasiveness of class in girls' physical activity in a rural town, *Sport, Education and Society*, 19(1), 1–18.

Stuij, M. (2015) Habitus and social class: a case study on socialisation into sports and exercise, *Sport, Education and Society*, 20(6), 780–798.

Sutton Trust (2014) *Research brief: extra-curricular inequality.* London: The Sutton Trust.

Vandermeerschen, H., Vos, S. and Scheerder, J. (2014) Towards level playing fields? A time trend analysis of young people's participation in club-organised sports, *International Review for the Sociology of Sport*, DOI: 10.1177/1012690214532450.

Vincent, C. and Ball, S. (2007) 'Making up' the middle-class child: Families, activities and class dispositions, *Sociology*, 41(6), 1061–1077.

Vincent, C. and Maxwell, C. (2016) Parenting priorities and pressures: Furthering understanding of 'concerted cultivation', *Discourse: Studies in the Cultural Politics of Education*, 37(2), 269–281.

Vincent, C., Rollock, N., Ball, S. and Gillborn, D. (2012) Being strategic, being watchful, being determined: Black middle-class parents and schooling, *British Journal of Sociology of Education*, 33(3), 337–354.

Weininger, E., Lareau, A. and Conley, D. (2015) What money won't buy: Class resources and children's participation in organized extracurricular activities, *Social Forces*, 94(2), 479–503.

Wheeler, S. and Green, K. (2014) Parenting in relation to children's sports participation: Generational changes and potential implications, *Leisure Studies*, 33(4), 267–284.

Wilkinson, R. and Pickett, K. (2010) *The spirit level.* London: Penguin.

Wilkinson, S. and Penney, D. (2014) The involvement of external agencies in extra-curricular physical education: reinforcing or challenging gender and ability inequities?, *Sport, Education and Society*, DOI: 10.1080/13573322.2014.956714.

Williams, B. and Macdonald, D. (2015) Explaining outsourcing in health, sport and physical education, *Sport, Education and Society*, 20(1), 57–72.

Williams, B., Hay, P. and Macdonald, D. (2011) The outsourcing of health, sport and physical educational work: a state of play, *Physical Education and Sport Pedagogy*, 16(4), 399–415.

15 The Swedish model for sport, recreation and health in times of change – a sustainable contract with the family of sport?

Suzanne Lundvall and Dean Barker

Introduction

The newly elected Swedish minister of public health and sports, Gabriel Wikström, is holding his first official speech to the Swedish Sports Confederation at a Sports Forum.[1] Wikström is a social democrat and 29 years old. He has one message: that the sports movement should help decrease existing health gaps in society. The audience looks somewhat puzzled; what has organized sport to do with health gaps? After the minister has left, a strategic discussion starts about the sports movement's assignment. Few of the delegates from the different sports federations rate the promotion of health as their main target. Instead, they are interested in attracting new members, keeping adolescents in sport longer, and securing the existence of non-profitable clubs as the foundation for a united popular movement vis-à-vis political decision-makers.

The speech of the sports minister points, on the one hand, to the expectations from the state on how organized sports and the Swedish Sports Confederation (Riksidrottsförbundet, RF) can promote public health. On the other hand it also points to concerns about public health and physical activity brought about by changes in society, neoliberal discourses and a strong belief in individual and market forces.

The purpose of this chapter is to examine how tensions around young people's recreational choices are played out in contexts shaped by discourses of health, physical activity and sport in a family context. The aim is to analyse young people's cultural practices in sport and physical activities in relation to symbolic and cultural boundaries. The concept 'family' is therefore broadened and understood as a social group constituted by a set of social practices, underpinned by a collective identity in relation to physical activity and health. Two 'family' concepts will be used; the *sports family* that relates to special sports federations and various sports, and the *sportive family* relating to the unit of families that actually participate actively in sports practice. This latter, the sportive family is in Sweden characterized by a nuclear family, a family with two parents and their biological children living together (Blomdahl, 1990).

In Sweden, sports for young people has traditionally been organized around a *Nordic model*, an agreement between the state and its citizens, where the majority of the different sports activities in sports clubs are planned and executed by leaders, coaches and parents that work voluntarily. This sports family consists of 70 different special sports federations. The newest special sports federation to be accepted by the general assembly in 2013, or 'to join the family', an expression used by the Sports Confederation (Riksidrottsförbundet, 2010, p17), was skateboarding. Approximately 42 per cent of the population between 7 and 70 years are members in sports clubs, and each week one quarter of the adult population is engaged in activities within the sports family. More than half of the children and adolescents up to the age of 16 years are members of the sports family in Sweden, and almost 80 per cent of their parents are, in one way or another, voluntarily engaged in the daily workings of the clubs (Wagnsson, 2009). The Swedish Sports Confederation (RF) defines itself as a democratic movement; the Swedish sports movement is part of our cultural heritage and an important aspect of our national identity. Thanks to the sports movement, millions of Swedish citizens have learned democratic procedures, respect for rules and fair play, have developed their leadership skills and improved their knowledge of dietary issues, physical exercise, health and well-being (Sports will, 2009, p11).

The Nordic model for the organizing of sports is partially due to a historically and culturally embedded public notion that participating in sport 'builds character', develops social skills, improves health – and keeps young people 'straight', and 'off the streets' (Norberg, 2004; Lindroth, 1974, 2004; see also Coakley and Pike, 2009).The assignment, often called the 'implicit contract', between the Swedish state and the sports movement is accordingly based on an old agreement. In exchange for state funding, the sports movement delivers recreational and competitive sport that supports social and moral development and physical competence. This contract, although implicit, acknowledge that the Swedish sports movement shall be accessible, based on equity and inclusion (SOU 2008: 59; Sports will, 2009). Inbuilt in the contract is to foster practical democracy, on the one hand, and competitiveness, on the other, values that are supposed to go hand in hand (Peterson, 2008). In the presence of a rapidly diversifying population in Sweden with expanding socio economical gaps (Sernhede, 2011), together with the increasing specialization and commercialization of sports, the accomplishment/success of the model is challenged. Hence, the aim of this chapter is to examine how tensions around young people's recreational choices are played out in contexts shaped by discourses of health, physical activity and sport in a family context.

The literature forming the basis for this chapter has a focus on families, health, recreation and sport and range from public health reports, youth research about health and well-being published by the Swedish Agency for Youth and Civil Society and sport research covering parents, young people and sports participation. The theoretical analysis has been inspired by Lamont and Molnár's (2002) concept of boundaries in order to increase our understanding of relational processes. Lamont and Molnár describe boundaries as defined by that which separates people or groups of people. Symbolic boundaries are represented by social actors categorizing objects, practices, time and space, whereas social boundaries are manifested in social difference (Lamont and Molnar, 2002). In focus when analysing symbolic boundaries are the creating, maintaining and contesting of institutionalized differences (e. g., class, gender, race, territorial inequality, etc.), and the capturing of dynamic dimensions of social or collective identity, cultural capital and membership (Lamont and Molnár, 2002). Symbolic resources are seen as conceptual distinctions, interpretive strategies and cultural practices/traditions generating feelings of similarity and social cohesion. Accordingly, the forming of the sports family as a pedagogical site is analysed through how values and perspectives on health, body and physical activity are structured as symbolic resources.

The positioning of the 'sports family'

To understand the delegates' reactions to the sports minister's speech, a short background of the Swedish model for organized sport and the Swedish society is needed. The *Nordic sport model* and the general discourse and philosophy around this model is a historical result of collective forces forming a popular movement of sport, marked by links to other voluntary popular social and political movements (Eichberg and Loland, 2010) in Sweden. The term 'popular movement' has strong links to what is seen as parts of civil society. In Sweden, popular movements contributed to the building of the 'welfare state' and the so-called '*folkhem*' during the first half of the 1900s. The term 'popular movement' covers three different dimensions: bodily movement, emotional movement and social movements: people participate in concrete bodily activities, they are moved by feelings, emotions, social interactions and relations, and, furthermore, social action and transactions occur when people meet in formal or informal networks oriented towards practical democracy. By defining the Swedish Sport Confederation as an independent non-governmental organization and part of the state's social and moral programme, state funding became possible in the early 1900s. But as several researchers note, the relations between the state and other parts of society are often complex and sometimes contrarious (Svedberg and Trädgårdh, 2007). Negotiations are typical features of these relations. Sweden is seen as one of the most individualistic countries in the world (Svedberg and Trädgårdh, 2007), but still in some sense embraces the idea of a 'folkhem': a collective product and symbol for welfare, equity and solidarity.

Sweden is consequently said to be a country governed by the state and shaped by social engineering, in concert with different agreements with the civil society (Svedberg and Trädgårdh, 2007). It is in this context that questions concerning the relationship between associations/organizations and problems/ issues affecting civil society emerge. Children's and youths' health and well-being is one such issue.

The sustainability of the popular movement of sport and with that the constru-ction of the sports family is based on the idea of contributing to public welfare by voluntary leadership and work, sports activities open for all, democracy and independency (Bergsgard and Norberg 2010). To belong to the cultural and social group of the sports family requires cultural capital within the sphere of leisure and sport that deals with educational capital, capital and skills attained in leisure practices, and the acquirement of the 'right' morals and tastes, the right kind of lifestyle (Tolonen, 2013). And as Macdonald and colleagues (2012) point out: *Sport is an embodied cultural practice that is invested with several biopolitical purposes beyond individual fulfillment* (MacDonald et al, 2012, p11). Examples of these investments are health, social cohesion and nation-building. People acquire capital and build identifications and values through a consciousness about distinctions and different kinds of capital and resources.

The 'will of inclusion' in the sports family, which strongly permeates the Nordic societies, is built on the assumptions of the inherited worthiness of sport, not least from a health and democratic development perspective. To some extent it becomes impossible to sit outside these circulated discourses. By joining the sports family each individual unit of family can take its responsibility and contribute to equity and solidarity and to the welfare of the nation. And as attainability in terms of sports for all is an important aspect of the state funding, there are few reasons to stay outside of the sports family. In the official policy document of Sports in Sweden, the sports family is described as follows:

> There is remarkable diversity in the Swedish sporting family. There are clubs that unite those lone wolves who, in rain and sleet, cover mile after mile of lonely roads, testing their own absolute limits. There are clubs that pay homage to team sports and collective ideas in which collabora-tion between individuals and the sum of individual skills determine the result. There is room for those who want to become stronger, improve their stamina, and develop their coordination, technique or tactics. But sports also form an important arena for social contacts in which old and young, able-bodied and disabled, men and women, native Swedes and immigrants, carefree keep-fitters and almost fanatically serious elite sportsmen and women can meet (Sports will, 2009, p14).

The quote acknowledges that there is room for everyone, regardless of moti-vation, background, special needs, etc. and that people are bound together through this family.

Governmental interventions for physical activity

The *Nordic sports model* has existed for over a century in Sweden, and has now moved into the post (post) modern era where physical inactivity, according to literature has become an important public health issue in relation to young people's health (Public Health Agency of Sweden, 2010, 2011, 2013/

2014). As a result of this trend, the Swedish sports movement has over the last decade been promoted as a crucial site for government intervention with several projects aiming at targeting new groups, promoting girls' sports and keeping young people practicing organized sports in their late teens. The site for this governmental intervention has been through the 'sports family', framed by the Sports Confederation and its special sports federation. The concrete action has been taken care of by local sports clubs as part of the sports family. In spite of these specific governmental interventions there has been a decline since 2002 both in the number of members in sports clubs and the total amount of executed sports activities. These trends suggest that interventions and extra financial support have not been successful (Swedish National Centre for Research in Sports, 2013). Evaluators have concluded that projects carried out in sports clubs strengthen already ongoing activities rather than being an engine for qualitative leaps in developing activities for engaging children and youth (Karp et al, 2014). These conclusions allude to the tensions that are played out in young people's recreational choices. For some groups of children and parents, the symbolic and social boundaries of the sports family seem to be transparent and a social group possible to bond and adhere to. The sportive families sit within the circulated discourses of the worthiness of sport. They appear to recognize and accept the structure, values and disciplining that goes with adult-governed pedagogical sites of sport practices (Karp, 2000; Augustsson, 2007; Svedberg and Trädgård, 2007; Eliasson, 2009; Wagnsson, 2009). For other units of families living within other family structures, the symbolic and social boundaries of the sports family are not that easy to transgress or connect to.

Added to the drawback of the interventions is also that sports profiled schools mainly attract students with Swedish background where the majority of parents are highly educated. Less than 5 per cent of the students come from ethnic minority groups (see, for example, Ferry, 2014). In other words, the symbolic and social boundaries of the sports family stretch over associations and into the education system as well. These findings evoke questions of the sustainability of the implicit contract between the state and the Sports Confederation; is it possible for this sports family to fulfil its role as a pedagogical site in the leisure sphere for the promoting of health and physical activity for all? This turns our interest towards leisure time as a site for health and recreational habits.

Leisure time as a site for health

Strangely enough, the relation between health, family and recreational habits during leisure time is not particularly well examined in Sweden. The attention is instead primarily focused on school and (psycho-social) health (SOU, 2001, 2010a, p79, 2010b, p80). What can be noted though is that the character of leisure time in Sweden – as in other countries globally – has changed in a relatively short period of time. New forms of communication and social media through internet have created a more disrupted landscape. According to the Swedish Agency for Youth and Civil Society (2007, 2011, 2012, 2014), former institutionalized and organized leisure time activities, often in interplay with associations, institutions and families, have lost their capacity to control time spent outside of school. Young people are spending more time at home, but are in touch with the world through the internet. These activities take place outside traditional disciplinary sites such as the school and even the family.

A recent study of almost 90,000 Swedish children and youth provides insights into the changing landscape of leisure time and recreational habits (Elofsson et al, 2015). Potentially problematic is that young people's recreation habits seem to be connected to aspects of self-experienced health and life quality. Few or no differences in health are reported between children and youth born in Sweden and children and youth born in Sweden with parents born abroad (Elofsson et al, 2015). And there are almost no differences between adolescents from underprivileged and privileged groups in terms of self-experienced health. Depending on country of origin, migration has resulted in differences in self-experienced health, especially among girls (Elofsson et al, 2015). Importantly though, groups of young people living in low status areas rate their *quality of life* lower than children and youth living in high status areas. Even more significantly for the purposes of this chapter, underprivileged groups state that school gives life meaning whereas adolescents in high status areas report that it is leisure time that gives meaning to life. Not surprisingly, children in high socio-economic status areas are very engaged in recreational activities, whereas children in low status areas would like to become engaged, but have problems finding their way into recreational activities (Elofsson et al, 2015; see also, e.g., Walseth, 2006a, 2006b, 2008). Problems are often due to a lack of activities, associations and sports clubs. Children and youth living with both parents, and with parents with a Swedish heritage/background, with above average material resources, are overrepresented in all kinds of different leisure time activities from arts schools to political engagement to sports involvement. This relationship is even stronger for children and young people engaged in sports activities as leisure time activities. There is also a significant difference in physical activity levels between the high and low privileged groups as much of the physical activity that young people do is within the frame of organized sport.

Accordingly, young people living in underprivileged areas are less satisfied with their leisure time situations, and are also less involved/engaged in the use of local and municipality activities and facilities. This can, in many cases, be related to the character of the place where they live. These places are often spoken of as 'white spots' as they are blank in numbers of associations and active sports club. If there are sports clubs active, the variations of sports are low, and soccer dominates (Lundvall, 2007, 2009). Hence, what children and youth do during their leisure time differs and becomes not only related to the resources of the families, but also to aspects of place, space and (class, ethnic) identity formation (Sernhede, 2011, Beach and Sernhede, 2011, Tolonen, 2013; see also, for example, Dagkas and Armour, 2012; and also Chapters 10, 13 and 14 in this volume). Low engagement and participation in sport may be a more complicated question than just lack of clubs. 'White spots' may also be a result of either a conscious act of resisting inclusion due to not being part of the circulating discourses of the worthiness of sport, or actually caused of being 'othered', excluded, not fully included in the sports family's 'will of inclusion' (Macdonald et al, 2012). Hence, to understand the engagement or non-engagement in the sports family and the participation in sports practices in underprivileged areas, several factors have to be considered.

Some commentators claim that young people's participation in sport and physical activities is a result of decisions negotiated within the context of their social environment, and mediated by the young person's views of self and their personal goals (Tolonen, 2013; see also Wright et al, 2003; Lee and Macdonald, 2010). By creating relations to different forms of activities and contexts, people develop feelings of belonging, and start to attach significance to different habits. In Bourdieu's terms, they acquire the taste for something. Developing a taste for something, or an orientation towards, for example, a physically active lifestyle has to do with symbolic and cultural resources; practices and traditions, but also with how symbolic and social boundaries between groups, place and space are experienced.

Belonging as part of symbolic values

An aspect of being a member of a social group is the kind of influence that is offered to young people when creating relations and meaning making, acknowledging similarities and differences. As described above, not all groups of children and adolescents experience access to the sports family, nor do they acquire feelings of belonging in organized sport. Often 'to belong to' is represented by feelings of being part of, to be counted on as a full member (Lundvall and Walseth, 2014). Feelings of exclusion, of not being invited into the family of sport, are expressed by feelings of not being seen, either by the coach or other team mates. In a study of two volleyball teams (coaches and players) situated in a larger city in Sweden, a common approach by the coaches was 'to make no distinction' between the players. The interviews with the players with diverse backgrounds revealed that this approach of ignoring intercultural perspectives, not being alert to when similarities and differences needed to be recognized and communicated led to feelings of being two groups of girls in the same team (Lundvall and Safizadeh, 2011). Other studies of inclusion of participants with diverse backgrounds suggest similar conclusions of 'not being part of'. Older adolescents with a diverse background that had gone through leadership courses in soccer for example, doubted their possibilities to succeed as coaches due to structural mechanisms and lack of social networks (Lundvall, 2007). Furthermore, parents with children participating in sports inclusion projects in underprivileged areas felt they were never asked to assist, or to contribute 'whatsoever' (Lundvall, 2007, 2009). The sports family seemed to be closed for those without the right symbolic and cultural resources. Bridging and bonding had difficulties to develop beyond the playing together and the realizing of shared values. This will impact on the feelings of belonging. Feelings of belonging can develop through participation in sport in different ways, either in terms of sharing and supporting: a will to become a part of a social practice, with its collective norms, rules and direct personal contact among members; and as a feeling of identity confirmation, a reciprocity, produced by participating that lead to a sense of meaningful participation (Lundvall and Walseth, 2014).

Despite the rapid development of technology and concurrent changes in the way that relations are formed, social context, families and friends still appear to be crucial for the meaning making of young people. To 'become' a sportive family is not only discursively produced as there is also a need of knowledge of the game, equipment, a car to help drive to matches, geographical knowledge of where the other teams' sports grounds are, the language to chit chat with other mums and dads on the side lines and so on.

In Swedish youth research and youth health politics, health and well-being are seen as aspects situated as a balance between body and psycho-social factors. These psycho-social factors are, for example, social relations, feelings of influence and belonging, school and work situation, economy and meaningful leisure time. Interestingly, the role of the sport and physical activity is hardly mentioned at all by youth research conducted by Swedish Agency for Youth and Civil Society.

One might well read this omission as a sign that children's and adolescents' health and wellbeing in relation to physical activity are taken care of, and that this 'care' is taken for granted. This assumption is surely tied to public perceptions of organizations in civil society generally and the Swedish Sports Confederation (and the social construction of the sports family), in particular. But as current literature on health, recreation, sport and physical activity suggests, we need a better understanding of the role social support plays in the context of health, recreation and physical activity; including how and when relations are built and by whom and where? (Bunke et al, 2013; Bunar, 2010). It is not physical health that is bothering young people's feeling of well-being and health. It is the experiencing of stress, loneliness, lack of relations that are troubling them (Public Health Agency of Sweden, 2010, 2011, 2013/2014). These are also common motives for leaving organized sports (see, for example, Coakely and Pike, 2009; Riksidrottsförbundet, 2010; Thedin Jakobsson et al, 2012).

Discussion

The social and symbolic group of the sports family faces a challenge. The construction of the sports family as a site for pedagogical work beyond individual fulfilment in relation to health, physical activity and sports is contested. That which in former times was a distinct trait of a popular movement characterized by bodily practicing under specific forms of freedom, practical democracy, the acquisition of social capital and responsibility might only be evident for some people. The Swedish 'sportive family' is becoming increasingly middle class. Organized adult-governed activities tend in this sense to be experienced as institutionalized activities surrounded by symbolic and social boundaries, distinguishing who has the right symbolic resources to belong to this specific social group of club members. Obviously, not all groups of adolescents, and especially not girls with minority background, find the accessibility or the feelings of belonging to the sports family as a pedagogical site for them.

The general belief in Sweden, like in other Western societies, is that sport is beneficial for many reasons. Sports policy-makers often assume that sport encourages desirable forms of citizenship, practical democracy in terms of influence, health, integration, exchange of intercultural knowledge, and formation and consolidation of social networks. However, sports research has seldom confirmed this view; rather, the research often challenges these assumptions (Dagkas and Armour, 2012; Coalter, 2007). Research has revealed that sport as a social and cultural practice rests upon Westernized ideals, a mode of 'whiteness' in the racial sense, and national identity. This Western-centric lifestyle is also accused of being built on an instrumental way of viewing body, bodily practices/exercise and health. The complexity of health and well-being in young people's and families' lives touches on bonding and bridging, on the building and creation of relations, a sharing of an individual but collective cultural identity. The last two decades with new public management politics has not only led to a more divergent society in Sweden. It has also resulted in a new market with commercialized sport for children and young, giving wealthy families new choices to support their children's physical activity. An even more intensified specialization at young age has also meant that groups of children drop out from sport as they are assessed as 'untalented'. These are new trends in Sweden. The global migration pattern underpins new culture interfaces where the taken for granted Nordic or Swedish sports model for physical activity, health and social development becomes stressed – as well as the will for inclusion.

The responsibility to individually and collectively take care of one's physical health has a long tradition in Sweden. To participate in bodily exercise has been part of the forming of the welfare state and the '*folkhem*' as part of a duty to contribute to public welfare, a collective identity shared with others; to learn the basics of how to live a healthy life. Swedes are regarded as a physically active nation (European Commission, 2010). Today, the former social democracy vision of a society built on 'equity and equality' is going through a process of instability, a disruption/turmoil, challenged by neoliberal discourses with a strong belief of the responsibility of the individual and market forces. This affects the sports movement where the investment values of early specialization, talent identification and commercialization challenges/ threatens the agreement between the state and the sports confederation. The symbolic and social boundaries that separate groups of families contain properties such as social, cultural and economic resources, and a collective understanding of what counts in the post (post) modern sports movement. To learn the consequences of selection and competition has become a dominant value within the sports family, relevant for a coming professional career (Wagnsson, 2009; Augustsson, 2007). And these experiences are seen by specific groups as valuable symbolic lessons, but difficult to combine with the view on health and well-being as represented by youth studies from the National Agency of Youth Affairs.

Conclusions

Several critical aspects emerge of how tensions around young people's recreational choices are played out in the context of health, physical activity and sport in Sweden. They touch on health and well-being as a rationale for the moving body, but they also touch upon emotional and social bonding and bridging. The question of why physical activity matters emerges as a crucial question to be answered and one that has important implications for policy and practice. The Swedish public health and sports minister's appeal to the sports family to help close health gaps in society is indicative of a sea change taking place around physical activity and Swedish sport. While sports parti-cipation in Sweden has long been seen from an instrumental perspective, the anticipated 'outcome' is shifting from 'civic participation in a democracy' to 'responsible care of the (biological) self'. This shift has already led to changes in the sports family and evidence suggests that boundaries are being redrawn. Far from closing gaps, we have proposed that broader neoliberal discourse and possibly even the health agenda itself is actually working to exclude a number of individuals and families from sport. Both survey data relating to demographics, and case study work with individuals and their families suggest that exclusion is happening along ethnic and class lines, a particularly con-cerning trend given that underprivileged members of society fare least well on most health indicators.

Health promotion is obviously an issue that the sports family will have to take seriously whether they want to or not. In the future, members of the various sporting bodies will need to meet politically mandated objectives in order to secure funding and support, if they do not already (implicitly, at least). Some kind of integration of health rationales with existing meanings of physical activity and its relevance is necessary. Fun, sense of community and belonging, fitness as opposed to health, and aesthetic experience all contribute to people's personal rationales for doing physical activity and sport. If and how these traditional dimensions can be connected with wider goals of improving population health are questions yet to be answered. It would seem to us that, first, how one answers these questions has much to do with how one defines health; and, second, connecting existing meanings of sports and health should be a conscious process rather than a process left to happen haphazardly and it is here that discursive change may prove generative rather than limiting.

Finally, as we have noted, within a context of increasing cultural heterogeneity, underprivileged families and families who do not conform to the nuclear model are less likely to become sportive families. We should add here that exclusion potentially has a secondary effect, if non-sportive families are stigmatized and labelled as unwilling to take part in the healthy practices of sport. In this sense, we do see a risk that sporting participation will become 'all but compulsory' and that non-participation will be seen as morally and economically irresponsible. Regardless of risks, the Swedish sports family will need to consider how they can be inclusive. While some information is emerging, there appears to be a need for more knowledge about how and why certain groups become sportive families and others do not. Within this complex and political context, future research can make a valuable contribution if the sports family shall continue to be an important pedagogical site for the contributing to health, social cohesion and practical democracy. One conclusion that emerges is that the sports family, as a social group of embodied cultural practice and part of a welfare state project, needs to be revitalized to allow new and other forms of symbolic resources and properties to grow in order to support a transgression of boundaries. In line with this is understanding more about what defines life quality and well-being in families' and young people's lives.

Note

1 The speech was held at a Sports Forum Meeting (9–10/11 2014) hosted by the Swedish Sports Confederation with delegates from the 70 different sports associations in Sweden. The topic for the Sports Forum was the strategic agenda for 2025.

References

Augustsson, C. (2007) *Unga idrottares upplevelser av föräldrapress* [*Children and youth in sport – experiences of parental pressure*]. PhD thesis. Karlstad: University of Karlstad.

Beach, D. and Sernhede, O. (2011) From learning to labour to learning for marginality: school segregation and marginalization in Swedish suburbs, *British Journal of Sociology of Education*, 32, (2), 257–274.

Bergsgaard, N. A. and Norberg, J. (2010) Sports policy and politics – the Scandinavian way, *Sport in Society: Cultures, Commerce, Media, Politics*, 13, (4), 567–582.

Blomdahl, U. (1990) *Folkrörelserna och folket*. [*The popular movements and the people*]. Stockholm: Carlsson. Stockholms universitet.

Blomdahl, U., Elofsson, S., Åkesson, M. and Lengheden, L. (2014) *Segrar föreningslivet? En studie av svenskt föreningsliv under 30 år bland barn och unga.* Rapport 2014: 15. [*Will the sports movement win? Report: Young Lifestyle.* 2014: 15]. Stockholm: Stockholms stad och Stockholms universitet.

Bunar, N. (2010) The geographies of education and relationships in a multicultural city – enrolling in a high-poverty, low-achieving school and choosing to stay there, *Acta Sociologica*, 53(2), 141–159.

Bunke, S., Apitzsch, E. and Bäckström, M. (2013) The impact of social influence on physical activity among adolescents – a longitudinal study, *European Journal of Sport Science*, 13, 1, 86–95.

Coakley, J. and Pike, E. (2009) *Sports in society: Issues and controversies.* London: McGraw-Hill Education.

Coalter, F. (2007) Sports clubs, social capital and social regeneration: 'ill-defined interventions with hard to follow outcomes'?, *Sport in Society: Culture, Commerce, Media, Politics*, 10(4), 537–559.

Dagkas, S. and Armour, K. (2012) *Inclusion and Exclusion through Youth Sport.* Oxon: Routledge.

Eichberg, H. and Loland, S. (2010) Nordic Sports – from social movements via emotional bodily movement – and back again, *Sport in Society: Culture, Commerce, Media, Politics*, 13(4), 679–690.

Elofsson, S., Blomdahl, U., Lengheden, L. and Åkesson, M. (2015) *Ungas livsstil i låg- och högstatusområden. En studie i åldersgruppen 13–16 år.* Stockholm: Stockholms stad och

Eliasson, I. (2009) *I skilda idrottsvärldar: barn, ledare och föräldrar i flick- och pojkfotboll.* PhD thesis. Umeå: Umeå universitet.

Ferry, M. (2014) *Idrottsprofilerad utbildning – i spåren av en avreglerad skola.* PhD thesis. Göteborg: Göteborgs universitet.

European Commission (2010) *Eurobarometer Sport and Physical Activity*, http://ec.europa.eu/public_opinion/archives/ebs/ebs_334_en.pdf.

Gottzén, L. and Kremer-Sadlik, T. (2012) Fatherhood and Youth Sports: A Balancing Act Between Care and Expectations, *Gender in Society*, 26 (4), 639–664.

Karp, S. (2000) *Barn, föräldrar och idrott. En intervjustudie om fostran inom fotboll och golf.* PhD thesis. Umeå: Pedagogiska institutionen, Umeå universitet.

Karp, S., Fahlén, J. and Löfgren, K. (2014) More of the same instead of qualitative leaps: a study of inertia in the Swedish sport system, *European Journal for Sport and Society*, 11(3), 301–320.

Lamont, M. and Molnár, V. (2002) The study of boundaries in the Social Sciences, *Annual Review of Sociology*, 28, 167–195.

Lee, J. and Macdonald, D. (2010) Are you just checking out our obesity or what? The healthism discourse and rural young women, *Sport Education and Society*, 15, 2, 203–221.

Lindroth, J. (1974) *Idrottens väg till folkrörelse.* PhD thesis. Uppsala: Uppsala univeritet.

Lindroth, J. (2004) *Ling – från storhet till upplösning i svensk gymnastikhistoria 1800–1950* [*Ling – from grandness to decline in Swedish history of Gymnastics*]. Eslöv, Sweden: Brutus Östlings bokförlag Symposion.

Lundvall, S. (2007) Handslagets speciella insatser med inriktning mot mångfald och integration, *Svensk Idrottsforskning* [*Journal of Swedish Sport Research*], 3/4, 66–69.

Lundvall, S. (2009) Idrott, mångfald och genus – hur blir svensk idrott mer färgrik och inkluderande? [Sport, multiculturalism and gender – How to make Swedish sport more including and colourful?] *Svensk Idrottsforskning* [*Journal of Swedish Sport Research*], 1, 27–30.

Lundvall, S. and Safizadeh, P. (2011) Möte mellan tillgänglighet och hinder – en explorativ studie om lokala idrottsföreningars arbete med mångfald och muslimska flickors tankar om sitt idrottsdeltagande, *i Svensk Beteendevetenskaplig forskning, SVEBI:s årsbok*, 49–70.

Lundvall, S. and Walseth, K. (2014) Integration and sports participation: Cultural negotiations and feelings of belonging, in *Women and sport, Scientific Report Series* http://www.sisuidrottsbocker.se/amnesomraden/kvinnorochidrott/ [accessed November 2014].

Macdonald, D., Pang, B., Knez, K., Nelson, A. and McCuaig, L. (2012) The will for inclusion. In S. Dagkas, and K. Armour (eds.) *Inclusion and Exclusion through Youth Sport*. Oxon: Routledge, 9–23.

Norberg, J. (2004) *Idrottens väg till folkhemmet. Studier i statlig idrottspolitik 1913– 1970*. PhD thesis. Stockholm: Stockholms universitet.

Peterson, T. (2008) When the field of sport crosses the field of physical education, *Educare*, 3(3), 83–97.

Public Health Agency of Sweden [Statensfolkhälsoinstitut] (2010) *Skolbarns hälsovanor i Sverige 2010*. Stockholm: Folhälsomyndigheten.

Public Health Agency of Sweden [Statensfolkhälsoinstitut] (2011) *Hälsa på lika villkor. Syfte och bakgrund till frågorna i nationella folkhälsoenkäten. Rapport 2011:09*.

Public Health Agency of Sweden [Statensfolkhälsoinstitut] (2013/2014) *Skolbarns hälsovanor i Sverige 2013/2014*. Stockholm: Folhälsomyndigheten.

Riksidrottsförbundet (2010) *Idrott och integration – en statistisk undersökning* [*Sports and Integration*]. Stockholm: Riksidrottsförbundet.

Sernhede, O. (2011) School, youth culture and territorial stigmatization in Swedish metropolitan districts, *Young*, 19(2), 159–180.

Sports will (2009) Riksidrottsförbundet.

SOU (2008) *Föreningsfostran och tävlingsfostran: en utvärdering av statens stöd till idrotten: betänkande*. Idrottsstödsutredningen. Stockholm: Fritze, p59.

SOU (2000) *Hälsa på lika villkor – nationella mål för folkhälsan*. Stockholm: Fritze, p91.

SOU (2010a) *Pojkars och flickors psykiska hälsa i skolan: en kunskapsöversikt*. Stockholm: Fritze, p79.

SOU (2010b) *Skolan och ungdomars psykosociala hälsa*. Stockholm: Fritze, p80.

Svedberg, L. and Trädgårdh, L. (2007) *Focus 07 – en analys av ungas hälsa och utsatthet*. Unga, civilsamhälletochvälfärd. Ungdomsstyrelsen [Swedish Agency for Youth and Civil Society]. Stockholm: Ungdomsstyrelsen, pp113–132.

Swedish Agency for Youth and Civil Society [Ungdomsstyrelsen] (2007) *Focus 07 – en analys av ungas hälsa och utsatthet*. Stockholm: Ungdomsstyrelsen.

Swedish Agency for Youth and Civil Society [Ungdomsstyrelsen] (2011) *När var hur – om ungas kultur*. Stockholm: Ungdomsstyrelsen.

Swedish Agency for Youth and Civil Society [Ungdomsstyrelsen] (2012) *Om deltagande i föreningsidrott Ung och fritid 2012*. Stockholm: Ungdomsstyrelsen.

Swedish Agency for Youth and Civil Society [Ungdomsstyrelsen] (2014) *Fokus14 – ungas fritid och organisering*. Stockholm: Ungdomsstyrelsen.

Swedish National Centre for Research in Sports [Centrum föridrottsforskning] (2013) *Statens stöd till idrotten – uppföljning 2014:1*. Stockholm: Centrum för idrottsforskning.

Swedish National Centre for Research in Sports [Centrum föridrottsforskning]. (2012) *Vem platsar i laget?* [*Who fits into the team?*]. Stockholm: Centrum för idrottsforskning.

Thedin Jakobsson, B., Lundvall, S., Redelius, K.,and Engström, L.-M. (2012) Almost all start but who continues? A longitudinal study of youth sport participation in Swedish sport clubs, *European Journal of Physical education*, 18 (1), 13–18.

Tolonen, T. (2013) Youth Cultures, Lifestyles and Social Class in Finnish Contexts, *Young*, 21(1), 55–73.

Wagnsson, S. (2009) *Föreningsidrott som socialisationsmiljö. En studie av idrottens betydelse för barn och ungdomars psykosociala utveckling*. PhD thesis. Karlstad: Karlstad University Studies.

Walseth, K. (2006a) Young Muslim Women and Sport: The impact of identity work, *Leisure Studies*, 25, 1, 75–94.

Walseth, K. (2006b) Sport and belonging, *International Review for the Sociology of Sport*, 41, 447–464.

Walseth, K. (2008) Bridging and bonding social capital in sport – experiences of young women with an immigrant background, *Sport, Education and Society*, 13, 1, 1–17.

Wright, J., Macdonald, D. and Groom, L. (2003) Physical Activity and Young People: Beyond Participation, *Sport, Education and Society*, 8(1), 17–33.

16 Family narratives of PE, physical activity and sport

Contingent stories

Fiona Dowling

Introduction

Imperatives to be physically active for the purposes of self-realization or preventive healthcare saturate public discourse in Norway as in other developed countries. Despite Norway's status as being one of the most egalitarian societies in the world with a greater distribution of wealth and access to higher education than most nations (SSB, 2013), social inequalities prevail with regard to participation in physical culture (Seippel et al, 2011; Vaage, 2004). By adopting a narrative approach and drawing upon Bourdieu's (1984) analytic tools of cultural and social reproduction, this chapter explores the processes by which young people and their families from a range of social class backgrounds either invest in and/or reject the dominant discourses about physical activity. It draws upon data from a qualitative study that focused upon parents'/guardians' and young peoples' narratives of physical education (PE) classes in schools and the stories they told about the meaning of physical activity (including organised sport, fitness training, outdoor pursuits) in their lives. What physical activity practices are valued and/or marginalized, and why? By reconstructing some of the participants' tales it aims to draw the reader into the complex socio-economic contingencies of families' narratives of engagement in physical culture.

Theoretical perspectives

A narrative approach recognizes that narration is fundamental to human meaning-making (Riessman, 2008). Individuals and families construct themselves and make sense of life experiences via the stories they tell to themselves and others. Individual and collective embodied experience is mediated and made 'real' via the linguistic shaping and telling of stories and the processes of their consumption. The meanings associated with physical activity are co-constructed and inevitably relational: tellers and 'listeners' are active meaning-making agents and 'small', or what we can call personal stories, are linked to 'big' or societal stories that are socio-economically and culturally situated (Phoenix, 2008). We do not all share the same repertoire of storytelling resources about the meaning of physical activity: the privileged have greater access to culturally preferred narratives than the socially marginalised (Gubrium and Holstein, 2009). Narratives are therefore also about power and the distribution of resources. Tales can be used to position people against their will, such as in the case of some current government narratives concerning the perceived obesity crisis that suggest overweight individuals are lacking self-control and have abhorrent fat, 'unhealthy' and immoral sedentary bodies (Burrows and Wright, 2007). In keeping with the idea that storytelling is a form of social action, stories about physical activity can thus be used not only to make sense of personal experiences (past, present and those imagined in the future) and one's position in the social world, but also as a means for families to pass on shared experiences and privileged values.

Family narratives are central to processes of socialisation or the accumulation of cultural capital (knowledge, skills, education), including narratives of physical capital (Bourdieu, 1984). Economic capital (wealth and income), social capital (membership in various groups or networks) and symbolic capital (reputation or honour) can interact in varying degrees with cultural capital with regard to narrating the practices of physical activity and sport. The field of the family forms individuals' 'habitus' (a socially constituted set of dispositions providing individuals with class-dependent, predisposed ways of categorising and relating to familiar and novel situations) and 'taste' (schemes of perception, thought and action, and a 'world view' that are reconciled with these dispositions) (Bourdieu, 1980, cited in Shilling, 2004). A 'taste' for sports participation is therefore inextricably linked to an individual's socially classed habitus and material constraints, although it is important to recognise that whilst deeply embodied it is not beyond transformation (Shilling, 2004). Organized sport or PE may, for example, represent fields that can provide sufficient unfamiliarity so as to challenge the taken-for-grantedness of the habitus (Bourdieu, 1994). By analysing the participants' socially classed physical activity narratives, we can thus illuminate how and in what ways their choice of social practices are linked to processes of power (how individuals or groups achieve their ends as against those of others) and whether, and how, they contribute to social reproduction or transformation. When reflecting upon the ways in which cultural and physical capital are accrued it is useful to keep in mind both the production of capital as 'the development of bodies in ways recognised as possessing value in social fields', as well as its potential for conversion in different fields such as work and education (Shilling, 2004, p474). A slim, fit body enjoys, for example, greater status than overweight, untrained bodies in postmodern societies: it has a greater 'exchange value' (Featherstone, 1991).

Research on families, social class and physical activity

Much of the international research on social class and young people's engagement in physical activity and PE/school sport has primarily focused on the views of the young people themselves albeit with parents' occupational and/or educational attainment level as a measure of their social class locations (e.g., O'Flynn and Petersen, 2007; Stuij, 2013; Quarmby and Dagkas, 2010, 2013). Pfister and Reeg (2006) and Macdonald et al's (2004) studies did, on the other hand, pay greater attention to the parents' attitudes. The German study concluded that the higher the parents' education, not least when both mother and father are academics, the more likely children are to be fit and competent movers, as well as have a normal body weight. They also identified links between the parents' own levels of physical activity and that of their offspring, and in particular the significance of fathers' activity levels and the way in which they more often acted as 'partners' in their children's sports participation (Pfister and Reeg, 2006). The Australian study also revealed the significance of 'intergenerational habitus' (Bourdieu, 1984) in parents' and children's physical activity patterns, in addition to peer networks, and not least, economic resources (Macdonald et al, 2004). Indeed, most of the parents, irrespective of their social class, perceived physical activity to be important for their children, not least for their health; but single parents and low-income families encounter a greater number of barriers that prevent them from providing such opportunities.

In England (Vincent et al, 2004) and in the US (Lareau, 2003), more general studies on parenting indicate that one such barrier might be related to class-contingent views of child-rearing and early socialization. For middle-class parents, physical activity and sports participation is part of the 'concerted cultivation' of their children's cultural capital whereas working class parents are more likely to rely on an attitude of the 'accomplishment of natural growth' (Lareau, 2003). The former is linked to a cultural repertoire exhibiting a strong sense of entitlement whereas the latter reflects a sense of constraint. Evans and Davies (2010) argue that the mushrooming of so-called private enterprise physical education, like toddler gymnastics groups or baby swimming classes, is symbolic of the hunger of the middle and upper classes to cultivate an appropriate embodiment in a postmodern society where ideal, fit, active bodies are highly valued. Stefansen and Aarseth's (2011) Norwegian study would indicate a similar trend and illustrates the degree and emotional magnitude to which middle class parents are willing to invest in their children's leisure pursuits.

With regard to the Norwegian sport and PE context, since the mid-1970s children/youth's competitive sport has been organised under the auspices of the Norwegian Confederation of Sports and the school PE curriculum has been framed within a broader notion of all-round physical education for health and recreation (Augestad, 2003). PE is a compulsory core subject throughout students' schooling, thus providing all young people with some form of learning and experience of physical activity. Sport, on the other hand, is a voluntary leisure activity (Seippel, 2002) that relies upon family interest despite generous public funding, with parents/guardians often acting as coaches or administrators for their children's teams. Although many young people are involved in a sport, their participation levels vary considerably according to gender and ethnicity: in 2010, three out of four 12-year-old boys/girls reported they are active in a club activity, but the number who drop out increases dramatically post 14 years old, particularly with respect to girls' participation, and in general, children/youth with an ethnic minority background are significantly less involved (http://ungdata.no/proc/print?id=22436&sibid=0&print=yes). Seippel et al (2011) revealed a significant relation between youths' perceived economic status (social class) and sports participation, although this data could not determine whether it was primarily economics or other lifestyle issues that affected this pattern. The narrative study presented below sheds some light onto these dynamics of families' socially classed engagement in physical activity.

Fragments of physical activity narratives from different social class locations

The narratives presented here have been crafted from qualitative data selected from in-depth interviews with ten young people from a range of social class backgrounds and their parents/guardians (six interviews with both mother and father; three interviews with fathers; one interview with a mother). The interviews were carried out separately, at a time and place chosen by the participant to enable her/him to feel more at ease and with the view to generating rich data. The data have been analysed for its content (what themes can be identified) (Riessman, 2008), as well as for, 'the circumstances of storytelling' (the way, and contexts of their mediation) (Gubrium and Holstein, 2009, p21).

Due to the confines of the chapter, the narratives are drawn from just two case families: a working-class and an upper middle-class family. While they cohere with some of the tales told in similarly socially positioned families, they are not intended to be representative. They are context-dependent reconstructions of particular families' narratives. The aim is for these authentic, life-like representations (Eisner, 1997) to invite the reader to revisit taken-for-granted notions of 'choice' about physical activity and illuminate the complexity beyond the single case. Following Polkinghorne (1995, p7), the narratives aim to unveil the participants' attempts to unravel, clarify and provide plots ('a type of conceptual scheme by which a contextual meaning of individual events can be displayed') that explain the decisions they make concerning participation in different forms of physical activity and PE or their rejection. The stories are crafted by the researcher but remain close to interview data. All names are pseudonyms.

Sheraz's and Sohails's narratives of physical activity

Sohail is 16 years old, the son of a first generation immigrant from Pakistan, Sheraz. They live together with Sohail's mother, sister and brother in a flat in an eastern suburb of a major city. The suburb is characterized as having a mixed socio-economic profile and is multicultural with approximately a 40 per cent immigrant population. Sohail is in the final year of middle school education. He has only lived in Norway for two years because he was sent with his mother and siblings to live in Pakistan for many years. Sheraz owns two corner shops and a taxi that he drives. He feels he belongs to the working class but he imagines a middle-class future for his children.

Fragments from Sohail's physical activity and PE narratives

I just love running! You see, in Pakistan we never did things like that! Doing warm-ups, that's so cool. I really like PE lessons though I'm not good at most things. Yunno football, volleyball, all that athletics stuff, jumping, hopping, yunno. Never done none of it before! I'm the worst in the class in football, 'coz they've all played loads, like. But running, the other day we had a competition – so cool! Prefer that than when I'm laughed at 'cause I can't do things. Know what I mean? They're all laughing and I'm dead embarrassed but they just don't get it, how difficult centring the football is. Sometimes I daren't take part, I just sort of pretend, like. Run 'round and not get noticed.

Yunno, once I did try to go to football training. Some of the lads accused me of always stayin' in, like. That I ought to train with them, have fun. But Dad wouldn't be having any of it. Said I'm not strong enough. He borrowed me my brother's hand weights, said I had to get stronger. It was after that he spoke to me uncle about the cricket team. I play cricket with me cousins and uncle, me brother. I'd played cricket in Pakistan so Dad said it would be better for me. There's this team of Pakistanis, play in the park in summer, like. Me Dad watches us when he's got time but he works most of the time. Shame we don't play at school 'cause then I'd show 'em! Then I could get a better grade, not just average. I'm trying to up me number of sit-ups and push-ups but I don't think I'll ever get a 6.[1] That's only for the likes of 'em on the football team, the sporty ones. And I need good grades to get into the best upper school. Mind you, maths is more important an' it's looking good, I got 6 mid-term!

... No I didn't mean PE's not important. It's good not to sit still all day, good to keep fit, for health and that. But – I can't really explain it, it's just better to get a good mark in maths. I go daily to homework help and there's no homework in PE, like, is there? Yunno. Me Dad wants me to be a doctor. I want to be an engineer. Me brother and sister are both good at school. I wanna do good, too.

...Yeah, it wasn't easy to start with but I've been on one of them special courses, learnt Norwegian, like. I also get homework help, as I told you. I have some mates now. One's from Poland, one's from Afghanistan, but most of 'em are like me, from Pakistan. I don't have any Norwegian friends, no. That's OK. I have to stay home a lot. Do homework or I'm on my PC, listen to music. In the summer we kicked a football around if weren't shouted at. Yunno it's not allowed in the flat gardens. Me Dad bought me a used bike so I cycled a bit with me mates here and there, to the shopping centre to hang out. They wanted to swim in the lake when it was dead hot, like, but I can't swim. Terrified me of water. Me mates, some of 'em go to boxing. I went about 5 times but it was tiring and boring. Me Dad said I had to stop. But I have the cricket. I've been made captain!

I'd like to dance, Hip Hop, yunno? But it's difficult with homework etc. I dance sometimes at family weddings, bangla like. ... No, I don't do sports in the winter. We did have two to three lessons once, borrowed some skis and skates. Cool! But I haven't tried after that, no. Like I told you, I train a bit of weights. When I'm old enough I want to go to the fitness studio with me brother. That's gotta be cool! Pump up me chest and biceps. Can protect myself, like. Me and me mates we arm wrestle. I'm getting stronger! We compete at push-ups sometimes. You've gotta look strong!

Fragments from Sheraz's physical activity and PE narratives

It's funny. I am liking now to be more busy and sweaty! I am training. A true Norwegian nearly! You know, when I am coming to Norway, I was a fit man. Army, you see. Army in Pakistan! Me, my father and his father before him. I am playing cricket, too! In the streets, in the park, wherever we can, you know! But arriving in Norway, no cricket in freezing cold! Just forest and I am not understanding all these people going into the forest. Why go into the cold forest? You see what I mean? Now I am understanding more, after 20 years! And now I am not working three jobs. When working three jobs you are not thinking about the fitness, eh? I am busy and tired. Supporting my family. Sending money back to Pakistan. Working, working. My wife and children are there. Duty. My wife has to look after her parents and the children are getting an excellent education at the private school in Islamabad. Very good education. English. I am not affording this in Norway but in Pakistan I am affording it. You know I owned a shop? Now a taxi! Good for the income, but not good for the heart! Now my Doctor telling me every time, are you exercising? Exercising, me! I say to him, do you think I have time to exercise?

This fitness project in my local community, it is very good. I learn to exercise again. The instructor's my sergeant major! Once a week in the school gym and I am doing sit-ups in the living room! Last week I took my wife for a walk near our home. She is saying me that she's too tired, climbing all the day the stairs at the work, but I insist! The children are doing some cricket and the older ones go to the fitness centre. But it's the education that comes first. Sohail, he is liking the cricket. It's good not to be on the streets, not to be forced into a street gang. Me and my wife we worry about the crime and Pakistani gangs. ... No, I'm not wanting Sohail to dance or play football. He's too weak and my wife's religious. He's not to be dancing with the girls, like the Norwegians, no! We think there are many opportunities here in Norway, big opportunities, so education's important. And we're not used to skiing and things like this. And it costs money with three children!

I am thinking as long as he's liking the PE it is OK with me. We don't really talk about it. He must not be getting the belly like mine, though! It's important with the education. I am not having the education, other than the basic. I ask him about maths and subjects like that. I am very strict I suppose. No chatting on the PC, things like that. Waste of time!

Anne's, Henrik's and Fredrikke's narratives of physical activity

Fredrikke is 16 years old and lives with her parents, Anne (housewife, previously a nurse) and Henrik (an architect). Fredrikke's sister is away studying at university. The family home is a large, detached house in a wealthy city centre suburb of a city. Here 16 per cent of the population are immigrants, half of whom come from western countries. Fredrikke attends a nearby upper school, studying for her baccalaureate. The family own a summer cottage at the coast and a cabin in the mountains.[2]

Fredrikke's narratives of physical activity

I simply love PE! It's a break from all the theory and you can just 'let go'. I like most things. Generally we have a lot of ball games, occasionally some gymnastics, but I try to do my best whatever it is! Everyone thinks PE's great fun, don't they? As well as learning different skills in the various activities, recently we've learned about nutrition. Really important stuff – learning for life! Everyone ought to eat healthy food and be active, so it's good to learn about it. ... What grade I get? Well, I had a 5 this term. I'd like to improve on that. I always try my utmost and I'm active out of school which is an advantage. ... Yes, my parents ask me what I've done. Not each week but they're interested to hear if I'm particularly keen to tell them something. They tend to help me with homework in other subjects, though.

But like I was telling you earlier, I've been very active as long as I can remember and my parents have always encouraged and supported me and my sister. They drove us to RG training,[3] especially Mamma. She got us started, I suppose. I was only three years old so I can't really remember. She wanted us to follow in her footsteps. They've supported my choice to start the dancing, too. I go to a private dance school now where you can try out all sorts of dance genres like funk, Hip Hop. It's fantastic! I can't say I miss all the travel with the RG competitions – quite often we had to fly and stay at hotels etc. It was fun but you get a bit fed up with it. But it's like I told you, I like to keep fit and healthy. All my friends do, too. They're all involved in some sort of sport. ... Now its winter we might go downhill skiing together, you know.

... We all walk the dog, but no, we don't exercise together apart from when we're at the cabin, downhill skiing, or at the coast in the summer when we might swim or sail together. Perhaps cycle. We're all active in our own way, I suppose. We do things together when we're abroad on holiday. We were in London at half-term and France last summer. That was fun!

Anne's and Henrik's narratives of physical activity

Yes, I suppose we're an active family, but we don't think about it really. Fredrikke's followed in my footsteps. I've driven her all over Norway to compete! Not to mention all the training!

I've done my fair share of driving, too, at least when my work load's permitted me, and don't forget Anne, I did sit in the sports club's governing body for years! And organised their jumble sales!

Yes, but you're often working and then you prioritise your squash! That's how it is. I go to the health studio 4 times a week, don't I! Recently I've hired a personal trainer to learn more about weight-training – fascinating! And I walk the dog daily 'cause I'm at home. You see, I stopped nursing some years ago to manage the family – follow up homework, take them to training, you know.

I'm often abroad with work, you see. I used to compete in sailing until I turned 30. National championships! Regional champion! Still participate in the Færder race.[4] Very social but it's a tough race! We had a summer cottage by the sea so sailing was part of growing up. Downhill skiing, too, when I was younger. Grew up in a family where skiing, mountain walking was the norm, you know! We used to play on skis in the woods behind the house or at our cabin in the mountains. Nowadays everything has turned so organised and commercial, more's the pity! I think you can learn a lot, though, from taking part in sport. Through RG the girls have learned to focus, concentrate and be organised. To stand on a stage, present themselves. I'm sure it spills over into school when they have to present work. ... Education is so very fundamental to life and of course it starts in the family. Learning begins early! Personally, I think PE could be removed from the curriculum, make way for the really important subjects like Norwegian, maths, languages. You can exercise after school, for goodness sake!'

I disagree, Henrik. They get to learn about muscles, training principles, that's a good thing. And they need a break from lessons and it gives Fredrikke energy to do homework. And we want her to do well at school, go onto study at university. Her grade in PE counts, so that's positive, too. A bonus she reaps from all her extra-curricula activity!

Reflecting upon the contingencies of the narratives

At first glance we might think that the physical activity narratives share a similar positive attitude towards the 'big' story (Phoenix, 2008) of physical activity. A closer inspection of the storytellers' logic reveals, however, significantly different habitus and taste that, in turn, reflect the two case families' socially classed doxa (Bourdieu, 1984). By paying attention to the 'small stories', we learn, for example, that Sheraz perceives PE as marginal to the 'real business' of his son's schooling and sports participation is viewed as a distraction from homework or time spent with the family. He imparts an instrumental view of physical activity (Shilling, 1993) to Sohail: Norwegian clubs are not for the 'likes of us' but cricket provides cultural ties with the Pakistani diasporic community and general fitness can prevent heart disease. As a first generation immigrant, Sheraz's social circumstances restrict his own and his wife's investment in physical culture; physical activity is marginalised in relation to family narratives of settling down in Norway, securing basic necessities and investing in the next generation's social mobility via education. Within a culture of natural growth (Lareau, 2003) Sohail is left to cycle or play outside his flat. His parents' cultural preferences, as well as economic means (disposable income and type of employment), limit the possibilities for him to participate in 'mainstream' organized sport. Though he sometimes longs to play football, Sohail reconciles himself with the seeming impossibility of his desire due to a perceived lack of agency. To date PE has not challenged his habitus nor seemingly expanded his physical capital and the family's narrative about physical activity does not equip him with adequate resources to be able to 'successfully' take part in PE. Logically from the storyteller's position, Sohail's makes sense of his life's experiences around a plot that awards greater significance to theoretical subjects (e.g., 'there's no homework help in PE') and explains his relative poor performance as due to his recent arrival in Norway ('never done games before'). Inadvertently, the narrative works to uphold a socially classed hierarchy of physical identities and keeps him on the margins of access to today's 'big' healthy, active lifestyles discourse.

In contrast, Fredrikke's physical capital has been concertedly cultivated (Lareau, 2003) from a young age across a range of fields (e.g., the family, institution of sport, private market) to the degree that school PE can almost appear superfluous. Henrik and Anne narrate tales of intergenerational habitus and a doxa that constructs physical activity as a meaningful human past time. They nurture their own physical capital but also contribute to Fredikke's sports club's voluntary workforce; they enjoy flexible working hours and a good economy that allow for this. When Fredrikke's taste for organized sport declines, they can afford to pay for an alternative activity as integral to their taken-for-granted active lifestyle among 'people like us'. Despite Henrik's marginalisation of PE in relation to other subjects, PE's grade is nevertheless valued for its potential conversion into education capital and the family's narrative is steeped in a sense of entitlement – less than a grade 5 is unthinkable. The family also recognise the importance of learning social skills and the social networks available via sport, as well as the potential to accrue health benefits and status attached to an ideal, fit body in contemporary society. The family's seemingly innocent physical activity stories work, in fact, to uphold the middle-class distinction that active lifestyles bestow and illustrate the power that culturally preferred narratives distribute (Gubrium and Holstein, 2009).

Concluding comments

Together, these family narratives of physical activity and PE provide sports organizations, policy-makers and the PE profession with useful tools for understanding the complex webs of power at play when inviting young people to enter physical activity arenas under well-intended, but wildly misleading slogans, like 'Sport for all' or 'meritocratic education'. They illustrate how families' social class locations interact with other markers, such as ethnicity, to influence 'choices' about participation in PE, physical activity and sport. The narratives show how families' habitus interact with current physical activity discourses to often reproduce, rather than transform, physical capital and demonstrate how young people cannot simply narrate investment in physical activity. Certainly, from a narrative perspective, an individual's sense of self is boundless and therefore open for change: our present selves are inevitably an expression of revising and editing the memories of the past within the self of the present, as well as containing elements of imagined futures (Gubrium and Holstein, 2009). Yet, a young person's ability to re-story her/his physical activity and PE narratives is inextricably bound to the structures in which s/he lives, not least socio-economic contingencies, and more often than not, is closely linked to her/his parents'/guardians' physical activity narratives.

Note

1 1 Norwegain students are assessed in PE from year 8. Grade 6 is the highest and 1 the lowest grade. Grades in PE count in a student's overall assessment grade with regard to upper school entrance and post-tertiary education.
2 Twenty per cent of households in Norway own second homes (http://forskning.no/hus-og-hjem/2008/06/bolig-i-hus-og-hytte).
3 RG training is defined as rhythmic gymnastics.
4 Yacht race that brings together some of the flashiest, most spectacular recreational boats in the North Atlantic area, as well as their skilled crews and affluent owners.

References

Augestad, P. (2003) *Skolering av kroppen. Om kunnskap og makt i kroppsøvingsfaget.* Doktoravhandling. Bø: Høgskolen i Telemark.

Bourdieu, P. (1984) *Distinction: A social critique of the judgement of taste.* London: Routledge.

Bourdieu, P. (1994) *In Other Words.* Cambridge: Polity Press.

Burrows, L. and Wright, J. (2007) Prescribing practises: shaping healthy children in schools, *International Journal of Children's Rights,* 15(6), 83–98.

Divine, F. and Savage, M. (2005) The cultural turn, sociology and class analysis. In: F. Divine, M. Savage, J. Scott and R. Crompton, eds. *Rethinking class. Culture, identities and lifestyle.* Basingstoke, Hampshire: Palgrave Macmillan, pp1–23.

Eisner, E. (1997) The new frontier in qualitative research, *Qualitative Inquiry,* 3(3), 259–273.

Evans, J. and Davies, B. (2010) Family, class and embodiment: Why school physical education makes so little difference to post-school participation patterns in physical activity schools in the West Midlands, *Physical Education Matters,* 3(2), 33–36.

Featherstone, M. (1991) The Body in Consumer Culture. In: M. Featherstone, M. Hepworth and B. Turner (eds.) *The Body: Social Process and Cultural Theory.* London: Sage Publications, pp170–196.

Gubrium, J. and Holstein, J. (2009) *Analyzing Narrative Reality.* London: Sage Publications.

Lareau, A.. (2003) *Unequal Childhoods: Class, Race, and Family Life.* Berkeley, CA: University of California Press.

Macdonald, D., Rodger, S., Ziviani, J., Jenkins, D., Batch, J. and Jones, J. (2004) Physical Activity as A Dimension of Family Life for Lower Primary School Children, *Sport, Education and Society,* 9(3), 307–325.

O'Flynn, G. and Petersen, E. B. (2007) The 'good life' and the 'rich portofolio': Young women, schooling and neoliberal subjectification, *British Journal of Sociology of Education,* 28(4), 459–472.

Pfister, G. and Reeg, A. (2006) Fitness as 'social heritage': A study of elementary school pupils in Berlin, *European Physical Education Review,* 12(1), 5–29.

Phoenix, A. (2008). Analysing narrative contexts. In: M. Andrews, C. Squire and M. Tamboukou (eds.) *Doing Narrative Research.* London: Sage Publications, pp64–77.

Quarmby, T. and Dagkas, S. (2010) Children's engagement in leisure time physical activity: exploring family structure as a determinant, *Leisure Studies*, 29(1), 53–66.

Riessman, C. K. (2008) *Narrative Methods for the Human Sciences*. London: Sage Publications.

Polkinghorne, D. (1995) Narrative configuration in qualitative analysis. In: J. Amos Hatch and R. Wisniewski (eds.) *Life history and narrative*. London: Falmer Press, pp5–23.

Seippel, Ø. (2002) Volunteers and Professionals in Norwegian Sports Organisations, *Voluntas: International Journal of Voluntary and Nonprofit Organisations*, 13(3), 253–270.

Seippel, Ø., Strandbu, Å. and Sletten, M. A. (2011) *Ungdom og trening. Endring over tid og sosiale skillelinjer. Rapport 3/11*. [*Youth and physical activity. Changes over time and social divisions. Report 3/11*]. Oslo: Norsk Institutt for forskning om oppvekst, velferd og aldring.

Shilling, C. (1993) *The Body and Social Theory*. London: Sage Publications.

Shilling, C. (2004) Physical capital and situated action: a new direction for corporeal sociology, *British Journal of Sociology of Education*, 25(4), 473–487.

Solesnes, O. (2010) Barnekroppen og idretten. Ein historisk analyse av barneidrett i Noreg1937–1976. In: K. Steinsholt and K. P. Gurholt (ed.) *Aktive liv: idrettspedagogiske perspektiver på kropp, bevegelse og dannelse*. Trondheim: Tapir forlag, pp51–69.

SSB (2013) *Likestilling – avhengig av hvor vi bor* [*Statistics Norway. Equality – depending where we live*], http://www.ssb.no/befolkning/artikler-og-publikasjoner/likestilling-avhengig-av-hvor-vi-bor.

Stefansen, K. and Aarseth, H. (2011) Enriching intimacy: the role of the emotional in the 'resourcing' of middle-class children, *British Journal of Sociology of Education*, 32(3), 389–405.

Stuij, M. (2013) Habitus and social class: A case study on socialisation into sports and exercise, *Sport, Education and Society*, http://dx.doi.org/10.1080/13573322.2013.827568.

Vaage, O. F. (2004) Mest mosjon og idrett blant de med høy inntekt og utdanning. *Samfunnsspeilet*, http://www.ssb.no/kultur-og-fritid/artikler-og-publikasjoner/mest-mosjon-og-idrett-bl.

17 Families, disability and sport

Hayley Fitzgerald

Introduction

> Cricket is a big family thing ... . It's only natural I like cricket, like it's always been round me. (Dave)

> When we're talking about football, dad'll treat us both the same. Like, will talk about my game and Wills', he's fair like that and you can see he's interested in both of us and I'm not missing out. When he starts talking to his mates he doesn't stop, god he goes on and on and I like it 'cause he's telling his mates about my football. (Tom)

> Me mum plays netball but apart from that we don't do sport. We're not into it. It's not what we're into at all. If there's nothing else on the telly, dad'll watch football but he's not bothered. He's into computers, that's what me and dad do. (Andy)

As these extracts illustrate the family can be a significant touchstone influencing and shaping young people's understandings and engagement in sport and leisure (Côté and Hay, 2002; Haycock and Smith, 2014). Dave is conscious that cricket forms a deep-rooted connection within his family and he believes it is inevitable that he is also immersed within this family activity. Similarly, Tom has a strong sense of the bond and pride football has stimulated between his brother and dad. In contrast, Andy is more interested in non-sporting leisure pursuits and seems influenced by his dad's interest in computers. Whilst the experiences of each of these boys are different they convey an awareness of the influence family has on their sporting interests. These accounts offer an alternative perspective to those often reported by parents, siblings and carers (Farrell and Krahn, 2014). Like Abbott (2013) I believe researchers have a responsibility to include, and listen to, the voices of young disabled people. This is a responsibility that sports researchers often fail to adequately address. Indeed, in this chapter I centralize the insights of three disabled boys and explore the interrelationships between family, disability and sport. In doing this their individual stories will help to shed light on how social and cultural factors contribute to shaping these young disabled people's sporting lives within the family.

The chapter begins by outlining how Bourdieu's conceptual tools can be effectively used to explore the embodied identities of young disabled people within the family. Following this, three short interview extracts are offered that reflect different pedagogical encounters influencing dispositions towards sport. The extracts feature Tom, Robin and Adam and provide a glimpse into the social arena of the family and the role sport plays in shaping relations and valuing different family members. Following each extract I offer a brief commentary about the boy's stories. A number of issues are highlighted including how sporting relations with other family members provide resources to construct deeply felt embodied values and this mediates the accumulation of (un) valued capital. In addition, I discuss how the presence of a young disabled person within the family seems to have nurtured, to a differing extent, new (disability) sport interests. In ending the chapter I argue that much more still needs to be learnt about different young disabled people living in diverse family contexts. These insights need to be more centrally located within research that is serious about better understanding family and sport.

Embodied identities and disability

Historically, disability has been understood in a number of ways, reflecting different social, cultural and political norms within society (Barnes et al, 1999; Shakespeare, 2014). While there are varied definitions and understandings of disability, two key models dominate; these are known as the medical model and the social model of disability. Both models continue to influence how disability is understood within society and each model has different implications for the way disabled people are positioned and perceived within sport and the family. The medical model focuses on the individual with the impairment and centralizes deficiency and abnormality (Oliver and Barnes, 2012). From this perspective, a disabled person may be deemed not able to engage in sport because of their impairment (e.g., physical, sensory or learning). The limitation to engagement in sport is situated with the disabled person. For example, a young disabled person using a wheelchair may find it difficult to play tag rugby on a grass surface in wet weather. Here the fault is with the young disabled person for not having the appropriate means for moving on this kind of surface. Typically, the family and parents take on the role of caring for and protecting young disabled people. This medical model understanding of disability and the role of parents are couched within powerful societal discourses that devalue disability and often construct minimal expectations of young disabled people (Kay and Tisdall, 2014). In contrast, the social model supports the view that disability is socially constructed and that it is society that disables people with impairments (Oliver and Barnes, 2012). That is, disability is defined as the restriction of opportunities to engage in community life because of physical and social barriers created by society. Applying the social model to sport would focus on the ways in which sport assumes a non-disabled norm in its structure, organization and delivery.

For example, not being able to perform a specific sport skill would be seen as a limitation of the sport (rules and practices), or failure of the practitioner to be flexible and account for the needs of disabled people. In relation to the example given earlier a social model approach would highlight how the practitioner was restricting the possibilities of the young disabled person playing tag rugby by not considering the use of an alternative accessible surface.

From a social model account the family serves as a resource that enables and nurtures the disabled young person in a way that supports a range of possibilities in sport and life more generally. Whilst both models provide a means for understanding disability within society (and sport) they have also been criticized for failing to adequately account for the lived experiences of disability. Edwards and Imrie (2003) have pointed to the utility of drawing on Bourdieu's work around the social construction of the body in order to provide a means of thinking beyond the biological reductionism of the medical model and the structural focus of the social model of disability. Indeed, elsewhere I have drawn on Bourdieu's thinking tools including practice, field, *habitus* and capital, to make sense of social experiences of young disabled people within PE and youth sport (see, for example, Fitzgerald, 2005, 2012; Fitzgerald and Kirk, 2009).

The origins of Bourdieu's uses of the *habitus* lie in the work of French anthropologist Marcel Mauss (1935/1973). Mauss's notion of 'techniques of the body' was deployed explicitly to challenge the idea that activities such as walking, marching, swimming and climbing were merely biomechanical. He argued instead that even though such activities may appear to be 'natural', they are in fact learned, and are thus embedded in social processes, processes that are socially sanctioned, purposeful and that have a history. Techniques of the body possess these key features and thus integrate the biological and the social. Over time, the provisional and always emerging outcome of this process of learning techniques of the body is the *habitus*. *Habitus* is, in Bourdieu's work, a central concept used as a means to bridge the relationship between agents and their social worlds (Bourdieu and Wacquant, 1992). Bourdieu (1998) considers the family is a key arena in which dispositions of the *habitus* associated with tastes, interests, behaviour and attitudes are embedded within young people's sense of self. In seeking to explore how disabled boys negotiate growing up in a non-disabled family I draw on data generated from discussions with three young disabled boys from the Midlands of England (Fitzgerald and Kirk, 2009b). Next, I offer three short accounts given by Tom, Robin and Adam.

Tom, his dad, brother and football

> When people say 'what's up with you?' I say nothing really. Well, I mean my legs are a bit wobbly but that's it. I can do everything. And these crutches, my crutches help me to get around quicker and make me more skilled and fast at football ... . I don't know what it is, I've always liked football, I watch [on the

TV] with me dad and brother, watch me brother and we all play. We've always done it. We watch England … . Well, my dad's into it so me and my brother are, it's always been like that. I guess it comes from dad. We're all into football. There's nothing else, it's football. My brother Will has played for longer, but he's older. Like from when we were really young we'd kick around, and then Will got in the school team, and now Washmoore FC. I've got my team, so we both play. Dad played but that was ages ago, he reckons he was good and we take after him. He just watches us now, he says he's too old to play. When we're talking about football dad'll treat us both the same. Like, we'll talk about my game and Will's, he's fair like that and you can see he's interested in both of us and I'm not missing out. When he starts talking to his mates he doesn't stop, god he goes on and on and I like it 'cause he's telling his mates about my football … . My team has CP players, they all wobble like me. Tim falls over a lot, he really goes for it, and then next thing, you see him, he's on the floor. Mike's the best, he's got good pace and has a solid tackle. My dad does the refereeing, we didn't have one so Geoff [coach] asked … . My dad takes me to training and games so he's there, so like he said yeah. He's like into football anyway, so he knows what he's doing. He had to do a course or he got a certificate, a proper one from the FA. I mean he's well into it, and I mean like is serious. He's not bad at it. I'm going to do it one day. (Tom)

It has been argued that sport can provide a means for developing father–child relationships (Kay, 2009) and also contribute to 'generative parenting' (Harrington, 2006). Indeed, Coakley (2006) suggests relationships fathers have with their family in leisure contexts reflect the construction of their own masculine identities. Here we see Tom's non-disabled family, particularly his father and brother, were keen football players and spectators. Tom also had this interest in football, which formed a significant touchstone in his relations with them. For Tom and his non-disabled family, football was an important feature of collective family life, which Tom embraced enthusiastically.

Interestingly, Tom's interest in disability football seemed to have been a catalyst for extending sporting interests within the family into this adapted version of football. In this family context, then, it would seem that sporting practices were not only those associated with a non-disabled norm but also included disability football. Tom's father, through his extended interest and participation in disability football had become what Shaw (2008) describes as an involved father. Tom is clearly impressed that his father was actively involved in his disability football. By engaging in disability football and having it as the focal point of conversations, it could be argued that Tom's father recognised a transfer value between non-disabled football and disability football. Indeed, Tom's father seems not to make any kind of distinction between either versions of football and valued them equally. This position is in contrast to a more common view that these are separate contexts of participation and have differential values afforded to them (DePauw, 1997; Fitzgerald and Kirk, 2009b). Tom's account illustrates how he is both aware and enthused that football is a mutual interest shared by his dad and brother.

Robin's family and wheelchair basketball

> Wheelchair basketball, it's a big thing with my family. Jack [brother] is mad about it, we all are. I've pretty much always played. I can't remember when I started; I know I was young, maybe eight. I play basketball at school but wheelchair basketball is better. It's a fairer game when you're all playing in a chair .... Mum went and got a coaching qual and coaches us. She's not bad and works us hard, she knows we want to win and will train us hard ... . On match days dad is the scorekeeper, a kind of official I suppose. He's not as important as mum though 'cause she's the coach. He tries not to shout from the side but can't help it ... . Jack, he'd like to be on the team. He wishes he was playing, I can tell. He loves the competition, being one of the boys, just like the rest of us. But he just hasn't got it. A few hours of training in a chair isn't any competition for those of us who've spent most of our lives in one. Now that prepares you. No amount of gym work is gonna get him that upper body strength. He'd need to spend hours in there. It makes him an easy target. You can spot him a mile off. And his chair skills are poor, he's so slow and clumsy. He's like half a yard behind every one else ... . My trophies are in the lounge, there's a shelf with them. Dad says he'll have to put a new one [shelf] up soon 'cause we're running out of space. Some of my dad's are up there but I've got more, he says he's proud of each one. When Jack's older he wants his to go with mine, he says he's going to get more than me. I know it sounds silly but my mum gets me to say what each are for. She says she doesn't want to forget if someone's around and they ask. Most of them say, but she still makes me do it. I don't mind, or sometimes she gets me to tell people, some of their friends can't believe the trophies I've won.

Like Tom's family, Robin's family seem to be sporty. They all seem to embrace Robin's interest in wheelchair basketball. In this context, Robin has been the catalyst for stimulating this new family interest and it has disrupted a non-disabled family sporting habitus previously evident within his family. Each family member has a role within wheelchair basketball and this pre-occupies much of their leisure time. In contrast to Tom's interest in football, Robin's wheelchair basketball interest was not confined to the males in the family. Indeed, Shaw's (2008) notion of an involved father is extended to also reflect his mum's contribution. To this end Robin acknowledges that his mum has the important role as the coach and this is valued by him and the players on this team. Robin's younger non-disabled brother, Jack, seemed to be a keen player and spectator. However, Robin positions Jack as 'less able' than him and his team-mates. For Jack the techniques of the body learned within the family and specifically associated with what are regarded as 'basic' mobility skills such as walking have little transfer value for wheelchair basketball. In contrast, for Robin in this specific sporting setting, and unlike many other situations he encountered (such as physical education), using a wheelchair regularly carries with it distinct physical capital that Robin rather than Jack possesses. At home Robin's wheelchair basketball achievements are visibly celebrated and this can be a source of discussion with visitors. It is interesting to note that Jack also aspires to have this kind of recognition. This visibility and recognition confirm the centrality and value that Robin and wheelchair basketball have within his family and sporting habitus.

Adam and his family

> Yes, my family's sporty; my brothers are mega, mega sporty. They do everything and are good. What it is, they pick sports up and they get good quickly. They get picked first all the time. I'm not like them. I do try in PE but I'm not the best. I like football mostly. I keep up with the Premier League and who is playing who, follow the results and know what I'm talking about. I watch the school team and could tell them a thing or two. Like last game, the defenders weren't disciplined and got in a bit of a mess. The midfield didn't work hard enough and left the forwards with too much work to do. It wasn't a good game ... . I hate [school] reports, if I could change one thing about school it'd be reports. It's not like I'm bad at school, I'm okay, my report is okay. I'd say my attendance is one of the best. It's just dad looks at PE first and my brothers, they're good at it so get As and I know I'll get C. I know before I look, I always get C ... . My brothers get loads of sports kit off mum and dad and not just at Christmas. At the start of the season they go down to Sports Soccer and get loads of stuff. I'm allowed to have a [replica] shirt, that's it. Mum and dad say I don't need all the kit 'cause I don't play. And I know I don't need like the pads and boots but it's what I feel and I want to feel like my brothers and it would be nice to wear sporty stuff like them. (Adam)

The extracts from Tom and Robin illustrate how the generation of capital through sport can be valued within the family. However, Adam's, enthusiasm for watching football and becoming a knowledgeable supporter seemed to him to be valued less than his brothers' successes at playing for the school team. In this family context, Adam believes his father values most capital associated with footballing performance. Adam seemed to have a strong sense that the physical capital his father valued was not evident through his school report, and this lack of achievement seemed to be exacerbated when comparisons were made with his bothers, who Adam perceived as attaining valued capital within his family. Barton (1993, 2009) and DePauw (1997) have argued that disabled people are often measured against idealized notions of normality and it was evident from Adam that he too was conscious of the ways in which sport gives prominence to a normative non-disabled body.

Being like his brothers by wearing the same clothes as them seemed to be something that was important in Adam's identity work. Indeed, this example serves to illustrate how Adam seeks to negotiate his (disabled) identity growing up in a non-disabled family in which sports participation is the norm. However, Adam's *habitus* was not compatible with that of other family members and, in part, resulted in his parents' reluctance to buy him the same sports kit as his brothers. It would seem that in Adam's case, and notwithstanding his family's acknowledgement of his enthusiasm and knowledge, he himself is applying a non-disabled masculine norm embodied by his brothers as the standard for judging himself (Wedgwood, 2014). While Adam invests in sport he is frustrated by the lack of recognition he receives from his family. In Adam's case it is worth considering how the sporting status afforded to him within his family will support, or deter, future engagement in sport?

Concluding remarks: boys, disability, family and sport

This chapter has sought to explore the ways in which three young disabled boys engage in the construction and constitution of legitimate and valued techniques of the body while growing up in a non-disabled family. A number of issues emerge from the extracts offered. First, for each of the boys specific sports were a shared interest among family members. This sporting relationship provided resources to construct deeply felt embodied values. Similar to wider research focusing on the family and sport it would seem that fathers were significant in guiding expectations about valued sports and this contributed to the embodied identities of the boys (Kay, 2009). Second, sporting practices within the boys' families seemed to be a key context from which to accumulate capital. In Tom's and Robin's cases there was parity of esteem with non-disabled sporting practices and comparable recognition associated with the gaining capital. For Adam, although sporting interests were shared, this did not afford him equivalent status with his siblings, particularly in relation to physical capital associated with playing football. Third, the presence of a disabled family member seems to have been a catalyst for new (disability) sport interests to be embraced within the family. For example, Tom's family extended their footballing interest to incorporate disability football. Robin's extract provides evidence of the reverse socialization of parents and a sibling into wheelchair basketball. In Robin's case the family, as a unit, seems to have taken a more active role in embracing an interest in wheelchair basketball. Whilst each of the boys has different experiences it is clear that much peda-gogical work is undertaken within the family that contributes to their learning about sport.

The interview extracts from the three boys open up a series of additional questions around disability, family and sport. In relation to a young disabled person within a family: what kind of stories would we hear from older young people who experience an acquired impairment? What stories would we hear from young people with different kinds of impairments? How would the stories differ if they came from young disabled people in a high performance national squad? How would a parent or other sibling with a disability con-tribute to the story? How would other differences relating to gender, ethnicity, sexuality and class also shape sports socialization and contribute to embodied identities? Of course, the families featured in this chapter seem to be very traditional in their composition. Therefore, questions remain around the nature of experiences and influences that differently constituted families may have. For example, how would dual-earning parents, reconstituted families brought about by remarriage, cohabitation and step-parenting, and families with same sex parents shape the sporting experiences of young disabled people? More broadly, if Tom, Robin, Adam, Dave and Andy were interviewed in 10, 15 and 20 years' time, what would we find about the continued influences of the family on sports participation through the life course? And how will these young people shape the families they may eventually nurture. There is clearly more we need to learn about families, disability and sport and in seeking these new insights researchers should recognize the valuable contributions young disabled people can make to these discussions.

References

Abbott, D. (2013) 'Who say what, Where, Why and How? Doing real-world research with disabled children, young people and family members', in T. Curran and K. Runswick-Cole (eds.) *Disabled Children's Childhood Studies. Critical approaches in a global context.* Basingstoke: Palgrave Macmillan, pp39–56.

Barnes, C., Mercer, G. and Shakespeare, T. (1999) *Exploring disability: A sociological introduction.* Cambridge: Polity Press.

Barton, L. (1993) Disability, Empowerment and Physical Education, in J. Evans (ed.) *Equality, Education and Physical Education.* London: Falmer Press, pp43–54.

Barton, L. (2009) Disability, physical education and sport: Some critical observations and questions, in H. Fitzgerald (ed.) *Disability and Youth Sport.* London: Routledge, pp39–50.

Bourdieu, P. (1998) *Practical reason: On the theory of action.* Cambridge: Polity Press.

Bourdieu, P. and Wacquant, L. J. D. (1992) *An invitation to reflexive sociology.* Cambridge: Polity Press.

Coakley, J. (2006) The good father: Parental expectations and youth sport, *Leisure Studies,* 25(2): 153–163.

Côté, J. and Hay, J. (2002) Family influences on youth sport performance and participation in J. M. Siva and D. Stevens (eds.) *Psychological foundations of sport.* Boston: Merrill, pp484–519.

DePauw, K. (1997) The (In)Visibility of DisAbility: Cultural Contexts and "Sporting Bodies", *Quest,* 49(4): 416–430.

Edwards, C. and Imrie, R. (2003) Disability and bodies as bearers of value, *Sociology,* 37(2): 239–256.

Farrell, A. F. and Krahn, G. L. (2014) Family life goes on: Disability in contemporary families, *Family Relations. Interdisciplinary Journal of Applied Family Studies,* 63(1): 1–6.

Fitzgerald, H. (2005) Still feeling like a spare piece of luggage? Embodied experiences of (dis)ability in physical education and school sport, *Physical Education and Sport Pedagogy,* 10(1): 41–59.

Fitzgerald, H. (Ed.) (2009) *Disability and youth sport.* London: Routledge.

Fitzgerald, H. (2012) The Paralympics and knowing disability, *International Journal of Disability, Development and Education,* 59(3): 243–255.

Fitzgerald, H. and Kirk, D. (2009) Identity Work: Young disabled people, family and sport, *Leisure Studies*, 28(4), 469–488.

Haycock, D. and Smith, A. (2014) A family affair? Exploring the influence of childhood sport socialisation on young adults' leisure-sport careers in north-west England, *Leisure Studies*, 33(3): 285–304.

Harrington, M. (2006) Sport and leisure as contexts for fathering in Australian families, *Leisure Studies*, 25(2): 165–183.

Kay, E. and Tisdall, M. (2014) 'A culture of participation' in S. Riddle and N. Watson (eds.) *Disability, Culture and Identity*. London: Routledge, pp19–33.

Kay, T. (Ed.) (2009) *Fathering through Sport and Leisure*. London: Routledge.

Mauss, M. (1973) Techniques of the bod, *Economy and Society*, 2(1): 70–88 (Original work published 1935).

Oliver, M. and Barnes, C. (2012) *The New Politics of Disablement*. Basingstoke: Palgrave Macmillan.

Shaw, S. M. (2008) Family leisure and changing ideologies of parenthood, *Sociology Compass*, 2(2): 688–703.

Shakespeare, T. (2014) *Disability Rights and Wrongs Revisited*. London: Routledge.

Wedgwood, N. (2014) 'My biggest disability is I'm a male!' The role of sport in negotiating the dilemma of disabled masculinity, in J. Hargreaves and E. Anderson (eds.) *Routledge Handbook of Sport, Gender and Sexuality*. London: Routledge, pp189–197.

18 Sport parent roles in fostering positive youth development

M. Blair Evans, Veronica Allan, Matthew Vierimaa and Jean Côté

Introduction

Parents are ambassadors for their children's sport involvement – making important decisions and promoting values that define how and when family members are involved in sport (Wuerth et al, 2004). Furthermore, parents are often assigned a spectrum of social roles in youth sport ranging from spectator to sport agent, financier, coach, equipment manager, and driver. The sum of these roles calls attention to a higher-order responsibility for parents to support young athletes through their skill development and to provide opportunities for personal development (Bailey et al, 2013). The investments that parents make are valued by social and cultural imperatives that underlie a tendency to judge parents according to their child's sport performance and character (e.g., Coakley, 2006). By constructing moral panics and ideals that define good parenting through how much capital is invested in youth sport (Dagkas and Quarmby, 2012), the resulting assumption is clear: Behind every good young athlete, there is a good parent.

One risk of such a perspective is that athletic performance gains priority over other developmental outcomes, and parents may be pressured to intensively guide their child's sport participation and push their child to succeed. When young athletes feel pressured to perform, low perceptions of autonomy emerge that prompt feelings of low competence and risk of burnout (Holt et al, 2009). Children may even be regarded as a second opportunity for parents to succeed by proxy, which, at an extreme, reflects a pathogenic pattern of behavior related to pressure, abuse, and conflict (e.g., denigration after poor performance; Tofler et al, 2005). In the perceived best interest for their child, parents often develop elevated expectations and put unnecessary pressure on performance.

With parents investing so much into sport, it is not surprising that they get a lot of bad press: News stories about inappropriate or abusive parent behaviours in the sport realm are routinely reported in the media. Nevertheless, parent involvement in sport is neither inherently positive nor negative, and the sport parent role is challenging and complex, involving competing pressures from sport organizations and communities (Harwood and Knight, 2014). With this in mind, we adopted principles of a personal assets approach to youth sport

(Côté et al, in press) to reveal how the value in sport parenting behaviours lie in their propensity to either support or harm quality relationships, activities and environments that are a foundation for positive youth development. This chapter will explore this proposition by describing the parenting role, how it changes from childhood to adolescence and across social settings, and how parents shape youth development.

What is the sport parent role?

The most comprehensive parent role is that of *socialisation*, whereby parents act as an agent for their child's involvement in sport by locating opportunities and 'signing their kids up' to participate (Wuerth et al, 2004). As an example, past research reveals that parent attitudes and dispositions toward sport are reflected in those of their children (e.g., parental perfectionism predicts child perfectionism in sport; Appleton et al, 2010). This intergenerational transfer may emerge from parent behaviours and attitudes that shape broader family cultures, which in turn creates expectations for sport involvement and define why sport participation is important. This process is highlighted in Wheeler's (2012) exploration of family habitus, and reveals the influence of the family in socializing young athletes into sport.

The sport parent role is also defined through *involvement*, by adopting instrumental roles within youth sport. Sport programs often rely on parents to take on coaching, volunteering, and fundraising activities. Although children report numerous benefits when their parents are highly involved (e.g., parent–coach role; Weiss and Fretwell, 2005), high involvement is neither positive nor negative in its own right. Indeed, positive outcomes may also emerge when parents adopt few social roles beyond providing transportation and watching their child play – especially as children attain higher levels of performance (e.g., Fraser-Thomas et al, 2008). As parents become involved in sport, they must nevertheless balance the broader family environment, and confront numerous setbacks related to the investment of time, finances, and personal health (Kirk et al, 1997). As a result, sport parent roles co-exist (and sometimes conflict) with different family demands and need to be adapted to different environments and contexts.

Shifting sport parent roles over time and across contexts

Not surprisingly, the direct role that parents have in the sport experience of their child (e.g. coaching, volunteering) decreases as athletes emerge from childhood into adolescence and young adulthood. This transition is shown across numerous contexts, and reflects the tendency for coaches and peers to take on more primary roles in sport involvement at older ages and at more elite levels (e.g., Chan et al, 2012). In contrast to the overall magnitude of parent involvement in youth sport, there is also evidence that parent roles and responsibilities evolve as children develop and attain higher levels of performance. Although parent roles within childhood sport may include aspects involving coaching and intensive involvement, the onset of adolescence and early adulthood often signals a transition to mentorship, guidance, and social support (Côté, 1999; Fraser-Thomas et al, 2013; Lauer et al, 2010). Such changes not only relate to development, but also to the nature of the program. As children transfer into more specialized and invested sport settings, a broader network of individuals in 'expert' roles shapes their sport pathway.

Similar to these changes over time, parenting roles in sport are also unevenly distributed according to gender. There is a tendency for parents to place greater importance on boys' sport participation, and for fathers' involvement in sport to more reliably transfer to children compared to mothers (Downward et al, 2014). Regarding what is appropriate for male or female parents, Coakley (2006) theorized about the nature of sport as a context for fathers to be involved in their child's life and to take on a domestic role while still retaining their masculinity. Consistent with this argument, the dominant sport fathering role has been defined in terms of simply being involved (e.g., share the sport experience) compared to mothering roles that outline more intensive support of the sport experience (e.g., responsible for child's development and providing support; Trussel and Shaw, 2012). Although gender roles are perhaps not universally applied across all social contexts (e.g., Chan et al, 2012), dominant gender expectations certainly emerge and influence the involvement of parents in sport.

Regarding the extent that parental roles differ as a reflection of cultural values, one initial difference relates to whether parents are able to provide the necessary support for sport participation. Cultural expectations that designate parents' responsibility for regulating their child's sport involvement may be difficult to live up to, specifically for those in a disadvantaged position (e.g., low socio-economic status, single parents; Dagkas and Quarmby, 2012). Although sport opportunities are ideally framed as a means of engaging disaffected or disadvantaged youth to facilitate positive youth development (e.g., Fraser-Thomas et al, 2005), access to sport programming for disadvantaged or ethnic minority families is limited. Even when governments subsidize youth sport involvement, low-income parents receiving financial assistance report that subsidies are often not enough to promote equal sport involvement and rarely cover the full cost of sport participation (Holt et al, 2011).

The experiences of youth from ethnic minority communities may also involve different parent influences (see Chapter 10 in this volume). As an example, Kay (2006) explored parental influence on young Muslim women participating in a UK sport program. At the intersection of cultures, traditions, and even generations – where sport participation was limited and only possible with parental approval – the women described how their sport involvement required them to navigate personal and cultural identities.

These parental influences are contrasted with those across developing regions, where sport for development programs are often implemented with a social objective to improve public health and education. As an example of parent influence across such contexts, Kay and Spaaij (2013) reflected on research from Zambia, Brazil, and India to explore how parent-child relationships form barriers to sport participation, or may even be a source of social issues that sport programs address. Whereas pressure to raise income or fulfil domestic caring duties may overshadow education and sport opportunities for impoverished Brazilian children, the large numbers of parent-less children in Zambia (i.e., combined effects of poverty, malaria, HIV/AIDS) experience little support for such opportunities. On the other hand, Kay and Spaaij (2013) reflected on positive outcomes from a sport for development program to address gender inequity in India, where girls who took part in a sport programme developed assertiveness and experienced shifts in family expectations for gender roles.

As such, parents are an important agent of change regarding their children's sport participation, regardless of differences in the structure of youth sport programs across dynamic cultural, political, and economic contexts. Grounded in this understanding about the magnitude of parent influence, the next section will focus on how this influence is exerted by discussing ways that parents may positively or negatively shape the development of young athletes.

Parenting and positive youth development

To explore how parents influence athletes' development, it is first essential to establish the developmental outcomes of youth sport involvement. Development in sport relates to the intent of sport involvement to cultivate performance in sport-specific skills, long-term participation in physical activity, and personal development (i.e., Côté et al, 2010). Indeed, sport is often explicitly structured in ways to improve performance by teaching skills and deselecting less-skilled participants from elite sport (e.g., Ford et al, 2009). Sport is also used to promote long-term engagement in physical activity and to limit issues such as childhood obesity (e.g, Janssen and LeBlanc, 2010).

In comparison, the perspective of sport as a personal development context focuses on opportunities for youth to improve life-skills related to personal beliefs, interpersonal skills, and community engagement (Benson, 2003). This is known as an asset-building approach and considers the social relationships and personal experiences of sport participation as opportunities to shape development. Youth sport researchers exploring pathways to ensure positive sport experiences have focused on this asset-building perspective, and how they are not only essential for personal development, but also for performance and participation outcomes (e.g., Fraser-Thomas et al, 2005).

Côté et al, (2010) specifically formed a conceptual framework defining the 4Cs (i.e., positive perceptions of competence, confidence, connection and character) as four vital psychosocial assets for promoting personal development, performance, and participation outcomes. This model was adapted from research defining psychosocial outcomes of school-based and extracurricular activities (Lerner et al, 2005) and defines asset-building according to the extent that youth derive increased perceptions of ability and likelihood of sport success, develop quality relationships and belongingness with others, and establish positive moral characteristics such as empathy and respect (Côté et al, in press). Adapting this positive youth development standpoint, the vital question addressed by researchers is shifting from *whether* youth experience positive development through sport, toward identifying the nature of sport experiences that make positive development most likely.

As a result, the vital question of relevance for parenting is: How do parents socialize their children into sport – and become involved directly in sport – in ways that promote development of personal assets? In the current chapter, we apply the personal assets framework (Côté et al, in press) to address this question. Specifically, Côté et al propose that personal assets are not inherently developed through sport participation alone. Rather, personal assets develop according to the extent that parents, sport programs, and communities provide opportunities for:

1   quality relationships;
2   appropriate settings; and
3   personal engagement in activities.

Although each of these processes involve complex decisions on behalf of parents, positive and negative parental actions related to each of these sources of influence are explored below.

Quality relationships

Perhaps most noticeably, the quality of parent–child relationships directly influences the developmental outcomes and personal assets that result from sport participation. Parent–child relationships within sport are importantly contrasted according to: active involvement in a programme; directive behaviours; support and praise; and pressure (Wuerth et al, 2004). In terms of parent behaviours that support positive outcomes, youth reported greater enjoyment of sport when their parents were highly involved in their sport, while being autonomy supportive and providing appropriate structure (e.g., guidelines; Holt et al, 2009). The concept of autonomy support has been particularly well documented in past research, representing a style of parenting that enables young athletes to feel that they have a choice (Holt et al, 2009).

Whereas a majority of parents are expected to apply appropriate levels of these behaviours, there is also the risk that parents damage their child's development by overemphasizing winning, holding unrealistic expectations, criticizing their children, and pushing their children to participate and compete (Gould et al, 2006; Sagar and Lavallee, 2010). Some parent behaviours have particular potential to erode the parent–child relationship and decrease enjoyment, including parent behaviours that draw attention to themselves (or their child), efforts to coach their child from the side lines, and arguing with coaches or officials (Knight et al, 2011). As athletes specialized and invested in a specific sport, Lauer et al (2010) furthermore revealed that athletes reported increased pressure from parents. Clearly, children who feel pressure to perform from parents may feel that they are being controlled and feel less satisfied with sport involvement.

Parents must sometimes contribute to programs in a volunteer role – indeed, many sport programs rely on parent contributions. Interestingly, a unique relationship emerges whenever parents assume coaching roles (Weiss and Fretwell, 2005). Whereas the parent–coach role has the potential to further strengthen parent–child bonds, the inability to separate coach–athlete and parent–child relationships can further erode the sport experiences of all members of the team. Irrespective of the specific roles adopted, however, it is important to realize that parent-child relationships are one of several vital sport relationships that, together, influence young athletes' experiences.

Personal engagement in activities

Parents influence the opportunities, encouragement, and support that their children have for meaningful engagement in an array of specific activities. This influence begins very early in development, as parents who provide children with ample opportunities to engage in active physical play help develop foundational motor and cognitive skills that are later essential for organized sport (e.g., balance, throwing; e.g., MacDonald and Parke, 1986). Athletes' early experiences and continued sport involvement are also shaped by parents, who determine which activities are engaged-in and to what extent (e.g., Bloom, 1985; Côté, 1999). While parents may make many sacrifices and invest sub-stantial time and resources into their children's sport participation, this tangible support appears to be a necessary condition for sport participation, rather than a factor that distinguishes differential sport development (Fraser-Thomas et al, 2013; Lauer et al, 2010).

Over time, parents' efforts to shape the scope and breadth of their children's sport involvement may be classified into pathways of either early specialization in a single sport, or early sampling in numerous sport activities. Early spe-cialization in a single sport beginning at a young age is, indeed, underpinned by conceptual arguments that elite performance in any skilled domain requires a vast amount of structured and deliberate practice starting early in development. Accordingly, early specialization is in some instance associated with elite sport performance (see Ford, et al, 2009). However, this pathway is also controversial because it poses risks in the form of decreased enjoyment, injuries, and burnout (e.g., Fraser-Thomas et al, 2008).

An early sampling approach, in contrast, is characterized by being involved in numerous organized sports and play activities throughout childhood, and is associated with long-term participation and personal development (e.g., Busseri et al, 2006; Fredricks and Eccles, 2004). Sampling can nevertheless be an early stage in the pathway to elite sport success (e.g., Côté, 1999; Memmert et al,

2010) and is aligned with autonomy supportive behaviours that eventually generate feelings that one's sport involvement is meaningful (Fraser-Thomas et al, 2013). With this in mind, parents should provide the necessary tangible support and encourage children to engage in diverse organized sport and play opportunities.

Appropriate settings

Finally and from a broader perspective, parents shape the physical and social environment of sport participation. Youth develop within a physical environment (e.g., large versus small sport clubs; urban versus rural regions) as well as a social environment (e.g., access to social ties such as close family and community members) that can be considered at both the macro- and micro-levels. At a macro-level, parents influence where their children grow up and the social environment they develop in. As an example, whereas urban and rural parents in Australia reported similar barriers to sport involvement (e.g., time commitments and program cost; Hardy et al, 2009), a distinguishing feature was that rural parents reported a limited variety of sport programmes. Although rural families may not have access to a wide variety of contexts, there are nevertheless benefits for young athletes in small communities. For example, residents of a small Canadian community described sport as a way to meaningfully engage in their community, and sport involved numerous play environments (e.g., recreational basketball with a range of ages and abilities; Balish and Côté, 2014). Although decisions such as where one lives clearly shapes athlete development, sport environments can nevertheless be adapted in ways that provide positive experiences, irrespective of community size (Balish and Côté, 2014)

In contrast, the micro-environment relates to the more direct family environment surrounding sport. To effectively juggle the myriad of sport activities of their active children, parents often go to great lengths to modify and adapt the family environment (Bloom, 1985). The related time commitment to be involved in sport, and to support sport involvement, often leads to substantial changes in the day-to-day life of the entire family (e.g., Kirk et al, 1997). As an example, Wheeler (2014) described the shifting nature of the 'weekend' for families in England and how organized sport was, for some families, an activity that consumed recreational time for members. The family environment and parents' involvement in sport thus shapes the way in which athletes construe their sport involvement and how they establish identities in and out of sport (Wheeler, 2012).

Translating research into positive parent influence

Contrasting the influence parents have on youth sport with the potential for misguided behaviours that harm youth development, sport parents represent a valuable conduit for translating youth development research. To initiate this type of action, however, it is arguably most necessary to conceptualize *what an effective sport parent does.* In line with contemporary definitions of youth development, Harwood and Knight (2014) theorized that effective sport parenting encompasses behaviours that increase 'the chances for children to achieve their sporting potential, have a positive psychosocial experience, and develop a range of positive developmental outcomes' (p2). In line with this definition, the authors identified six postulates regarding behaviours that relate to parenting expertise, including:

1 selecting appropriate sport opportunities and providing social support;
2 parenting in an authoritative or autonomy-supportive manner;
3 coping well with the emotional demands of competition and serving as an emotionally intelligent role model;
4 fostering healthy relationships with coaches, officials, and other parents;
5 effectively managing the changing demands from sport organization(s);
6 adapting involvement according to the child's developmental stage.

Although each postulate reflects a range of potential behaviours, Figure 18.1 provides case examples that underscore the relevance of each postulate within six specific sport parenting experiences. By exploring the complexities of sport parenting, the cases also reveal the perils of creating moralistic beliefs for what parents should do, because parent behaviours are fundamentally context-bound and the 'right' actions are rarely clear (e.g., what it means to be autonomy-supportive differs across situations). Ultimately, these postulates serve as a foundation to build parent-training programs with the foremost goal of enhancing sport parenting knowledge and relevant cognitive, social, and emotional skills.

As an example of how a parenting intervention may target one or more of Knight and Harwood's (2014) postulates, the working with parents approach (Lafferty and Triggs, 2014) was designed to help parents cope with emotions and develop positive relationships in sport. The intervention aimed to ensure a supportive sport experience by first educating parents to enhance understanding of the sport itself, how performance is developed, and what role sport parents have. The second and overarching goal of the program was to establish parents' sense of how their emotional reactions influence their child's sport experience, and form coping strategies to regulate their emotions around sport. Despite limited evidence related to the efficacy of parent training programmes, grounding interventions within best-available research will, at the very least, provide theoretical support for their potential to stimulate youth development.

In contrast with theory-generated programs that are largely grounded in the academic realm (such as the example above), an array of publically funded and for-profit programs are applied in the broader public realm, with varying levels of theoretical support. As an example, Table 18.1 describes publically available programmes (e.g., workshops, online modules, courses) involving sport parent education from across Canada and the United States. These programmes primarily adopt educational approaches for shaping parent

Appropriate activities

Joan is a single mother of Devlin, a Canadian grade 11 high-school student and skilled volleyball player. Because her birthday falls in late September and the age cutoff for high school sport is on 1 September, Devlin has the choice of joining the junior team (i.e., younger students, where she would be a 'starter') or the senior team (i.e., talented senior students, where she would have fewer playing opportunities). What team does Joan encourage her daughter to join?

Autonomy support

Chang has started playing tennis at his school, and would like to make his school's competitive team. He has started searching online for training techniques and saving money to buy equipment. When his parents notice his intrinsic drive to develop his skill, how do they react?

Emotional control

Tanya and Donald's 13-year-old daughter Sonya is attending her first national figure skating competition. If she wins the competition, she will be considered an up-and-coming Olympic contender and will be provided with funding to secure a renowned coach. How do they interact with Sonya and her coach on the days leading up to the event?

Fostering healthy relationships with coaches

Thomas is a former professional soccer player and has enrolled his son in a soccer program for 9-year-olds. The team's coach is another parent who often makes mistakes with skill development and strategy. How does Thomas approach the situation?

Adapting involvement and coping with changing demands

Bjorn enjoys running with his 15-year-old-daughter Melissa and has always coached her on technique and guided her training. Now that Melissa is reaching an elite level and has joined a running team, she relies on Bjorn less frequently and even ignores his advice. How will Bjorn adapt his involvement with Melissa's running?

Figure 18.1 Five case examples of the complex situations that parents encounter

behaviours by providing information about parenting roles and the needs of young athletes. In contrast, some programs adapted more diverse approaches to change parent behaviour, such as through conveying standards for parent behaviour through codes of conduct or rules. Nevertheless, evidence is still needed to reveal the benefits of using sport parent programming.

Moving forward, the focus of research and practice on sport parent programming should be to produce positive long-term outcomes for parents and young athletes, while also being consistently used in settings that reach individuals who are in greatest need of the programming. This comprehensive characterization emerged through the work of Glasgow, Vogt and Boles (1999), who created a framework to evaluate public health interventions that considered whether they are generalizable and practical for long-term change (e.g., is an intervention low cost, and are organizations willing to use them over a

Table 18.1 Overview of Example Parent Training Programmes from Canada and the United States

Parent Training Programme	Overview
Respect in Sport Parent Programme http://respectinsport.com/parent-p rogram/	*Online training and certification programme* Empowers parents to ensure their child's safety, encourages effective communication, and creates a standard of respectful behaviour
Positive Sport Parent http://www.positivesportparent.com	*Online resources and live information sessions* Educates parents on a range of sport topics to encourage their children to achieve their full potential through positive sport experiences
Parents Association for Youth Sports Course http://www.nays.org/parents/	*Video-based educational programme* Educates youth sport parents about their roles and responsibilities as well as ways in which they can ensure their child's sport experience is enjoyable
YESports Mastery Approach to Parenting in Sports http://www.y-e-sports.com/ParentE ducation.html	*Online self-instruction video* Designed to get parents and coaches on the same page for the benefit of children by fostering a mastery motivational climate
Canadian Sport for Life: A Sport Parent's Guide http://canadiansportforlife.ca/resour ces/sport-parents-guide	*Handbook* Enhances parents' understanding of the needs of young athletes throughout the various stages of development
SportSafe (British Columbia): The Parent Contract http://www.cscd.gov.bc.ca/sport/p rograms/sportsafe.htm	*Code of conduct (signed by parents)* Outlines acceptable rules for behaviour in youth sport; emphasizes the importance of children's enjoyment

long period of time). By forming effective programming that is adopted and extends to those in greatest need, sport parent research will ideally promote sport environments that have the greatest likelihood of producing positive developmental experiences.

Conclusion

Although parents are expected to have an interest in optimizing their child's sport experience, the prevalence of examples that demonstrate negative parental influence make it important to promote parenting behaviours that enable positive youth development. Drawing conclusions regarding which specific behaviours to promote as 'ideal' is, nevertheless, a complex task because parent-child relationships are coloured by the socio-cultural contexts that comprise sport environments. As an example, the behaviours of Canadian parents enrolling their six- or seven-year-old children in competitive hockey is a phenomenon that reflects Canadian ideals, where 'good' Canadian parents are expected to enrol their child in hockey. Furthermore, the sport system is structured such that elite selection processes often begin separating children at early ages – so there is a competitive advantage to specializing in a single sport during early childhood. In this light, parent behaviours should be seen as operating within a broader social system.

Even across social contexts, however, several propositions have garnered strong evidence. First, parents should be involved in the sport setting to some degree and should develop positive relationships that ultimately prompt their child to feel supported and autonomous. Parents also need to find a way of supporting their children in forming positive relationships with peers, coaches and other members of the sport community. Children should be provided with opportunities to experience a spectrum of sport activities – ranging from play to deliberate practice – and ideally will participate in sport within a supportive social and physical environment.

References

Appleton, P. R., Hall, H. K. and Hill, A. P. (2010) Family patterns of perfectionism: An examination of elite junior athletes and their parents, *Psychology of Sport and Exercise*, 11, 363–371.

Bailey, R., Hillman, C., Arent, S. et al (2013) Physical activity: An underestimated investment in human capital, *Journal of Physical Activity and Health*, 10, 289–308.

Balish, S. and Côté, J. (2014) The influence of community on athletic development: An integrated case study, *Qualitative Research in Sport, Exercise and Health*, 6, 98–120.

Benson, P. L. (2003) Developmental assets and asset-building communities: Conceptual and empirical foundations. In R. Lerner and P. L. Benson (eds.) *Developmental Assets and Asset Building Communities: Implications for Research, Policy and Practice*. New York: Kluwer, pp19–43.

Bloom, B. S. (1985) *Developing Talent in Young People*. New York: Ballantine.

Busseri, M. A., Rose-Krasnor, L. and Willoughby, T.et al (2006) A longitudinal examination of breadth and intensity of youth activity involvement and successful development, *Developmental Psychology*, 42, 1313–1326.

Chan, D. K., Lonsdale, C. and Fung, H. (2012) Influences of coaches, parents, and peers on the motivational patterns of child and adolescent athletes, *Scandinavian Journal of Medicine and Science in Sports*, 22, 558–568.

Coakley, J. (2006) The good father: Parental expectations and youth sports, *Leisure Studies*, 25, 153–163.

Côté, J. (1999) The influence of the family in the development of talent in sport, *The Sport Psychologist*, 13, 395–417.

Côté, J., Bruner, M. W., Erickson, K. et al (2010) Athlete development and coaching. In J. Lyle and C. J. Cushion (eds.) *Sport Coaching: Professionalism and Practice*. Oxford: Elsevier, pp63–79.

Côté, J., Turnnidge, J. and Vierimaa, M. (in press) A personal assets approach to youth sport. In A. Smith and K. Green (eds.) *Handbook of Youth Sport*. London: Routledge.

Dagkas, S. and Quarmby, T. (2012) Young people's embodiment of physical activity: The role of the 'pedagogized' family, *Sociology of Sport Journal*, 29, 210–226.

Downward, P., Hallmann, K. and Pawlowski, T. (2014) Assessing parental impact on the sports participation of children: A socio-economic analysis of the UK, *European Journal of Sport Science*, 14, 84–90.

Ford, P. R., Ward, P., Hodges, N. J. et al (2009) The role of deliberate practice and play in career progression in sport: The early engagement hypothesis, *High Ability Studies*, 20, 65–75.

Fraser-Thomas, J., Côté, J. and Deakin, J. (2005) Youth sport programs: An avenue to foster positive youth development, *Physical Education and Sport Pedagogy*, 10, 19–40.

Fraser-Thomas, J., Côté, J. and Deakin, J. (2008) Understanding dropout and prolonged engagement in adolescent competitive sport, *Psychology of Sport and Exercise*, 9, 645–662.

Fraser-Thomas, J., Strachan, L. and Jeffery-Tosoni, S. (2013) Family influence on children's involvement in sport. In J. Côté and R. Lidor (eds.) *Conditions of Children's Talent Development in Sport*. Morgantown, WV: Fitness Information Technology, pp179–196.

Fredricks, J. A. and Eccles, J. S. (2004) Parental influences on youth involvement in sports. In M. R. Weiss (ed.) *Developmental sport and exercise psychology: A lifespan perspective*. Morgantown: Fitness Information Technology, pp145–164.

Glasgow, R. E., Vogt, T. M. and Boles, S. M. (1999) Evaluating the public health impact of health promotion interventions: The RE-AIM framework, *American Journal of Public Health*, 89, 1322–1327.

Gould, D., Lauer, L., Rolo, C. et al (2006) Understanding the role parents play in tennis success: A national survey of junior tennis coaches, *British Journal of Sports Medicine*, 40, 632–636.

Hardy, L., Kelly, B., Chapman, K. et al (2009) Parental perceptions of barriers to children's participation in organized sport in Australia, *Journal of Paediatrics and Child Health*, 46, 197–203.

Harwood, C. G. and Knight, C. J. (2014) Parenting in youth sport: A position paper on parenting expertise, *Psychology of Sport and Exercise*. Advance online publication. doi:10.1016/j.psychsport.2014.03.001.

Holt, N. L., Kingsley, B. C., Tink, L. N. et al (2011) Benefits and challenges associated with sport participation by children and parents from low-income families, *Psychology of Sport and Exercise*, 12, 490–499.

Holt, N. L., Tamminen, K. A., Black, D. E. et al (2009) Youth sport parenting styles and practices, *Journal of Sport and Exercise Psychology*, 31, 37–59.

Janssen, I. and LeBlanc, A. G. (2010) Systematic review of the health benefits of physical activity and fitness in school-aged children and youth, *International Journal of Behavioural Nutrition and Physical Activity*, 7, 1–16.

Kay, T. (2006) Daughters of Islam: Family influences on Muslim young women's participation in sport, *International Review for the Sociology of Sport*, 41, 357–373.

Kay, T. and Spaaij, R. (2013) The mediating effects of family on sport in international development contexts, *International Review for the Sociology of Sport*, 44, 77–94.

Kirk, D., O'Connor, A., Carlson, T. et al (1997) Time commitments in junior sport: Social consequences for participants and their families, *European Journal of Physical Education*, 2, 51–73.

Knight, C. J., Neely, K. C. and Holt, N. L. (2011) Parental behaviors in team sports: How do female athletes want parents to behave?, *Journal of Applied Sport Psychology*, 23, 76–92.

Lauer, L., Gould, D., Roman, N. et al (2010) Parental behaviors that affect junior tennis player development, *Psychology of Sport and Exercise*, 11, 487–496.

Lerner, R. M., Lerner, J. V., Almerigi, J. et al (2005) Positive youth development, participation in community youth development programmes, and community contributions of fifth grade adolescents: Findings from the first wave of the 4-H Study of Positive Youth Development, *Journal of Early Adolescence*, 25, 17–71.

Lafferty, M. E. and Triggs, C. (2014) The Working with Parents in Sport Model: A practical guide for practitioners working with parents of elite young performers, *Journal of Sport Psychology in Action*, 5, 117–128.

MacDonald, K. and Parke, R. D. (1986) Parent–child physical play: The effects of sex and age of children and parents, *Sex Roles*, 15, 367–378.

Memmert, D., Baker, J. and Bertsch, C. (2010) Play and practice in the development of sport-specific creativity in team ball sports, *High Ability Studies*, 21, 3–18.

Sagar, S. S. and Lavallee, D. (2010) The developmental origins of fear of failure in adolescent athletes: Examining parental practices, *Psychology of Sport and Exercise*, 11, 177–187.

Tofler, I. R., Knapp, P. K. and Lardon, M. T. (2005) Achievement by proxy distortion in sports: A distorted mentoring of high-achieving youth. Historical perspectives and clinical intervention with children, adolescents, and their families, *Clinics in Sports Medicine*, 24, 805–828.

Trussell, D. E. and Shaw, S. M. (2012) Organized youth sport and parenting in public and private spaces, *Leisure Sciences*, 34, 377–394.

Wheeler, S. (2012) The significance of family culture for sports participation, *International Review for the Sociology of Sport*, 47, 235–252.

Wheeler, S. (2014) Organised activities, educational activities and family activities: How do they feature in the middle-class family's weekend?, *Leisure Studies*, 33, 215–232.

Weiss, M. R. and Fretwell, S. D. (2005) The parent-coach/child-athlete relationship in youth sport: Cordial, contentious, or conundrum?, *Research Quarterly for Exercise and Sport*, 76, 286–305.

Wuerth, S., Lee, M. J. and Alfermann, D. (2004) Parental involvement and athletes' career in youth sport, *Psychology of Sport and Exercise*, 5, 21–33.

Index

Page numbers in italic refer to figures. Page numbers in bold refer to tables.